SpringerBriefs in Criminology

Dis-Connect. Artist: Sarah Tucker; Prisoner 82888
This painting highlights the urgent need for outsiders to acknowledge, understand, and respect the journey of prisoners, both socially, culturally, and humanely. Despite being home to the most incarcerated people in the world—its First Nations peoples—Australia continues to lack a human rights charter and remains largely indifferent to these critical issues. This dis-connect is represented in the extension of hands from opposing places that bridge environments, space, time, and culture while searching for unity. The colours are the ochres of the First Nations flag, juxtaposing shades of grey that dissect Australia's colonial history
Mediums: Acrylic paint on canvas

SpringerBriefs in Criminology present concise summaries of cutting edge research across the fields of Criminology and Criminal Justice. It publishes small but impactful volumes of between 50-125 pages, with a clearly defined focus. The series covers a broad range of Criminology research from experimental design and methods, to brief reports and regional studies, to policy-related applications.

The scope of the series spans the whole field of Criminology and Criminal Justice, with an aim to be on the leading edge and continue to advance research. The series will be international and cross-disciplinary, including a broad array of topics, including juvenile delinquency, policing, crime prevention, terrorism research, crime and place, quantitative methods, experimental research in criminology, research design and analysis, forensic science, crime prevention, victimology, criminal justice systems, psychology of law, and explanations for criminal behavior.

SpringerBriefs in Criminology will be of interest to a broad range of researchers and practitioners working in Criminology and Criminal Justice Research and in related academic fields such as Sociology, Psychology, Public Health, Economics and Political Science.

Sarah Tucker • Johannes M. Luetz

Therapeutic Prison Art Interventions

Empirical Perspectives

Sarah Tucker
School of Social Sciences, Arts,
Design & Architecture
University of New South Wales
Sydney, NSW, Australia

School of Social Sciences
Christian Heritage College
Brisbane, QLD, Australia

Johannes M. Luetz
Graduate Research School
Alphacrucis University College
Brisbane, QLD, Australia

School of Law and Society
University of the Sunshine Coast
Maroochydore, QLD, Australia

School of Social Sciences
University of New South Wales
Sydney, NSW, Australia

ISSN 2192-8533   ISSN 2192-8541 (electronic)
SpringerBriefs in Criminology
ISBN 978-3-031-85990-8   ISBN 978-3-031-85991-5 (eBook)
https://doi.org/10.1007/978-3-031-85991-5

Johannes M. Luetz The Open Access (OA) production of this book was made possible by additional contributions of donors who are acknowledged on page xxvii.

© The Editor(s) (if applicable) and The Author(s) 2025. This book is an open access publication.

Open Access This book is licensed under the terms of the Creative Commons Attribution 4.0 International License (http://creativecommons.org/licenses/by/4.0/), which permits use, sharing, adaptation, distribution and reproduction in any medium or format, as long as you give appropriate credit to the original author(s) and the source, provide a link to the Creative Commons license and indicate if changes were made.
The images or other third party material in this book are included in the book's Creative Commons license, unless indicated otherwise in a credit line to the material. If material is not included in the book's Creative Commons license and your intended use is not permitted by statutory regulation or exceeds the permitted use, you will need to obtain permission directly from the copyright holder.
The use of general descriptive names, registered names, trademarks, service marks, etc. in this publication does not imply, even in the absence of a specific statement, that such names are exempt from the relevant protective laws and regulations and therefore free for general use.
The publisher, the authors and the editors are safe to assume that the advice and information in this book are believed to be true and accurate at the date of publication. Neither the publisher nor the authors or the editors give a warranty, expressed or implied, with respect to the material contained herein or for any errors or omissions that may have been made. The publisher remains neutral with regard to jurisdictional claims in published maps and institutional affiliations.

This Springer imprint is published by the registered company Springer Nature Switzerland AG
The registered company address is: Gewerbestrasse 11, 6330 Cham, Switzerland

If disposing of this product, please recycle the paper.

Dedicated to Aunty Koomba, Angie Sinclair, Sister Kate, Heather Ferguson, Mrs Mac, and all the AMAZING, RESILIENT, CAPABLE prisoners who have taught me so much.

Foreword

Although this may seem unorthodox, let me begin by saying what this Foreword does *not* do. It does not review the benefits of art and art therapy inside, nor does it provide many empirical and theoretical perspectives. There is no need for this. Plenty of publications [*now*] provide this; and not to put too fine a point on it, so does this book [*sorry; I don't mean to get ahead of myself*]. What this Foreword *does* do is narratively create a context—through storytelling, narratives, and summaries—that ultimately crescendos into why *this* book is so important.

I've been an art therapist for over 30 years, during which I have been involved with forensic systems in one form or another. Like many art therapists, I experienced difficulty validating our work in others' eyes, or finding supportive data that underscored the importance of what we did. Nowhere was this more true than within correctional settings. When I began as a rehabilitation therapist/art [*it was what was on the right of that slash that was important; this was the designation that indicated I was an* art *therapist*] in a Northern California prison, there were few resources available on the benefits of art therapy in prison. I was familiar with one case study of a woman in prison (Levy, 1978), and one chapter by an art therapist and psychologist about art therapy in jail (Day & Onorato, 1989). That was it. Then, word came out—a book was to be published about art therapy in prison. I eagerly awaited its release. In 1994, Liebman's *Art Therapy with Offenders* was published in the United Kingdom. It provided chapters written by other art therapists that introduced the reader to what it was like working inside.

Still, while I greatly appreciate Liebman and her contributions, and have come to respect and admire her as a colleague, this book didn't scratch all of my itches. Although it covered the *what*, for me, it didn't necessarily dig deep enough for me to understand the *how* and the *why*. I also came to realize that it didn't necessarily account for the various cultural differences between the United States and the United Kingdom. As a result, seeing such a need, I took Dr. Gladys Agell's advice [*the Director of the art therapy program I attended*]: "Don't say … do." I put together a panel for the 1994 American Art Therapy Association conference held in

Chicago. Our focus was on the specific benefits of art therapy inside the walls (Gussak, Dorwin, & Hall, 1994). This was soon followed by more presentations, an invitation to put together the first book about art therapy in North American correctional systems, *Drawing Time* (1997), and several more publications.

Around the turn of the century [*21st—I'm not that old*], I accepted a position at Florida State University. My interest in Corrections began to wane. I thought I had reached saturation. However, upon arriving at FSU, I had an interesting interaction with …

> … Dr. Sally McRorie, the chairperson for my department …[who], set up a meeting with me to discuss my research agenda … After being involved with prison work for quite a while, I had wanted to get away from corrections. So, during our conversation, I suggested ways in which I might pursue an entirely different research agenda … After letting me ramble for around 23 minutes, she finally spoke up: "Yeah, that's fine … but what about that art therapy in prison stuff? Now, that's sexy." (Gussak, 2019, p. vii)

Alas, this got me thinking—and eventually I came to realize, that up until that time, while I was focusing on theoretical perspectives and vignettes that supported the *how* and the *why*, I never explored the *"but, did it really?"* In other words, there was no robust empirical support that demonstrated such effectiveness. This led to a number of quantitative and mixed-method studies that examined the efficacy of art therapy in men's and women's prisons.

Several experimental/control group, pre/posttest empirical studies/designs conducted in the early 2000s demonstrated that art therapy was indeed effective in improving mood, locus of control, socialization, and problem-solving for those who were incarcerated (Gussak, 2004, 2006, 2007, 2009). This further led to more examinations, publications, and presentations, national and international collaborations, contributions to others' books, and presentations with a rich global reach, and a follow-up text in 2019 [*if you call 22 years later a follow-up*], *Art and Art Therapy with the Imprisoned: Re-creating Identity* (Gussak, 2019). Ultimately, after reaching the right people, this culminated in the development of a state-wide art therapy in prison program, in which 4 [soon to be 5] art therapists provide services to youthful offenders in 9 [soon to be 10] prisons (Hart et al., 2023; Soape et al., 2022), which, in turn, yielded some more rich empirical and qualitative support. Additionally, the tendrils further expanded, and I was soon collaborating with arts and art therapy programs around the world.

Why do I recount all of this? What is the point, other than my own self-aggrandizement? It's simply to stress, *this takes a long time.*

Let me tell another story [*sigh—another one?*]. After 18 months of developing the contract between Florida State University and the Florida Department of Corrections to institute this unique partnership to bring art therapy inside, I was ready to hire art therapists. Given that they would be employed by the university, I needed the signature of the then-Department Chairperson. Three weeks later, after we were able to hire the clinicians, I thanked and informed him that we were moving forward. He exclaimed, "that was fast." My response? "Yeah, it only took 25 years."

This leads me to the significance of this book [*finally*] that you now hold in your hands [*or are reading on your Kindle—who am I to judge?*].

I have had the good fortune to (virtually) meet Sarah Tucker over a year ago, when she reached out to discuss some of her innovative ideas and examinations about the benefits of the arts inside prison. During our unfortunately infrequent but certainly stimulating and exciting conversations, I learned a great deal about her, her work, her drive to make this work happen, and her research agenda that culminated in this text. And then, I got to read this book.

This somewhat brief book is rich with details on the Australian prison system and how art and art therapy can facilitate change for those inside; it will indeed be a valuable resource for not just clinicians but everyone who is involved with the carceral systems. And, while it provides some empirical data—and granted, it is from a small sample that doesn't necessarily provide generalizability, but *that's beside the point*—it also provides narratives and vignettes that remind us of the people behind the numbers.

Thus, while empirical evidence is clearly important, we can't truly understand who the incarcerated truly are and what they really experience without *their* voices. We need the narratives and descriptions in order to humanize the resultant data. And who better to help convey and amplify those voices than someone who has been on both sides of the wall?

One thing I have been very careful about—and it took me many years to gain this understanding—is recognizing that, as an outsider, I need to respect the subculture that is established inside by those incarcerated, and not insinuate my own sense of correctness and privilege. I often tell my students, we are like ambassadors entering such environs in which it is vital to listen and learn from those who are a part of them. As someone who was formerly incarcerated, Sarah Tucker recognizes how fundamental it is to honor the identities of those inside and not capitulate to the labels placed on them by a dominant society. Thus, even when drenched in statistics, we continue to get a glimpse of those behind them.

Thus, as this book demonstrates, as we move forward in this much-needed exploration, we could certainly benefit from collaborating with those who have experienced both the inside *and* the outside culture.

In addition, while I have spent years exploring the benefits of art therapy within prisons, it eventually dawned on me that I was doing the same thing that frustrated me about Liebman's (1994) book, as indicated above. As her book seemed to primarily focus on a specific cultural and geopolitical system, my work initially focused on art therapy in the United States' systems, from which I tended to generalize my theoretical understandings and empirical findings to *all* correctional systems. The judicial and correctional systems within the United States are quite different from those in other countries—quite frankly, I have learned how different *each state* is from one another. My awareness of how cultural differences impact correctional systems developed; as my collaborations with people throughout Western and Eastern cultures expanded, I learned to move away from Americentric perspectives; I have learned to learn.

This book reminds me of this so clearly. In speaking with Sarah Tucker, I came to understand how different things were down under. This book provides valuable content and context on the experiences of those inside the Australian system.

And yet, what was also striking was that while some of this was foreign, some of it was indeed familiar. What I mean is that while institutions are culturally and politically influenced, there remain universal constructs—regardless of where they are, *all* prisons are dehumanizing and objectifying, and that the label *prison inmate* strips away identity, providing almost insurmountable obstacles in re-integrating back into society upon release. Sarah Tucker's program reflects and underscores Australia's specific cultural mores. Yet her focus remains on addressing each individual as a separate, significant being. As she strives to reverse the labels that the settings institute through art, she provides a useful blueprint for reversing stigmatization that *all*—art therapists, mental health clinicians, and correctional personnel—can follow regardless of where they are in the world.

As is clear to any of you holding this book [*or swiping through on your* Kindle], this book is somewhat abbreviated; indeed, in some ways, I was left hungry for more. Yet, what is important is that the authors got this book out *now*. As I continue to encourage many of my colleagues, particularly those in corrections, it is important to disseminate their information promptly. We need more, and we need it now. While the authors may not have put the final punctuation mark at the end of the research, they are indeed contributing to the *beginning* of these important conversations on the value of providing these services inside, to reach those who some in society have deemed unworthy of our reach. I expect there is a great deal more in Sarah Tucker and Johannes Luetz and that they will continue with these explorations long after this book is released. Simply put, they were smart to begin wading in *now* instead of waiting until later to dive into the deep end.

We are indebted to Sarah Tucker and Johannes Luetz, and people like them, who take the risk to put their information out there so that others can benefit from it—and I don't mean just those who offer the services or those who conduct the research. I mean those forgotten people inside who will receive such services because they are helping spread the good word.

Florida State University   Professor David E. Gussak
Tallahassee, FL, USA   (PhD, ATR-BC, HLM)
November 2024

References

Day, E. S. & Onorato, G. T. (1989). Making art in a jail setting. In H. Wadeson, J. Durkin and D. Perach (Eds.), *Advances in art therapy* (pp. 126–147). Wiley.

Gussak, D. (2019). *Art and art therapy with the imprisoned: Re-creating identity.* Routledge.

Gussak, D. (2009). The effects of art therapy on male and female inmates: Advancing the research base. *The Arts in Psychotherapy, 36*(1), 5–12. 10.1016/j.aip.2008.10.002

Gussak, D. (2007). The effectiveness of art therapy in reducing depression in prison populations. *International Journal of Offender Therapy and Comparative Criminology, 51*(4), 444–460. 10.1177/0306624X06294137

Gussak, D. (2006). Effects of art therapy with prison inmates: A follow-up study. *The Arts in Psychotherapy, 33*(3), 188–198. 10.1016/j.aip.2005.11.003

Gussak, D. (2004). Art therapy with prison inmates: a pilot study. *The Arts in Psychotherapy, 31*(4), 245–259. 10.1016/j.aip.2004.06.001

Gussak, D., Cowie, J., Dorwin, R., & Hall, N. (1994). Breaking through barriers: The advantages of art therapy in forensic settings. *Proceedings of the 25th annual conference of the American art therapy association,* p. 122.

Hart, M., Soape, E., Barlow, C., Torrech-Perez, M., Gussak, D. E., & Schubarth, A. (2023). Expanding the IDEA: Ongoing- and evolving-evaluation of an art therapy in prisons program. *International Journal of Offender Therapy and Comparative Criminology.* 10.1177/0306624X231213313

Levy, B. (1978). Art therapy in a women's correctional facility. *Art Psychotherapy, 5*(3), 157–166. 10.1016/0090-9092(78)90006-6

Liebmann, M. (1994). *Art therapy with offenders.* Jessica Kingsley Publishers.

Soape, E., Barlow, C., Gussak, D. E., Brown, J., & Schubarth, A. (2022). Creative IDEA: Introducing a statewide art therapy in prisons program. *International Journal of Offender Therapy and Comparative Criminology, 66*(12), 1285–1302. 10.1177/0306624X211013731

Institutional Review Board Statement

This study was designed and conducted according to the guidelines of the National Statement on Ethical Conduct in Human Research (2007) (National Statement (2007) developed jointly by the National Health and Medical Research Council (NHMRC), the Australian Research Council (ARC), and Universities Australia and published by the Australian Government (2007) https://www.nhmrc.gov.au/about-us/publications/national-statement-ethical-conduct-human-research-2007-updated-2018 (accessed 7 April 2023). Effective January 1, 2024, the National Statement on Ethical Conduct in Human Research 2007 (updated 2018) has been revoked and updated, whereupon the study applied the ethical guidance from the 2023 National Statement. https://www.nhmrc.gov.au/about-us/publications/national-statement-ethical-conduct-human-research-2023 (last accessed October 2, 2024). The study was approved by the CRA Human Research Ethics Committee (HREC no. EC00354) on November 9, 2020, and October 19, 2021, and by the Uniting Care Queensland Human Research Ethics Committee (HREC Ref.: Tucker_20221221) on February 9, 2023. This study is the first ex-prisoner-led research on therapeutic art delivery in Australia to receive support from a correctional agency to move forward with data collection in art therapy. The data discussed in this research were collected in 2023. The study design was informed by a multi-year pilot conducted across several prison centers.

Note About Supplementary Chapters

This book features three supplementary chapters. The materials provided therein will be useful resources for educators, art therapists, prison managers, and other stakeholders seeking to implement similar future therapeutic art programs in a variety of national and international judicial settings.

Supplementary Chapter 1: Visual Vignette (A): Group Artwork

This visual vignette documents group artwork. Numerous inmates discarded valuable work due to shame or restrictions on keeping items in their cells. Some of these pieces were salvaged and are included in this supplementary chapter with the participants' consent. Other artworks were retrieved by the inmates from the rubbish bin with the encouragement of other group members and/or the facilitator. This vignette provides a snapshot of some of the salvaged artworks and the context surrounding their creation.

Supplementary Chapter 2: Visual Vignette (B): Single Case Study

This visual vignette documents a single case study. In contrast to Supplementary Chapter 1, which features the work of multiple inmates, this chapter traces the unique journey of a single inmate who successfully participated in the "Change the Design of Your Life" (CDL) program. It features selected art exercises from the CDL workbook that was specifically created by the first author for this research. Aligning with the program design, the participant responded to input and artwork, reflecting consistent improvements.

Supplementary Chapter 3: Research Instruments and Additional Resources

The final supplementary chapter comprises a compendium of resources from this research. Featured resource materials include the mixed-methods research instrument that also invites visual responses from the participants (Appendix 1), the AART Instrument, which was used to collect data in the public art exhibition (Appendix 2), the Certificate of Completion that program participants received on the day of graduating from the program (Appendix 3), the list of art supplies used in this research (Appendix 4), and selected commentary from members of the public (Appendix 5).

Key Terms Used in This Book

Lockdown: Correctional centers can be "locked down" to accommodate a security incident, staff training days, other staff shortages, health emergencies (e.g., during the COVID-19 pandemic), cell searches, or infrastructure renovations.

Parole: "The conditional release of a prisoner after they serve part of their sentence in a prison. While on parole, they are supervised in the community until the end of their sentence" (Queensland Government, 2018a, para. 1).

Probation: "A community-based order that courts may use as an alternative to, or along with, a prison sentence" (Queensland Government, 2018b, para. 1).

PTSD: Post-traumatic stress disorder is frequent in prison. Lifetime prevalence ranges from 17.8% (male inmates) to 40.1% (female inmates). Despite these high rates, PTSD in prison is widely disregarded, under-researched, and under-diagnosed (Belet et al., 2020).

Recidivism: Refers to a foundational concept in criminology research, referring to a person's relapse into criminal behavior, typically "after the person receives sanctions or undergoes intervention for a previous crime" (NIJ, 2024, para. 1; Cowling, 2023, p. 2). Operational definitions of recidivism can vary considerably between countries, states, and/or jurisdictions and hamper effective cross-country comparisons, including on account of divergent data frameworks, at times involving reimprisonment, reconviction, or persons being detained or remanded in custody, and different lengths of follow-up periods (Yukhnenko et al., 2023). Despite these differences and difficulties, a recent international study on recidivism rates globally cross-referenced 33 countries and found that "in released prisoners, 2-year reconviction rates ranged from 17.6% in Norway to 54.9% in Australia" (Yukhnenko et al., 2023, p. 3). Crucially, according to the Australian Law Reform Commission (ALRC, 2018), controlled and funded by the Australian Government, the proportion of Aboriginal and Torres Strait Islander prisoners with a prior record of imprisonment is even higher across all Australian States and Territories, ranging between 68% (Victoria) and 85% (Australian Capital Territory):

> Nationally, the proportion of prisoners with a prior record of imprisonment was very high: three quarters (76%) of Aboriginal and Torres Strait Islander prisoners and half (49%) of non-Indigenous prisoners in 2016 had been in custody on at least one previous occasion. (ALRC, 2018, p. 120)

Global recidivism rates are considerable (Yukhnenko et al., 2020, 2023), with estimates typically interpreted as an important proxy for the effectiveness of rehabilitation and post-release programs (Cowling, 2023). High rates of prior imprisonment are also reflected in this study, wherein 86.7% of all participants indicated that their current imprisonment was not their first time in prison (Sect. 6.2; Tables 6.2 and 6.3). High recidivism rates suggest that alternative forms of therapy, rehabilitation, and reintegration are needed. This study advocates for creative methods of reducing recidivism rates in Australia and beyond.

References

ALRC—Australian Law Reform Commission. (2018). *Pathways to justice—An inquiry into the incarceration rate of Aboriginal and Torres Strait Islander Peoples.* Australian Government. https://www.alrc.gov.au/wp-content/uploads/2019/08/final_report_133_amended1.pdf

Belet, B., D'Hondt, F., Horn, M., Amad, A., Carton, F., Thomas, P., Vaiva, G., & Fovet, T. (2020). Trouble de stress post-traumatique en milieu pénitentiaire [Post-traumatic stress disorder in prison]. *L'Encephale, 46*(6), 493–499. 10.1016/j.encep.2020.04.017

Cowling, C. (2023). *Reducing recidivism: A focus on rehabilitation instead of punishment.* Lexington Books.

NIJ—National Institute of Justice. (2024). *Recidivism.* https://nij.ojp.gov/topics/corrections/recidivism

Queensland Government. (2018a). *Applying for parole.* https://www.qld.gov.au/law/sentencing-prisons-and-probation/sentencing-probation-and-parole/applying-for-parole

Queensland Government. (2018b). *Probation.* https://www.qld.gov.au/law/sentencing-prisons-and-probation/sentencing-probation-and-parole/probation

Yukhnenko, D., Farouki, L., & Fazel, S. (2023). Criminal recidivism rates globally: A 6-year systematic review update. *Journal of Criminal Justice, 88,* 102115–102115. 10.1016/j.jcrimjus.2023.102115

Preface

As I (Sarah) write this, surrounded by the artworks produced over decades by myself and prisoners and reflecting upon this book publication, what emerges is an enduring theme. Despite the consistent, sometimes pervasive life disruptions I have faced and overcome, it has been the ability to explore the inner self visually that has allowed me to creatively resolve challenging situations and experiences.

The desire to produce art in response to the multifaceted effects that incarceration has had on me personally and socially—by any means—becomes a cathartic process. Prison remains in the shadow of my life; it continues to rear its ugly head in the form of job rejections, inquisitions upon applications, additional police checks, required referees, certifications, international visa restrictions and refusals, targeted security checks, and additional administrative documents and procedures—along with a morbid curiosity from the general public that feeds off human misfortune.

Over recent years, the term "Lived Experience" has been popularized (and exploited) by the corporate media as a convenient way to refer to (often hard-earned) perspectives gained from life experiences. This has led to a sense in the broader society that the experiences have been "lived" and "completed." However, this idea falls short of reflecting the daily and ongoing struggles of ex-prisoners. There is a sense of a pervasive social misperception that there is a kind of "complete freedom" upon release and leaving the prison gates behind. This notion is incorrect. Limited by comprehensive community restrictions, prisoners who have served an extensive sentence face an increased risk of morbidity and significantly reduced opportunities. Despite public discourses suggesting justice systems are interested in engaging ex-prisoners to consult on their successful reintegration experiences, such interest often seems feigned and/or tokenistic, and the overall uptake of inviting ex-prisoner perspectives remains minimal.

"Life" post-prison is rather a "Living Experience." Social demands for harsher, more punitive justice result in new laws, draconian methods, and regressive practices that complicate (and compromise) judicial systems and limit access to interventions, both middle (mid-sentence) and end-of-pipeline (upon release). Increasing demands for police checks for employment (typically within fields of work beneficial to the wider community, such as the evidence-based therapies underpinning the mental health sector), limit opportunities to leverage the "living experience" potential of ex-prisoners, diminishing prospects for reducing recidivism.

Notably, inequality and gender divisions are particularly pronounced post-release. Female ex-prisoners commonly face sensationalized and negative media coverage, impacting (and forever tainting) their social identity. With Indigenous women being incarcerated at alarming rates, disconnecting important cultural ties and family bonds, there is a sense that the cycle of recidivism has not (yet) been challenged at the core. Even as I write this (end of August 2024), there is a push to lower the age of criminal responsibility in Australia's Northern Territory to the age of ten.[1]

Set against this background, I vividly remember the story told to me of falling deeply in love with paint, color, and visual expression at the age of three. Intermingled with the reminders of prison is the tangible memory of the anguish I experienced when being stripped of my art supplies and left in the void of my own mind while facing periods of solitary confinement. It is that anguish that motivates me to see all prisoners entitled to the basic human right to express themselves—by whatever means—specifically art.

As I (Johannes) reflect on Sarah's journey, I can say that watching her create, teach, exhibit, and gift art liberally to the world around her has become a definitive highlight for me. For the years I have known Sarah, art has been the center of her life, the focus of her joy, and the backbone of her resilience. I have felt privileged to observe this time and again.

I have watched her initiate multiple art exhibitions, including for the purposes of this research (Chap. 6). I have listened to her deliver invited keynote addresses at public art exhibitions organized by "Art from Inside"[2] (Figs. 1, 2, and 3). I have heard (and watched) her deliver highly engaging invited guest lectures to students (I remember these guest lectures vividly—I was the one who invited her to give them and always marveled at her commitment and personal investment that expressed itself through little gifts, prizes, and "student surprises" that she brought into her lectures and then threw across the lecture room to delighted students who knew the correct answer). I was also privileged to stand beside her when we co-delivered a conference paper (Autoethnographic Reflections on Prison Art Therapy and Holistic Inmate Resilience and Rehabilitation) at the 10th International Criminal Justice Conference in Melbourne, Australia (November 21–24, 2022). And I was there with her in some difficult moments when she felt dismayed after overhearing another human utter an expression of contempt in her direction (I especially remember one time when I felt utterly aghast and incredulous after she showed me an email she had just received). In all these moments, I learned so much about "Living Experience."

---

[1] https://www.sbs.com.au/news/article/youth-advocates-say-jail-terms-for-10-year-olds-would-be-a-disaster-for-northern-territory/t3ocjolmb

[2] https://artfrominside.org.au

Fig. 1 "Art from Inside" Prisoner Art Exhibition 2020 (Photo used with permission: https://artfrominside.org.au/about/) (Photo: Martin Howard / Art from Inside)

Fig. 2 Keynote at "Art from Inside" 2022 (Photo: Wendy Barron de Luetz)

More than anything else, however, I remember witnessing how skillfully and deferentially she engaged with prisoners "inside"—and ex-prisoners "outside." The absolute highlight was watching her command the respect of fifteen male inmates in a high-security prison in Australia—a sight indelibly etched in my memory. How she read the room, how she stooped down to the level of the prisoners seated at tables and creating art—how she cared, supported, and encouraged them in their

Fig. 3 Keynote at "Art from Inside" 2022 (Photo: Johannes M. Luetz)

(sometimes feeble) attempts at creating art—beyond words. What stands out to me in all these experiences with Sarah over the years is how art fundamentally "fueled" her resilience and inspired her to keep going—even when the world around her suggested that throwing in the towel was the thing to do. Relatedly, I can say with confidence that it was her love for art that underpinned her readiness to undergo as many research ethics committee reviews as were ultimately required (we can't count them off on the fingers of one hand, and they took upward of four years to complete—stretched long by bureaucratic due processes and the myriad uncertainties linked to COVID-19 and associated prison lockdowns and endless research delays). In all of this, it was Sarah's love of art that sustained her tenacity and gave her the resilience to find the will to keep going—even when circumstances and people around her suggested (and sometimes demanded) that she quit. This book is incontrovertible evidence that she did not quit.

These experiences and memories shout one message: Art in prison is powerful. Art in prison is under-appreciated. Art in prison is under-implemented. It gives voice to the voiceless. It renders visible the invisible. It returns the color where adverse life experiences have whitewashed it away. Art in prison is all this—and so much more: it heals emotional pain, soothes distress, reduces agitation, comforts the soul, calms intense emotions, relieves anxiety and boredom, aids self-regulation, facilitates self-expression, gives voice to inner experiences, enables reflection, encourages introspection, uncovers suppressed emotions, articulates trauma, externalises inner conflict, reframes narratives, reinterprets the past, reimagines the future, rebuilds identity, restores dignity, affirms personhood, reclaims voice, fosters agency, nurtures resilience, and strengthens social bonds; it humanizes—by affirming individuality beyond institutional identity; it builds bridges to the outside world—through art exhibitions; and it supports prospects of rehabilitation and social reintegration—by cultivating commitment to perseverance and practising the art of finishing.

Art is an under-recognized means to break the cycle of recidivism—the revolving door of prisons. Art offers beauty, meaning, and freedom *from* prison—during, after, and beyond the context of incarceration. To this end, I hope that one day, art therapy in prisons will become a mainstream feature in judicial centers across Australia and beyond. To the world, art might just be a craft. To a prisoner, art might just be the world.

As we (Sarah and Johannes) introduce the contents of the book, some notes about the featured artworks are in order. This book explores how art therapy can contribute to prisoner welfare, including inmate emotional well-being. For the purposes of this research, the concept of "art" is comprehended in a broad and inclusive manner. As such, art may comprise paintings, drawings, experimental/abstract, craft, coloring-in, collages, card-making, script-writing, architectural drawings, illustrations, shadings, and sketches, among others. As the availability of resources can be subject to change according to different prisons' security ratings, it is useful to accommodate a flexible approach to art that may be adjusted to suit a range of prison centers and varying inmate skills and interests.

Some explanatory notes about the use of language in this book are appropriate. The research documented in this book has arisen from the first author's experiences as an inmate, ex-prisoner, artist, art teacher, prisoner support worker, and researcher. These multiple roles include her "lived experiences" (past) and "living experiences" (ongoing) and have informed the use of language in this book.

The authors are aware of some of the debates surrounding "labeling theory" and the effects language may have on prisoners (Aldington et al., 2020; Bidwell & Polley, 2023; Braithwaite, 1989; Cullen & Johnson, 2016). Brownlee (2017) argues that generic terms like "perpetrator," "offender," and "criminal" carry misguided connotations and perpetuate unfair and unfounded assumptions about people's dispositions and inclinations. According to Cullen and Johnson (2016), the labeling of prisoners may even be associated with criminogeny[3] and is therefore opposed to furthering the aims of deterrence. More specifically, Cullen and Johnson (2016) purport that "labelling and treating people as 'offenders'—especially sending them to prison—sets in motion a number of processes that increase, rather than decrease, criminal involvement" (p. 94). Contrastingly, Bidwell and Polley (2013) advocate for the use of "progressive language" (p. 314), which Tran et al. (2018) have

---

[3] Criminogeny, derived from "crimin-" (relating to crime) and "-geny" (origin), is a term used in the field of criminology to refer to the study of the origins or causes of criminal behaviors (Akers & Sellers, 2012).

characterized as "humane and constructive language that promotes respect, dignity, understanding, and positive outlooks" (p. 4).

As experienced by the first author, living in close quarters in prison with other people sometimes opens opportunities to become lifelong "mates," thus making the term "inmate" an appropriate terminological option. By using the terms "inmate," "prisoner," "artist," and "program participant" interchangeably, the authors wish to use and propagate language that is respectful and stigma-free and allows inmates to feel accepted, respected, and supported.

Accordingly, the book uses the terms "Indigenous" and "Aboriginal" in direct reference to the Australian First Nations peoples. It follows established guidelines in the use of culturally appropriate language and terminology and uses capital letters for First Nations, Aboriginal, Indigenous, and Torres Strait Islander/s. Capital letters also apply to Traditional Owners, Custodians, Law, Culture, Kinship, Elders, and Country (Australian Government, 2022).

There is also an important personal and experiential dimension to these matters. The first author recognizes the impacts of her own Indigenous ancestry and, despite being Caucasian in appearance (as are a large part of the Stolen Generations[4]), there is an intense personal identification with Australian Aboriginal Culture, Kinship, and Country. Despite being brought up European, she finds a compassionate, empathetic, and familiar place learning from and with the Indigenous. Notably, while the first author was in prison, initially as an inmate and then later as a teacher, she was honored to be taught important aspects of Cultural Art that were permissible to be taught by Cultural Law. The second author, for his part, also shares these sentiments and esteems the Indigenous, including in areas of traditional spirituality and sustainability (Luetz, 2024).

This book proudly celebrates prisoner artwork. It is the first book on prison art therapy research in Australia using mixed methods led by an ex-prisoner. Moreover, it

- Documents and celebrates prisoner art and life from the "inside."
- Intersects the criminal–criminologist paradigm and engages diverse stakeholder groups.
- Validates therapeutic art in prisons and addresses a major gap in the literature.
- Builds on 5 years of piloting and publicizes findings and experiences from the "inside."
- Showcases a prison art program that overcomes the limitations of previous approaches.
- Presents authentic prisoner perspectives using sensitively attuned art therapy delivery.
- Highlights the significance of Indigenous art and identity within the prison milieu.

---

[4] In Australia's historical context, the term "Stolen Generations" refers to the practice of the white assimilation policy used to impose colonization. Tragically, this entails the forcible removal of Indigenous children from their families. https://bth.humanrights.gov.au/significance/historical-context-the-stolen-generations

All prisoner artists gave fully informed consent to participating in this research and having their artwork published. Crucially for the authors, it was established early on with the prisoners that their artwork would not be profited from. Therefore, honoring this commitment, including to publicize their perspectives widely and freely for the benefit of other inmates and in support of enhancing rehabilitation outcomes, it was deemed vital to adopt a fully Open Access (OA) publishing model so that the book may be made freely available to the widest possible readership and exert influence in Australia and beyond.

Correspondingly, the two authors are immensely grateful to the School of Social Sciences, University of New South Wales, for funding the Open Access publication of this book—thereby enabling the voices of prisoner-artists to be freely heard and their artwork openly celebrated. Finally, the authors also thank the publisher SAGE for permission to reprint, in slightly revised form, a part of their jointly authored peer-reviewed journal article entitled "Art Therapy in Australian Prisons—A Research Agenda,"[5] published in 2023 under a Creative Commons 4.0 license in the *International Journal of Offender Therapy and Comparative Criminology*. That methodological publication can be seen as a vital stepping stone to this book. This book is the first to publish the empirical data from this study.

Building on these prefacing comments, it is our joy and privilege to present to you *Therapeutic Prison Art Interventions: Empirical Perspectives*.

Australia
Brisbane, Australia
November 2024

Sarah Tucker
Johannes M. Luetz

References

Aldington, C., Wallace, J., & Bilby, C. (2020). Out-casted/Re-casted: Towards a lexicon for restorative artmaking and co-creation. In G. Varona Martínez (Ed.). *Arte en prisión. Justicia restaurativa a través de proyectos artísticos y narrativos*, Editorial Tirant lo Blanch, 159–203.

Akers, R. L., & Sellers, C. S. (2012). *Criminological theories: Introduction, evaluation, and application* 6. Oxford University Press.

Australian Government. (2022). *Public Service Commission First Nations Vocabulary: Using culturally appropriate language and terminology*. Australian Public Service Commission. 27 July. https://www.apsc.gov.au/working-aps/diversity-and-inclusion/diversity-inclusion-news/first-nations-vocabulary-using-culturally-appropriate-language-and-terminology

Bidwell, L., & Polley, L. (2023). 'Mind your language': What people in prison think about the language used to describe them. *Howard Journal of Crime and Justice*, 62(3), 313–324. https://doi.org/10.1111/hojo.12515

Braithwaite, J. (1989). *Crime, shame and reintegration*. Cambridge University Press.

---

[5] https://doi.org/10.1177/0306624X231165350

Brownlee, K. (2017). *Stop labelling people who commit crimes 'criminals'*. Aeon Media Group. https://aeon.co/ideas/stop-labelling-people-who-commit-crime-criminals

Cullen, F. T., & Jonson, C. L. (2016). *Correctional theory: Context and consequences*. Sage.

Luetz, J. M. (2024). Can Indigenous ecotheology save the world? Affinities between traditional worldviews and environmental sustainability. *Climate and Development*, *16*(8), 730–738. https://doi.org/10.1080/17565529.2024.2305883

Tran, N.T., Baggio, S., Dawson, A., O'Moore, E., Williams, B., Bedell, P., Simon, O., Scholten, W., Getaz, L. & Wolff, H. (2018). Words matter: A call for humanizing and respectful language to describe people who experience incarceration. *BMC International Health and Human Rights*, *18*(41). 10.1186/s12914-018-0180-4

A Huge Shout-Out to All Generous Donors!

The authors thank the School of Social Sciences, University of New South Wales, for generously supporting the Open Access publication of this book, making its contents freely accessible to a global audience and ensuring the unrestricted sharing of prisoner voices and artwork with the widest possible readership.[1]

---

[1] https://www.springernature.com/gp/open-science/journals-books/books/pricing

Tonight
I composed a picture
a mental melody
you weren't here
to see/hear it
so I'll paint/sing it
for you later
meanwhile
this documents your absence
(Stuart James Placing, 1978)

Acknowledgments

The First Author

In 2018, I (Sarah) grappled with the challenge of advocating for prisoners and their artistic aspirations when an Australian correctional agency decreased access to art. My empathy for the incarcerated stemmed from a personal understanding of their internalized pain, drawn from my own past experiences. Finding myself in a situation where reaching out seemed like the only option, I made a pivotal phone call, connecting with Dr. Johannes Luetz.

In my words, Dr. Luetz discerned a shared understanding of my lived experience and a common desire for humane prison research. With empathy, patience, and encouragement, he guided me through the complex landscape of government intricacies, policies, human rights violations, and societal biases against former offenders. Despite facing tears, setbacks, and years of dedication, this project wouldn't have come to fruition without his unwavering support and the mutual learning we experienced. I am profoundly grateful for his dedicated efforts, and he has become a revered colleague investigator.

Kudos to the awesome Senior Librarian "dude", Stephen Morton, from Christian Heritage College (CHC), for aiding my unique information requests, supporting me through electronic, and economic disadvantages, and just being an all around cool dude!

I offer my humble thanks to the various friends who have supported me, the dogs I lost, and the ones I gained during this process.

And most of all I thank my partner, who not only supported this project from the start, but he believed in it—and most of all me—easing the long arduous nights, the self-doubt, and then making it all worthwhile; he is my best friend, and love of my life.

Placing, S. J. (1978). *Walled Garden: Poems from NSW Prisons*. Ball & Chain Press, N.S.W. Department of Corrective Services. Sydney. NSW.

The Second Author

As the co-author and co-investigator, I asked Sarah Tucker, the first author and principal investigator, for permission to respond to her kind note of thanks.

I vividly remember Sarah's call to me in 2018. I was instantly taken by her research idea and instinctively willing to support it. I had no idea it would take until the end of February 2024 to complete this research. It has been an extraordinary journey as a research supervisor, and I wish to acknowledge and thank Sarah for:

- Her preparedness to undergo as many research ethics committee reviews as were ultimately required. We can't count them off on the fingers of one hand.
- Caring so genuinely for the welfare of prisoners. On two occasions, I had the privilege to see her engaging about fifteen male prisoners in her therapeutic art program in a men's high-security prison and was impressed at how good she is at what she does: how she reads the room; how she commands the prisoners' respect; how she cares for them; and how she cares for art and art therapy on the "inside"—beyond words.
- Her perseverance through two years of COVID-linked research delays, including her tenacity and resilience to find the will to keep going when circumstances and people around her suggested throwing in the towel would be the thing to do.
- Her willingness to lead two peer-reviewed articles that arose from her work, in addition to the current book:

> Tucker, S., & Luetz, J.M. (2023). Art Therapy in Australian Prisons—A Research Agenda, *International Journal of Offender Therapy and Comparative Criminology*. https://doi.org/10.1177/0306624X231165350
>
> Tucker, S. & Luetz, J.M. (2021). Art Therapy and Prison Chaplaincy—A Review of Contemporary Practices Considering New Testament Teachings. In J.M. Luetz & B. Green (Eds.), *Innovating Christian Education Research—Multidisciplinary Perspectives* (pp. 239–269). Springer. https://doi.org/10.1007/978-981-15-8856-3_15

During her time of "waiting" for the various permissions and approvals that were needed to finalize her Master of Social Science Leadership, to which this thesis research pertains, Sarah moved house twice, completed two other postgraduate degrees (Graduate Certificate in Applied Neuroscience; Christian Heritage College; completed in 2021; Graduate Certificate in Criminology; Griffith University; completed in 2022), and is currently pursuing a further degree to obtain her accreditation as an art therapist.

Sarah, what can I say? I had no clue it would take all these years to get this thesis research completed. All I can say is that I am impressed by what you accomplished. I hope it will inspire many others to continue what you started and that one day art therapy in prisons will become a mainstream feature in correctional centers across Australia and worldwide. Sarah, thank you for the privilege of learning from you and with you.

Both Authors

First, the authors wish to thank Reverend Steven Fincham (Uniting Care Prison Ministry and former State Coordinator of the State Chaplaincy Board) for his unwavering support of this research over many years. Second, they thank Professor Emerita Eileen Baldry AO FASSA FRSN, former Deputy Vice-Chancellor Equity

Diversity and Inclusion and Professor of Criminology at the University of New South Wales, Sydney, for offering constructive suggestions on draft versions of our research design and for writing the book's postscript. Third, a special note of thanks goes to several individuals who have offered constructive comments on draft versions of data collection instruments: Barbara Kienast (Senior Project Manager and voting member of the BioDesk Institutional Biosafety Committee), Reverend Doctor Geraldine Wheeler (for sharing her expertise in the interpretation and analysis of visual art), Reverend Professor Emeritus Philip Hughes and Reverend Doctor Peter Armstrong (for contributing their expertise on human research ethics), and Gilbert Deem (late ex-inmate, for offering invaluable "insider" perspectives on draft iterations of our questionnaire design). Fourth, a note of thanks goes to Uniting Care Prison Ministry Queensland for supporting this research through the acquisition of prison art supplies that are essential for the running of the art therapy programs. Fifth, huge thanks to Professor David E. Gussak ATR-BC HLM, Florida State University Graduate Art Therapy Program and Project Coordinator FSU/FL Department of Correction Art Therapy in Prisons program, for offering generous support, advice, and insight and for writing the book's Foreword. Sixth, the authors express a big note of thanks to Karen du Plessis for assistance with data analysis. Last but by no means least, the authors express their sincere thanks and appreciation to the dozens of inmates who have participated in this research, including during the five years of piloting that led up to it—thank you all!

Contents

1	Introduction: Research Background and Intended Contribution	1
2	Australian Prison History Matters: Selected Evolutionary Perspectives	7
3	Australian Prison Populations Today: Statistics and Trends	11
4	Prison Art Therapy: Overview of Previous Studies and Initiatives	15
5	Materials and Methods	25
6	Results and Key Findings	37
7	Discussion	69
8	Concluding Synthesis	85
9	Supplementary Chapter 1: Visual Vignette (A): Group Artwork	93
10	Supplementary Chapter 2: Visual Vignette (B): Single Case Study	107
11	Supplementary Chapter 3: Research Instruments and Additional Resources	135
	Postscript	145
	Index	149

List of Figures

Fig. 1	"Art from Inside" Prisoner Art Exhibition 2020 (Photo used with permission: https://artfrominside.org.au/about/) (Photo: Martin Howard / Art from Inside)	xxi
Fig. 2	Keynote at "Art from Inside" 2022 (Photo: Wendy Barron de Luetz)	xxi
Fig. 3	Keynote at "Art from Inside" 2022 (Photo: Johannes M. Luetz)	xxii
Fig. 6.1	Participant P15 responding to Question 6.2	40
Fig. 6.2	Control group participant C2 responding to Question 5.2 (pretest above, posttest below); no significant change in expression is observed	49
Fig. 6.3	Participant P2 responding to Question 5.1 (pretest above, posttest below)	49
Fig. 6.4	Participant P2 responding to Question 5.2 (pretest above, posttest below)	50
Fig. 6.5	Participant P9 responding to Question 5.2 (pretest above, posttest below)	50
Fig. 6.6	Participant P14 responding to Question 5.1 (pretest above, posttest below)	51
Fig. 6.7	Participant P12 responding to Question 5.1 (pretest above, posttest below)	51
Fig. 6.8	Participant F14: Week 2 progress illustrates unique expression of female art	52
Fig. 6.9	Poster advertising the research art exhibition at a community radio (Photo: Sarah Tucker)	53
Fig. 6.10	Art exhibition, September 11–13, 2023 (Photo: Sarah Tucker)	54
Fig. 6.11	Members of the public completing the AART instruments used in this research (Photo: Johannes M. Luetz)	54
Fig. 6.12	Artist: P1	55
Fig. 6.13	The art of reading people is a key focus of the art program (workbook pp. 13–15)	56
Fig. 6.14	Artist: P2	57

Fig. 6.15	Artist: P4	58
Fig. 6.16	Artist: P9	59
Fig. 6.17	Artist: P12	60
Fig. 6.18	Draft of final (intended) artwork	60
Fig. 6.19	Artist: P14	61
Fig. 6.20	The final artwork placard reflects considerable self- and life awareness.	62
Fig. 6.21	Artist: P15	63
Fig. 6.22	Researcher journal with locking mechanism (Photo: Sarah Tucker)	66
Fig. 7.1	Participant CONT-02 responding to Question 6.4 (pretest above, posttest below)	71
Fig. 7.2	Nearly completed final artwork produced by non-completing P8	72
Fig. 7.3	Control group participant C2 responding to Question 6.5 (pretest above, posttest below). The responses signify a clear request to be included in the full CDL art program.	75
Fig. 7.4	CDL Participant 11 responding to Question 5.1 (pretest), outlining the Australian Indigenous flag, which symbolizes the Indigenous People, the sun under which they live, and their Country—his "biggest dream". The outline represents the significant collective desire for independence, recognition, and treaty	78
Fig. 7.5	(**a**, **b**, **c**, **d**) Images created by CDL Participant 11 reflect his ancestral connection to Indigenous Australian themes and/or colors. Top left: A rudimentary color wheel showcases skill in color mixing methods. Top right: An incomplete but accurately brush-lined image of an Australian native plant sacred to smoking ceremonies known as "Saltbush" (Atriplex nummularia) shown in its natural habitat, the Australian scrub. To the top left of the "Saltbush" is a swatch of painted color, which is impressionistic of the weather changing in the Australian outback. Bottom left: A pencil sketch of a turtle with Australian Indigenous tribal markings on its shell. Bottom right: A black silhouette fine-lined brushed painting of a native Australian plant known as a "Black Boy" (Xanthorrhoea preissii) or in some Aboriginal Australian dialects as "Wardnu". This silhouette is set against the outline of the Australian central outback landscape in a similar style to famous Indigenous artist Albert (Elea) Namatjira	79
Fig. 7.6	Control group participant P10 responding to Question 5.1 (posttest), "the biggest dream." A line drawing of the Aboriginal Australian flag is stylized to mimic movement in the wind. To the right, there's a stylized pen outline of a soccer ball. These two images significance for Indigenous males. The images symbolize the dream of many to emulate their hero,	

List of Figures xxxix

	Wiradjuri man Harry Williams, the first Indigenous member of the Australian national soccer team to play in a FIFA World Cup in 1974	80
Fig. 9.1	P9 Progress work from Session 1.5 (see Table 6.1)	94
Fig. 9.2	P14 Progress work from Session 1.5 (Table 6.1)	94
Fig. 9.3	P15 Progress work from Session 2.5 (Table 6.1)	95
Fig. 9.4	Participants' color theory progress work	96
Fig. 9.5	P2 Preliminary understanding of primary and secondary colors	97
Fig. 9.6	P11 Final attempt	98
Fig. 9.7	P9 Final color wheel	98
Fig. 9.8	P1 Final color wheel	99
Fig. 9.9	Inmate responses to discussion on fight and flight processes (see Table 6.1)	99
Fig. 9.10	P2 Preliminary sketches for final piece	100
Fig. 9.11	P2 Preliminary sketches for final piece	101
Fig. 9.12	P1 Preliminary ideas manifesting during Sessions 4.0–6.0 (Table 6.1)	102
Fig. 9.13	P1 Preliminary ideas manifesting during Sessions 4.0–6.0 (Table 6.1)	103
Fig. 9.14	P1 Preliminary sketch for final piece	104
Fig. 9.15	Qualitative data analysis	105
Fig. 10.1	Drawing basic shapes: Pencil example exercises from Session 1	108
Fig. 10.2	First page of inmate's sketchbook: Pencil exercises drawing basic shapes	109
Fig. 10.3	Questionnaire answer reflecting the program participant's excitement and high motivation	110
Fig. 10.4	Inmate sketch of a "safe place"	110
Fig. 10.5	Drawing facial shapes	111
Fig. 10.6	Inmate developing facial features	112
Fig. 10.7	Exercises focusing on eye details	112
Fig. 10.8	Exercises emphasizing other facial features	113
Fig. 10.9	Inmate demonstrating their expanding skills	114
Fig. 10.10	Exercises focusing on human skulls	115
Fig. 10.11	Inmate sketching an anatomic form	116
Fig. 10.12	Exercises focusing on expression and facial and neck anatomy	117
Fig. 10.13	Inmate responses focusing on expression and facial and neck anatomy	118
Fig. 10.14	Exercises focusing on diverse styles and emotional expressions	119
Fig. 10.15	Inmate showing improvements in illustration skills	119
Fig. 10.16	Portrait of program facilitator produced by inmate in class	120
Fig. 10.17	Exercise to illustrate white on black	121
Fig. 10.18	Inmate's first attempt at white on black technique	122

Fig. 10.19	White on black portrait exercise	123
Fig. 10.20	Inmate's first portrait attempt (black on white)	123
Fig. 10.21	Inmate's second portrait attempt (white on black)	124
Fig. 10.22	Illustration of an Indigenous male Elder	124
Fig. 10.23	Inmate's first response to the exercise	125
Fig. 10.24	Inmate's second response to the exercise	126
Fig. 10.25	Inmate's third response to the exercise	126
Fig. 10.26	Monochrome portrait produced by the facilitator using instant coffee	127
Fig. 10.27	Inmate's response to the instant coffee exercise	128
Fig. 10.28	Golden ratio example illustration	128
Fig. 10.29	Inmate's response to working with patterns and the golden ratio	129
Fig. 10.30	Inmate's color wheel exercises	130
Fig. 10.31	Inmate's work associating colors, emotions, and actions	131
Fig. 10.32	Storyboard depicting "Rodney Respect 100%" leaving prison on release day	131
Fig. 10.33	Inmate's response to storyboard exercise	132
Fig. 11.1	Sample prisoner buy-up form showing art supplies available (2019). Prisoners need to fill in the form as shown and submit it for approval to the administration	140

List of Tables

Table 6.1	Data collection dates	38
Table 6.2	Complete commencing cohort of CDL program participants (P)	38
Table 6.3	Complete commencing cohort of control group participants (C)	39
Table 6.4	CDL program participants **(pretest)**	41
Table 6.5	CDL program participants **(posttest)**	41
Table 6.6	Control group **(pretest)**	42
Table 6.7	Control group **(posttest)**	42
Table 6.8	CDL program participants **(pretest)**	43
Table 6.9	CDL program participants **(posttest)**	43
Table 6.10	Control group **(pretest)**	44
Table 6.11	Control group **(posttest)**	44
Table 6.12	CDL program participants **(pretest)**	45
Table 6.13	CDL program participants **(posttest)**	46
Table 6.14	Control group **(pretest)**	46
Table 6.15	Control group **(posttest)**	47
Table 6.16	Data analysis derived from the AART Instrument ($n = 28$)	64
Table 11.1	CDL art supply list	141

About the Authors

Sarah Tucker (first author) is an experienced prison art therapy facilitator. In seeking to promote rehabilitation, healing, reconciliation, and recidivism prevention for offenders and society, Sarah draws on her own experiences of incarceration for background and inspiration. She served four years at Adelaide Women's Prison from 1996 until 1999. After more than two decades outside of prison and then stepping back in as an art teacher, facilitator, prisoner advocate, and briefly as an Indigenous Peoples Chaplain, she is well acquainted with both prison culture and the myriad systemic issues facing institutional incarceration today. From 2017 to 2023, she taught art therapy classes to incarcerated people in the State of Queensland while documenting and publishing her empirical research. Having grown up in poverty and then completing high school while living on the streets, Sarah is accustomed to having to overcome acute struggles, social exclusion, and cultural hurdles for herself and others. To survive the experiences that led her to prison and a post-prison life, she immersed herself in outlaw motorcycle club business management and street life, including employing and teaching numerous street youth and fundraising for youth events. Uniquely, it is her extensive life in the arts and as a tattoo artist for 25 years that gives her such broad insight and perspective toward societies forgotten and underground, leading her into interesting and unexplored research territories and topics. Sarah has experience working with various creative therapeutic interventions, including facilitating children's group therapy art workshops, individual therapy, and trauma-informed creative therapy practices. She has several undergraduate and postgraduate degrees: Bachelor of Visual Arts, University of New England (2001); Graduate Certificate in Applied Neuroscience, Christian Heritage College (2021); Graduate Certificate in Criminology, Griffith University (2022); and Master of Social Science Leadership, Christian Heritage College (2024); Associate Degree of Arts Therapy, IKON Institute (2024). To expand on this research, Sarah is currently pursuing a PhD at the University of New South Wales (UNSW), School of Social Sciences, Arts, Design & Architecture, Sydney, Australia.

Johannes M. Luetz (second author; Professor, BA/USA, MBA/Germany, PhD/Australia) is a senior social scientist based in Brisbane, Australia. He is the Director of Graduate Research and Research Development at Alphacrucis University College and serves as the institution's Chair of Human Research Ethics. He has lived and worked across countries and continents and conducts interdisciplinary humanitarian research at the science–faith, interfaith, and science–policy interface. He has consulted for World Vision, conducting research on disaster preparedness, poverty, and social exclusion, including raising awareness of the growing effects of environmental change on vulnerable communities in Asia, Africa, and Latin America. As a social scientist, Johannes has affiliations with the University of New South Wales (UNSW Sydney), where he is Adjunct Associate Professor in the School of Social Sciences, and with the University of the Sunshine Coast (USC Maroochydore), where he is Adjunct Professor in the School of Law and Society. He is Deputy Editor of the *International Journal of Climate Change Strategies and Management* and serves on the editorial boards of several international academic journals, including *Humanities and Social Sciences Communications* (nature portfolio). He has more than 100 academic publications to his credit, and his integrative research has led to several authored and edited books, including major international volumes, encyclopedias, and handbooks. Johannes is well acquainted with academic publishing. He is passionate about social justice, equality, and rehabilitation and has visited prisons in Australia, Latin America, and Europe.

Chapter 1
Introduction: Research Background and Intended Contribution

This study on contemporary art therapy in Australian prisons arises from the first author's unique experiences and perspectives as both an artist and a former inmate. As such, the research is uniquely shaped and informed by her perspectives; its inception and implementation arose from her lived (and living) experiences. This opening section, therefore, prefaces the Introduction with selected brief autobiographical information, which contextually frames the remainder of this chapter and the research presented herein.

As a prison art therapy facilitator working in conjunction with an Australian correctional agency, the principal researcher seeks to promote rehabilitation, healing, reconciliation, and recidivism prevention for both offenders and society. To this end, she draws on her own personal experiences of incarceration for background and inspiration. After nearly three decades outside of prison and then stepping back in as an art tutor and First Peoples Chaplain, she is well acquainted with both prison culture and the myriad systemic issues facing institutional incarceration today. Having developed and implemented the "Change the Design of Your Life" (CDL) art therapy program in two prisons in Australia (2018–2019), she has witnessed a high proportion of participants complete the 8-week program and then continue with their art, assimilating it as an intervention and relapse prevention tool. After 5 years of piloting, some observations noted have been: (1) inmates have grown in self-confidence through self-awareness and accountability; (2) engagement with art has reduced involvement in violence and prison drug culture; (3) some inmates have discovered art as a tool they can share with their own family members and children, thus assisting them with re-connection; and (4) art therapy has resulted in changing habitual behaviors and has strengthened cognition, especially for inmates with lower levels of education. Given these positive preliminary results, prisoner artwork might be progressively acknowledged and leveraged by community corrections as a vital, albeit underappreciated, tool for interaction and communication. More recently, the principal investigator has turned her experiences into an empirical higher education research project where she systematically analyzed the effectiveness of art therapy for prisoner rehabilitation. Having grown up in poverty and then

© The Author(s) 2025
S. Tucker, J. M. Luetz, *Therapeutic Prison Art Interventions*, SpringerBriefs in Criminology, https://doi.org/10.1007/978-3-031-85991-5_1

completing high school while living in the streets, the first author is accustomed to having to overcome acute struggles, social exclusion, and cultural hurdles for herself and others. Uniquely, it is her extensive life in the arts and as a tattoo artist for 25 years that gives her such broad insight and perspective toward societies forgotten and underground, leading her into unconventional and unexplored research territories and topics. Furthermore, with an Indigenous Australian background, she is uniquely positioned to identify and empathize with Aboriginal inmates who comprise a significant proportion of prisoner populations today (more on this in Chaps. 2, 3, and 7). It is this unique background that gives rise to the current research.

Australia has a rich art history that has been influenced by both Indigenous and migrant peoples for generations and therefore offers manifold opportunities for meaningful engagement (Bonython, 1976; Stanhope et al., 2020; Whitelaw, 1991). Even so, art therapy in prisons remains widely under-researched in Australia and beyond and represents a major gap in the literature (Cohen-Liebman, 2016; Cohen-Liebman & Gussak, 2001; Giles et al., 2016; Hass-Cohen & Carr, 2008; King, 2016; Vito et al., 2007). Although Gussak did some empirical studies in the early to mid-2000s that are noted in Chap. 4, art therapy has never been implemented widely for rehabilitative purposes to the extent that this would be desirable (e.g., Bolwerk et al., 2014; Cohen-Liebman & Gussak, 2001; D. Gussak, 2004, 2006, 2007, 2009a, 2009b). This limited uptake is regrettable. Given the diverse benefits that art therapy can have on inmate well-being and prisoner rehabilitation, mainstreaming prison art therapy is highly propitious (Schwartz et al., 2020; Tucker & Luetz, 2021). Despite the fact that "art therapy, and the art therapist, can be a tool for social change" (Green, 2019, p. 17), to date, there are no recorded studies in Australia which have investigated the therapeutic benefits of art in prison populations with measured outcomes (Djurichkovic, 2011). Literary analysis suggests that research tends to be hampered by limitations in methodological approaches that are suited to prison environments (Day, 2020; Richards & Ross, 2001; Wener, 2012). By engaging "inside" with inmates over the course of several weeks, this therapeutic art research addresses this knowledge gap.

Appropriate delivery of art therapies within prisons needs to consider the cross-disciplinary fields required to evaluate art therapies appropriately to reach evidence-based conclusions (Gussak, 2016; Kapitan, 2011). Although studies of this nature are yet to be implemented widely, it holds promise for future research by offering a stronger evidence base underpinning art therapy within prisons. Much prison research lacks longitudinal data due to the transient lifestyles of prisoners and relies heavily upon government-acquired statistics and data that can be devoid of human connection and interaction (Cunneen et al., 2013; Richards & Ross, 2001). This research design has been purposely created to increase response and participation rates while avoiding both impact bias and self-selection bias (Martin et al., 2018; Ngauja, 2016; Olsen, 2011).

Building on 5 years of piloting, this research transcends disciplinary boundaries by integrating qualitative and quantitative data collection and analysis within a carefully tailored mixed-methods research design (Chen & Luetz, 2020; Creswell & Creswell, 2018). By combining divergent methodologies to foster new knowledge and insights, this research embodies a prototype that promises to overcome the limitations of previous prison research (Banks et al., 1971; Banuazizi & Movahedi, 1975; Douglas et al., 1992; Haney et al., 1972; Richards & Ross, 2001; Tolich, 2014; Vito et al., 2007). This study aims to facilitate creative interventions through sensitively attuned art therapy delivery. Benefits are anticipated to accrue to diverse stakeholder groups, including inmates, chaplaincy and parole services, voluntary facilitators, policymakers, criminologists, prisoner advocacy groups, and taxpayers, among others.

This book is structured as follows. Beginning with a brief overview of the historical evolution of the prison system in Australia, Chap. 2 establishes the contemporary incarceration context. It will argue that imprisonment in Australia cannot be meaningfully comprehended apart from its historical evolutionary background. Thereafter, Chap. 3 presents contemporary statistics and trends and discusses the levels of educational attainment of prisoner populations in Australia. This context is deemed essential to comprehend both the opportunities and limitations, and constraints inherent in art therapy program delivery in Australia. Next, Chap. 4 offers a review of past prisoner art therapy initiatives in Australia. Importantly, this section shows the scarcity of engagements in this area to date. Thereafter, Chap. 5 presents the multidimensional approaches, materials, and methods. This chapter includes study context (Sect. 5.1), research design and aims (Sect. 5.2), data collection and outcome measures (Sect. 5.3), data analysis, triangulation, and synthesis (Sect. 5.4), and finally, proposal development, pretesting, retesting, and calibrating (Sect. 5.5). Next, Chap. 6 presents the results and key findings. This includes an overview of the prison centers (Sect. 6.1), the prisoner demographics (Sect. 6.2), results from the questionnaires, grouped according to quantitative (Sect. 6.3), qualitative (Sect. 6.4), and visual results (Sect. 6.5), findings from the public art exhibition (Sect. 6.6), and researcher reflections on journaling (Sect. 6.7). Thereafter, Chap. 7 offers a critical analysis of four key themes: Australia's prison environments (Sect. 7.1), how therapeutic art can offer a reduction in inmate violence (Sect. 7.2), wider correlations of the cascading benefits art programs offer to non-program participants (Sect. 7.3), and finally, how Indigenous identity is bound to artistic expression (Sect. 7.4). Finally, Chap. 8 recapitulates and synthesizes the main contribution of this research, discussing key findings (Sect. 8.1), limitations and opportunities for future research (Sect. 8.2), and recommendations for research, policy, and practice (Sect. 8.3).

This book also features three supplementary chapters. The materials provided therein will be useful resources for educators, art therapists, prison managers, and other stakeholders seeking to implement similar future therapeutic art programs in a variety of national and international judicial settings. Supplementary Chapter 1: Visual Vignette (A) documents group artwork (Chap. 9). Numerous inmates discarded valuable work due to shame or restrictions on keeping items in their cells. Some of these pieces were salvaged and are included in this supplementary chapter with the participants' consent. Other artworks were retrieved by the inmates from the rubbish bin with the encouragement of other group members and/or the facilitator. This vignette provides a snapshot of some of the salvaged artworks and the context surrounding their creation. Next, Supplementary Chapter 2: Visual Vignette

(B) documents a single case study (Chap. 10). In contrast to Supplementary Chapter 1, which features the work of multiple inmates, this chapter traces the unique journey of a single inmate who successfully participated in the "Change the Design of Your Life" (CDL) program. It features selected art exercises from the CDL workbook that was specifically created by the first author for this research. Aligning with the program design, the participant responded to input and artwork, reflecting consistent improvements. Finally, Supplementary Chapter 3: Research Instruments and Additional Resources comprises a compendium of resources from this research (Chap. 11). Featured resource materials include the mixed-methods research instrument that also invites visual responses from the participants (Appendix 1), the AART Instrument, which was used to collect data in the public art exhibition (Appendix 2), the Certificate of Completion that program participants received on the day of graduating from the program (Appendix 3), the list of art supplies used in this research (Appendix 4), and selected commentary from members of the public (Appendix 5).

References

Banks, C. W., Haney, C., Jaffe, D., & Zimbardo, P. (1971). *The Stanford prison experiment. A simulation study of the psychology of imprisonment*. web.stanford.edu/dept/spec_coll/uarch/exhibits/Narration.pdf

Banuazizi, A., & Movahedi, S. (1975). Interpersonal dynamics in a simulated prison: A methodological analysis. *The American Psychologist, 30*(2), 152–160. https://doi.org/10.1037/h0076835

Bolwerk, A., Mack-Andrick, J., Lang, F. R., Dörfler, A., & Maihöfner, C. (2014). How art changes your brain: Differential effects of visual art production and cognitive art evaluation on functional brain connectivity. *PLoS One, 9*(7), e101035. https://doi.org/10.1371/journal.pone.0101035

Bonython, K. (1976). *Modern Australian painting, 1970/1975*. Rigby.

Chen, J.-M., & Luetz, J. M. (2020). Mono-/Inter-/Multi-/Trans-/Anti-disciplinarity in Research. In W. Leal Filho, A. Marisa Azul, L. Brandli, P. Gökcin Özuyar, & T. Wall (Eds.), *Quality education* (pp. 1–17). Springer Nature.

Cohen-Liebman, M. S. (2016). Forensic art therapy: Epistemological and ontological underpinnings. In D. E. Gussak & M. L. Rosal (Eds.), *The Wiley handbook of art therapy* (pp. 469–477). John Wiley & Sons.

Cohen-Liebman, M., & Gussak, D. (2001). Investigation vs intervention: Forensic art therapy and art therapy in forensic settings. *American Journal of Art Therapy, 40*, 123–135.

Creswell, J. W., & Creswell, J. D. (Eds.). (2018). *Research design: Qualitative, quantitative and mixed methods approaches* (5th ed.). Sage.

Cunneen, C., Baldry, E., Brown, D., Brown, M., Schwartz, M., & Steel, A. (2013). *Penal culture and hyperincarceration: The revival of the prison*. Routledge.

Day, A. (2020). At a crossroads? Offender rehabilitation in Australian prisons. *Psychiatry Psychology and Law, 27*(6), 939–949.

Djurichkovic, A. (2011). *Art in prisons: A literature review of the philosophies and impacts of visual arts programs for correctional populations*. Report for Arts Access Australia. UTS Shopfront Student Series no 3. UTSePress https://opus.lib.uts.edu.au/bitstream/10453/19836/7/Art%20in%20Prisons.pdf

References

Douglas, J., Burgess, A., Burgess, A., & Ressler, R. (1992). *Crime classification manual. A standard system for investigating and classifying violent crimes*. Jossey-Bass.

Giles, M., Paris, L., & Whale, J. (2016). The role of art education in adult prisons: The Western Australian experience. *International Review of Education, 62*(6), 689–709. https://doi.org/10.1007/s11159-016-9604-3

Green, J. (2019). *Cultivating emotional wellbeing: Museums & art therapy* (Order No. 13900279). ProQuest One Academic (2295447226).

Gussak, D. (2004). Art therapy with prison inmates: A pilot study. *The Arts in Psychotherapy, 31*(4), 245–259.

Gussak, D. (2006). Effects of art therapy with prison inmates: A follow-up study. *The Arts in Psychotherapy, 33*(3), 188–198.

Gussak, D. (2007). The effectiveness of art therapy in reducing depression in prison populations. *International Journal of Offender Therapy and Comparative Criminology, 51*(4), 444–460.

Gussak, D. (2009a). Comparing the effectiveness of art therapy on depression and locus of control of male and female inmates. *The Arts in Psychotherapy, 36*(4), 202–207.

Gussak, D. (2009b). The effects of art therapy on male and female inmates: Advancing the research base. *The Arts in Psychotherapy, 36*(1), 5–12.

Gussak, D. E. (2016). Art therapy in the prison milieu. Part V: Practicing art therapy in interdisciplinary settings. In D. E. Gussak & M. L. Rosal (Eds.), *The Wiley handbook of art therapy* (pp. 478–486). Wiley.

Haney, C., Banks, C., & Zimbardo, P. (1972). Interpersonal dynamics in a simulated prison. *International Journal of Criminology and Penology, 1*(1), 69–97.

Hass-Cohen, N., & Carr, R. (2008). *Art therapy and clinical neuroscience*. Jessica Kingsley Publishers.

Kapitan, L. (2011). *Introduction to art therapy research*. Routledge.

King, J. (2016). *Art therapy, trauma and neuroscience. Theoretical and practical perspectives*. Routledge.

Martin, M. S., Crocker, A. G., Potter, B. K., Wells, G. A., Grace, R. M., & Colman, I. (2018). Mental health screening and differences in access to care among prisoners. *The Canadian Journal of Psychiatry, 63*(10), 692–700. https://doi.org/10.1177/0706743718762099

Ngauja, S. B. (2016). *Understanding my role as an art therapist in the prison system* (Order No. 10190737). ProQuest Dissertations & Theses Global. (1873209553).

Olsen, R. (2011). Self-selection bias. In P. J. Lavrakas (Ed.), *Sage research methods: Encyclopedia of survey research methods* (p. 4). Sage.

Richards, S. C., & Ross, J. I. (2001). Introducing the new school of convict criminology. *Social Justice, 28*(1), 177–190. https://www.jstor.org/stable/29768063.

Schwartz, M., Russell, S., Baldry, E., Brown, D., Cunneen, C., & Stubbs, J. (2020). *Obstacles to effective support of people released from prison: Wisdom from the field*. https://unswprimo.hosted.exlibrisgroup.com/permalink/f/a5fmj0/unsworks_modsunsworks_71832

Stanhope, Z., Bernal, A., Wright, S., & Almiron, F. J. (Kapwa). (2020). *Unfinished Business: The Art of Gordon Bennett*. Queensland Art Gallery.

Tolich, M. (2014). What can Milgram and Zimbardo teach ethics committees and qualitative researchers about minimizing harm? *Research Ethics, 10*(2), 86–96. https://doi.org/10.1177/1747016114523771

Tucker, S., & Luetz, J. M. (2021). Art therapy and prison chaplaincy—A review of contemporary practices considering New Testament teachings. In J. M. Luetz & B. Green (Eds.), *Innovating Christian education research—Multidisciplinary perspectives* (pp. 239–269). Springer. https://doi.org/10.1007/978-981-15-8856-3_15

Vito, G., Maahs, J., & Holmes, E. (2007). Criminology: Theory, research and policy. In *Crime and criminology* (2nd ed., Chapter 1, pp. 3–27). Jones and Bartlett Publishers.

Wener, R. (2012). *The environmental psychology of prisons and jails: Creating humane spaces in secure settings*. Cambridge University Press.

Whitelaw, B. (1991). *The art of Frederick McCubbin*. National Gallery of Victoria.

Open Access This chapter is licensed under the terms of the Creative Commons Attribution 4.0 International License (http://creativecommons.org/licenses/by/4.0/), which permits use, sharing, adaptation, distribution and reproduction in any medium or format, as long as you give appropriate credit to the original author(s) and the source, provide a link to the Creative Commons license and indicate if changes were made.

The images or other third party material in this chapter are included in the chapter's Creative Commons license, unless indicated otherwise in a credit line to the material. If material is not included in the chapter's Creative Commons license and your intended use is not permitted by statutory regulation or exceeds the permitted use, you will need to obtain permission directly from the copyright holder.

Chapter 2
Australian Prison History Matters: Selected Evolutionary Perspectives

Australia's contemporary prison system cannot be meaningfully understood apart from the country's history, which saw a significant proportion of early Australian settlers transported from Britain as convicts. Between 1787 and 1868, many tens of thousands of convicts were shipped from Britain and Ireland to Australia (Plowright, 2020). It is estimated that approximately 20% of the Australian population may be descended from convicts who originally arrived during the colonial period (Shaw, 1966). Although these historical realities are readily acknowledged, Australia's incarceration history has been far from romantic (Baldry & Cunneen, 2014; Cunneen et al., 2013). This chapter covers selected evolutionary perspectives on Australia's contemporary prison history.

Australian prisons are as young as their host country, which was birthed at the time of colonization (Coyle, 2009; O'Toole, 2006). Hill (2019) has documented how sweeping shifts of free thought brought on by the Age of Enlightenment in England progressively altered social morale and thereby set the conditions for rapid increases in survival crime. This situation expanded poverty and enlarged the socio-economic divide across England and London, more specifically. These socioeconomic conditions thereby laid the foundations for alternative methods of punishment, eventually leading to prisoner population increases, public executions, floggings, and ultimately, transportation to the British Empire's offshore colonies (Cunneen et al., 2013; Grant & Jewkes, 2015; Hill, 2019; Walsh, 2006). Hill (2019) covers the birthing of the Transportation Act of 1717 in his investigation into Australia's penal history through a detailed account of the political and theological motivations that underpinned the pilfering and exploration quests of that era (Harding et al., 2019). Following the American War of Independence, King George began transporting convicts to *Terra Nullius*[1] (Hill, 2019). Upon arrival of the prison hulk ships,

---

[1] The Latin expr. *Terra nullius* ('tɛrə nʌ' laɪəs/, plural terrae nullius) means "nobody's land." Evidently, in relation to Australia this term is a flagrant misnomer, given that the continent, Tasmania, and several smaller islands have historically comprised many dozens of "language, social or nation groups of Aboriginal Australia" (Australian Institute of Aboriginal and Torres

hostilities promptly ignited toward the traditional owners and inhabitants. Indigenous Australians were viewed by the Anglophones as "the least enlightened and ignorant on earth" (Hill, 2019, p. 116). Up until 1868, approximately 168,000 convicts were transported to Australia (Harding et al., 2019). A condescending perception persists to this day within streams of Anglophone Australian collective culture (Baldry & Cunneen, 2014; Kendall et al., 2020). Even though public executions were soon discontinued for colonizers and Anglophones, these punitive methods continued against Indigenous Australians as a means of pacification for the ensuing colonialization until the mid-1800s (Anderson, 2015; Cunneen et al., 2013; O'Toole, 2006). This double standard of prisoner (mis) treatment has persisted over time and still influences the Australian prison culture and management today (Gage, 2009; Russell & Baldry, 2020).

Regrettably, prison ruins are far too often misrepresented as a kind of progressive colonial history of Australia, sometimes even being revered as tourist attractions (Russell & Baldry, 2020). Relatedly, Finnane (1991) and Grant and Jewkes (2015) mention the eighteenth-century radial architectural design of many Australian prisons, which has been characterized as psychologically oppressive, specifically for Indigenous Australians (Grant & Jewkes, 2015). Furthermore, Grant and Jewkes (2015) also reflect upon the punitive models of prisoner re-education, which was aimed at exacting maximum punishment to break the human spirit of free will.

More recently, the World Wars exerted a strong social influence toward a prolific military presence within government-employed agencies, which have introduced conditions that permit officers to follow through with a dominant military-styled regime of control over the inmates (Kennedy, 1988; Nagle, 1978). This has nurtured and sustained a culture of punishment over rehabilitation that remains within the bloodlines of prison culture today (Schwartz et al., 2020; Stephenson, 1982).

References

Anderson, S. (2015). Punishment as pacification: The role of Indigenous executions on the South Australian frontier, 1836–1862. *Aboriginal History Journal, 39*, 3–26.
Australian Institute of Aboriginal and Torres Strait Islander Studies. (1996). *Map of Indigenous Australia*. Retrieved August 18, 2021, from https://aiatsis.gov.au/explore/map-indigenousaustralia
Baldry, E., & Cunneen, C. (2014). Imprisoned Indigenous women and the shadow of colonial patriarchy. *Australian and New Zealand Journal of Criminology, 47*(2), 276–298. https://doi.org/10.1177/0004865813503351
Coyle, A. (2009). *A human rights approach to prison management: Handbook for prison staff* (2nd ed.). International Centre for Prison Studies.
Cunneen, C., Baldry, E., Brown, D., Brown, M., Schwartz, M., & Steel, A. (2013). *Penal culture and hyperincarceration: The revival of the prison*. Routledge.

Strait Islander Studies [AIATSIS], 1996, para. 1); https://aiatsis.gov.au/explore/map-indigenous-australia (last accessed on April 9, 2023).

References

Finnane, M. (1991). After the convicts: Towards a history of imprisonment in Australia. *Australian and New Zealand Journal of Criminology, 24*(2), 105–117. https://doi.org/10.1177/000486589102400205

Gage, S. (2009). Boggo road prison: From riots to ruin. .

Grant, E., & Jewkes, Y. (2015). Finally fit for purpose: The evolution of Australian prison architecture. *The Prison Journal, 95*(2), 223–243. https://doi.org/10.1177/0032885515575274

Harding, R. W., Rynne, J., & Thomsen, L. (2019). History of privatized corrections. *Criminology and Public Policy, 18*(2), 241–267. https://doi.org/10.1111/1745-9133.12426

Hill, D. (2019). *Convict colony: The remarkable story of the fledgling settlement that survived against the odds*. Allen & Unwin.

Kendall, S., Lighton, S., Sherwood, J., Baldry, E., & Sullivan, E. A. (2020). Incarcerated Aboriginal women's experiences of accessing healthcare and the limitations of the 'equal treatment' principle. *International Journal for Equity in Health, 19*, 48. https://doi.org/10.1186/s12939-020-1155-3

Kennedy, J. J. (1988). *Commission of review into corrective services in Queensland*. Final Report.

Nagle, J. (1978). *Report of the royal commission into NSW prisons*. Sydney, NSW. Royal Commission into New South Wales Prisons (1976–1978). Parliament of New South Wales. G46890D-1

O'Toole, S. (2006). *The history of Australian corrections*. University of NSW Press.

Plowright, M. (2020). *Were your ancestors transported to Australia as convicts?* Migration Museum. https://www.migrationmuseum.org/were-your-ancestors-transported-to-australiaas-convicts/

Russell, S., & Baldry, E. (2020). *The Booming Industry Continued: Australian Prisons. A report*. 22 p. University of New South Wales. https://www.cclj.unsw.edu.au/article/report-booming-industry-continued-australian-prisons-2020-update

Schwartz, M., Russell, S., Baldry, E., Brown, D., Cunneen, C., & Stubbs, J. (2020). *Obstacles to effective support of people released from prison: Wisdom from the field*. https://unswprimo.hosted.exlibrisgroup.com/permalink/f/a5fmj0/unsworks_modsunsworks_71832

Shaw, A. G. L. (1966). *Convicts and the colonies: A study of penal transportation from Great Britain and Ireland to Australia and other parts of the British Empire*. Faber.

Stephenson, J. R. (1982). *Nor iron bars a cage*. Boolarong Publications.

Walsh, T. (2006). Is corrections correcting? An examination of prisoner rehabilitation policy and practice in Queensland. *Australian and New Zealand Journal of Criminology, 39*(1), 109–133.

Open Access This chapter is licensed under the terms of the Creative Commons Attribution 4.0 International License (http://creativecommons.org/licenses/by/4.0/), which permits use, sharing, adaptation, distribution and reproduction in any medium or format, as long as you give appropriate credit to the original author(s) and the source, provide a link to the Creative Commons license and indicate if changes were made.

The images or other third party material in this chapter are included in the chapter's Creative Commons license, unless indicated otherwise in a credit line to the material. If material is not included in the chapter's Creative Commons license and your intended use is not permitted by statutory regulation or exceeds the permitted use, you will need to obtain permission directly from the copyright holder.

Chapter 3
Australian Prison Populations Today: Statistics and Trends

Against the background presented in Chap. 2, the decade 1994–2004 saw Australian prison populations increase by 43%, with the upsurge considerably exceeding the 15% background increase in the Australian population (Australian Bureau of Statistics [ABS], 2004). Since then, the prisoner population has increased further, from 24,171 in 2004 (ABS, 2004) to 40,591 in 2022 (ABS, 2022; ALRC, 2018). Indigenous Australians have been particularly afflicted. In the words of the Australian Human Rights Commission, "First Nations Australians are the most incarcerated people in the world, making up just three percent of our population, but 29 percent of the prison population" (Australian Human Rights Commission [AHRC], 2021, para. 8). Sadly, despite COVID-19 leading initially to a reduction in the prisoner population overall, Indigenous incarceration has since increased further (see Sect. 7.4). According to recent figures available from the Australian Bureau of Statistics (ABS), the proportion of Aboriginal and Torres Strait Islander prisoners has steadily increased,[1] rising from 29% of all Australian prisoners (30 June 2020) to 30% (30 June 2021), 32% (30 June 2022), 33% (30 June 2023), and 36% (30 June 2024) (ABS, 2021, 2022, 2023, 2024, 2025). Tragically, this upward trend is unchanged. According to the latest figures currently available from the ABS (2025),

> From 30 June 2023 to 30 June 2024, Aboriginal and Torres Strait Islander prisoners increased by 15% (2019) to 15,871 […] The age-standardised imprisonment rate increased from 2266 to 2559 prisoners per 100,000 Aboriginal and Torres Strait Islander adult population. At 30 June 2024, Aboriginal and Torres Strait Islander prisoners accounted for 36% of all prisoners; 76% (12,120) had experienced prior adult imprisonment.

The numbers in these statistics underscore the growing need to develop and implement alternative rehabilitative methods and community interventions.

---

[1] www.abs.gov.au/statistics/people/crime-and-justice/prisoners-australia/latest-release#aboriginal-and-torres-strait-islander-prisoners.

3.1 Statistics on Inmate Education and Cognitive Disparity

One of the most prominent issues restricting inmate rehabilitation is cognitive learning ability. Statistics published in 2019 show that 33% of inmates had not completed year 10, 17% had completed year 8 or under, and 2% reported no schooling or access to schooling specifically in remote regions, while less than 19% had completed the equivalent of year 12 (Australian Institute of Health and Welfare [AIHW], 2019). Statistics further reflect that tertiary education is uncommon: diploma 4.4%, bachelor's degree 1.5%, and postgraduate study 0.5% (Baldry et al., 2018). Additionally, many prisoners experience social exclusion and are therefore more likely to have experienced abuse, neglect, and childhood trauma, in addition to mental health problems with insecure housing and unstable relationships (Guthrie et al., 2013; Morgan, 2018; Simpson et al., 2021; Social Exclusion Unit, 1997). It has been noted for decades that such cyclic and interlocking disadvantages are a major characteristic of prison populations (Centre for Policy Development, 2020; Gage, 2009; United Nations Office on Crime and Drugs, 2010).

3.2 Additional Issues and Challenges

Geographical issues compound the problem. For example, Queensland has inadequate support for remote Indigenous communities, in addition to complex legal systems, leaving Indigenous inmates poorly supported through the prison systems (Baldry et al., 2012, 2013; Black, 1987; French & Keyzer, 2012). Although census information has supported better statistical understandings by highlighting the myriad of cognitive and social difficulties faced by prisoners, this area remains widely misunderstood by external academics and researchers. According to Hayman (2012), "Australian policymakers rely heavily on international research, including research in the United States demonstrating a compelling link between education and training and reductions in recidivism" (p. 41). In 2012, Hayman reported that Australian inmate populations were ahead of US vocational training engagements by nearly 20%. Notwithstanding, overall incarceration rates in that era were significantly lower than today (27,000 in 2012 compared to 40,591 in 2022) (ABS, 2022). This suggests that less overcrowding in prisons during this earlier era permitted more ease and better access to education (Harmes et al., 2019; Hayman, 2012). Less overcrowding is generally beneficial for prisoner well-being for a range of reasons, including in areas of health and mental health (Belet et al., 2020; CSAC, 2018; Schlosser, 1998).

In summary, there are clear suggestions from research that the delivery of education, while positively correlated with reductions in recidivism, is enduringly low in Australian prisons (Newton et al., 2018). This means that alternative methods of educational engagement with prisoners are needed to address current gaps. This is explored next.

References

ALRC—Australian Law Reform Commission. (2018). *Pathways to justice—An inquiry into the incarceration rate of Aboriginal and Torres Strait Islander Peoples.* Australian Government. https://www.alrc.gov.au/wp-content/uploads/2019/08/final_report_133_amended1.pdf

Australian Bureau of Statistics. (2004). *Prisoners in Australia, 2004; No. 4517.0 – archived issue originally released 23/12/2004.* https://www.abs.gov.au/AUSSTATS/abs@.nsf/Look up/4517.0Main+Features12004?OpenDocument=

Australian Bureau of Statistics. (2021). *Prisoners in Australia, Reference period 2021.* https://www.abs.gov.au/statistics/people/crime-and-justice/prisoners-australia/2021

Australian Bureau of Statistics. (2022). *Prisoners in Australia, Reference period 2022.* https://www.abs.gov.au/statistics/people/crime-and-justice/prisoners-australia/2022

Australian Bureau of Statistics. (2023). *Prisoners in Australia. ABS. Reference period 2023.* Released 25/01/2024. https://www.abs.gov.au/statistics/people/crime-and-justice/prisoners-australia/2023

Australian Bureau of Statistics. (2024). *Prisoners in Australia, Reference period 2023.* https://www.abs.gov.au/statistics/people/crime-and-justice/prisoners-australia/latest-release

Australian Bureau of Statistics. (2025). *Prisoners in Australia. ABS. Reference period 2024.* Released 19/12/2024. https://www.abs.gov.au/statistics/people/crime-and-justice/prisoners-australia/latest-release

Australian Human Rights Commission. (2021, April 14). *Stop mass incarceration to prevent deaths in custody.* Race Discrimination. https://humanrights.gov.au/about/news/mediareleases/stop-mass-incarceration-prevent-deaths-custody

Australian Institute of Health and Welfare. (2019). *The health of Australia's prisoners 2018.* Australian Government. https://www.aihw.gov.au/getmedia/2e92f007-453d-48a1-9c6b-4c9531cf0371/aihw-phe-246.pdf.aspx?inline=true end text

Baldry, E., Dowse, L., & Clarence, M. (2012). People with intellectual and other cognitive disability in the criminal justice system. University of New South Wales. https://www.facs.nsw.gov.au/__data/assets/pdf_file/0005/591368/189-Intellectual_and_cognitive_disability_in_criminal_justice_system-accessible.pdf

Baldry, E., Clarence, M., Dowse, L., & Trollor, J. (2013). Reducing vulnerability to harm in adults with cognitive disabilities in the Australian criminal justice system. *Journal of Policy and Practice in Intellectual Disabilities, 10*(3), 222–229. https://doi.org/10.1111/jppi.12039

Baldry, E., Bright, D., Cale, J., Day, A., Dowse, L., Giles, M., Hardcastle, L., Graffam, J., McGillivray, J., Newton, D., Rowe, S., & Wodak, J. (2018). A future beyond the wall: Improving post-release employment outcomes for people leaving prison final report. *UNSW Sydney.* https://doi.org/10.26190/5b4fd2de5cfb4

Belet, B., D'Hondt, F., Horn, M., Amad, A., Carton, F., Thomas, P., Vaiva, G., & Fovet, T. (2020). Trouble de stress post-traumatique en milieu pénitentiaire [Post-traumatic stress disorder in prison]. *L'Encephale, 46*(6), 493–499. https://doi.org/10.1016/j.encep.2020.04.017

Black, S. (1987). *Low literacy and crime: A case study of the relationship* (pp. 31–39). Australian Crime Prevention Council.

Centre for Policy Development. (2020). *Partners in crime: The relationship between disadvantage and Australia's criminal justice system.* cpd.org.au/2020

CSAC—Corrective Services Administrators' Council. (2018). *Guiding principles for Corrections in Australia.* State Government of Victoria. https://www.corrections.vic.gov.au/guiding-principles-for-corrections-in-australia

French, P., & Keyzer, P. (2012, May 30). *The impact of mental impairment legislation for people with cognitive impairment: The Aboriginal Disability Justice Campaign.* Forum, Monash University. https://www.monash.edu/law/research/centres/castancentre/publicevents/events/2001-2014/2012/aboriginal-disability-justice

Gage, S. (2009). Boggo road prison: From riots to ruin. .

Guthrie, J., Levy, M., & Fforde, C. (2013). Investment in prisons: An investment in social exclusion? Linking the theories of justice reinvestment and social inclusion to examine Australia's propensity to incarcerate. *Griffith Journal of Law & Human Dignity, 1*(2), 254–281.

Harmes, M. K., Hopkins, S., & Farley, H. (2019). *Beyond incarcerated identities: Identity, bias and barriers to higher education in Australian prisons 2019*. University of Southern Queensland.

Hayman, G. W. (2012). *Turning prisons into learning communities: A new vision for corrections education* (Order No. 3541666). ProQuest One Academic (1115149061)

Morgan, A. (2018). How much does prison really cost? Comparing the costs of imprisonment with community corrections. Australian Institute of Criminology, Research Report 5, ISSN (Online) 2206-7280. https://www.aic.gov.au/sites/default/files/2020-05/rr_05_240418_2.pdf

Newton, D., Day, A., Giles, M., Wodak, J., Graffam, J., & Baldry, E. (2018). The impact of vocational education and training programs on recidivism: A systematic review of current experimental evidence. *International Journal of Offender Therapy and Comparative Criminology, 62*(1), 187–207. https://doi.org/10.1177/0306624X16645083

Schlosser, E. (1998). The prison-industrial complex. *Atlantic Monthly, 282*(6), 51–77.

Simpson, P. L., Guthrie, J., Jones, J., & Butler, T. (2021). Identifying research priorities to improve the health of incarcerated populations: Results of citizens' juries in Australian prisons. *The Lancet Public Health, 6*(10), e771–e779. https://doi.org/10.1016/S2468-2667(21)00050-5

Social Exclusion Unit. (1997). *HL Deb 09 December 1997*. vol 584 cc20-2WA. api.parliament.uk

United Nations Office on Crime and Drugs. (2010). *Handbook for prison leaders. Criminal Justice Series*. United Nations.

Open Access This chapter is licensed under the terms of the Creative Commons Attribution 4.0 International License (http://creativecommons.org/licenses/by/4.0/), which permits use, sharing, adaptation, distribution and reproduction in any medium or format, as long as you give appropriate credit to the original author(s) and the source, provide a link to the Creative Commons license and indicate if changes were made.

The images or other third party material in this chapter are included in the chapter's Creative Commons license, unless indicated otherwise in a credit line to the material. If material is not included in the chapter's Creative Commons license and your intended use is not permitted by statutory regulation or exceeds the permitted use, you will need to obtain permission directly from the copyright holder.

Chapter 4
Prison Art Therapy: Overview of Previous Studies and Initiatives

A review of the literature shows that art therapy programs are very sparse across the Australian prison landscape (Russell & Baldry, 2020; Sarre, 2010). While there has been "little systematic evaluation" (Djurichkovic, 2011, p. 1) of prison art programs worldwide, Gussak's (2016) work in American forensic environments has been a cornerstone (Gussak & Rosal, 2016) for the development and implementation of art therapy programs across the USA (Prison Arts Collective, 2020; Prison Fellowship, 2018; Sydes et al., 2017), and this work has been a relevant platform for the Australian prison art therapy context.

Rothwell (2016) encourages allied health teams and organizations to be actively involved in client-centered Gestalt therapy, which minimizes power imbalances, counter-transference, and vicarious trauma. Leveraging inmates' natural inclination for art creation in the correctional environment proves promising for addressing mental illnesses, enhancing anger management, and mitigating neurological struggles from brain injury, substance abuse, and intellectual challenges (Cohen-Liebman, 2023; Rothwell, 2016). Relatedly, the European models of restorative justice also offer progressive alternative approaches to implementing rehabilitation using arts and creative therapies (Aldington et al., 2020). Such approaches have also had a considerable influence across the Spanish-speaking world (Varona Martínez, 2020). Regrettably, Australia remains in the ideological shadows of the punitive and retributive US-American prison and justice system (Seiter, 2017). This is explored through the eyes of the American artist Jesse Krimes,[1] who uses his experience as a prisoner-artist in the US incarceration system for his own intra- and interpersonal exploration. Relevant experiences and his artwork produced in prison have been featured in the documentary "Art and Krimes by Krimes" (Nahimas, 2021). Similarly, Raymond Watson,[2] an Irish poet, artist, and ex-prisoner, uses art for personal therapeutic effect (Watson, 2013). Such stories of individual success through

---

[1] https://www.jessekrimes.com/.
[2] https://thehandsofhistory.com/raymond/.

the restorative power of art are inspiring in their context. Notably, these narratives and approaches focus solely on the individual and do not feature the cascading benefits of implementing therapeutic art in the wider prison context.

Moreover, going beyond the prison context, international literature also shows many positive outcomes of art as a therapeutic resource in extreme environments of war, racial division, and resistance to injustice, including as a bridge across cultural differences and as a tool of empowerment for the marginalized (Berman, 2019). Berman's community art counseling training center "Lefika La Phodiso"[3] is a response to the trauma of a post-apartheid South Africa and is relevant in its use of art therapy techniques to combat the aftermath of communities and individuals scarred by colonial violence and incarceration.

As with the Torch Program in Australia,[4] there are several restorative justice programs implementing post-release community art initiatives, including Mural Arts Philadelphia[5] and the Kostler Art Program in the United Kingdom.[6] The Evidence Library of the National Criminal Justice Arts Alliance houses key documents and research on the impact of creative arts-based projects, supporting a range of interventions within the criminal justice system across the United Kingdom and beyond.[7] Despite these and other promising art therapy initiatives, the Ethical Principles for Art Therapists (AATA, 2013) assert that there are notable research gaps in evidence-based art therapy practices, a point similarly underscored by McMillan (2003), Djurichkovic (2011), and Gussak (2016).

Historically, although American trends in correctional settings have been closely replicated, art as a therapy has been left behind. In 2003, at the International Forum on Education in Correctional Settings Australia (IFECSA), McMillan (2003) argued for the necessity of creative arts programs in Australian Prisons (Djurichkovic, 2011). Despite repeated calls for rehabilitation-focused art in prisons, there has been very little uptake. For example, currently, in Queensland, there are very basic art certifications offered through government-funded Technical and Further Education (TAFE). According to Hayman (2012), this government-funded TAFE education is not specifically geared toward the unique needs of prisoners. This point has been noted by Craig et al. (2013):

> The vast majority of mentally disordered offenders come from very poor material, emotional and social conditions, and expecting an over intellectualized model of any kind to help them shows a massive ignorance and disrespect for the difficult lives our clients have. (p. 153)

---

[3] https://lefikalaphodiso.co.za/about-us/.
[4] https://thetorch.org.au.
[5] https://www.muralarts.org/program/restorative-justice/.
[6] https://koestlerarts.org.uk/.
[7] https://artsincriminaljustice.org.uk/evidence-library/.

4.1 External Providers of Prison Art Initiatives

TAFE certifications do not focus on self-expression or rehabilitation but are aimed primarily at maintaining enrolment numbers (Cale et al., 2019; Hayman, 2012; Newton et al., 2018). Importantly, these TAFE certificates do not function within a personal accountability paradigm, and their success has been questioned (Eileen Baldry, personal communication, 15 March 2021; Cale et al., 2019).

A review of the literature suggests that there is an overwhelming need for more and better data on prison art therapy in Australia, with indications that programs require better facilitation and need to be far more cognizant of the manifold limitations associated with prison environments (Auty & Liebling, 2020; Belton & Barclay, 2008; Cohen-Liebman & Gussak, 2001; Craig et al., 2013; Dawe, 2007; Day et al., 2004, 2011; Djurichkovic, 2011; Giles et al., 2016; Gussak, 2004, 2006, 2007, 2009a, 2009b, 2013, 2016; Hopkins et al., 2019; Howells et al., 1997, 2004; Junge, 2006; Wright, 2005). Furthermore, according to Junge (2006), much of the available prison research is methodologically flawed and requires a more holistic systems approach. Similarly, the Arts Council of Australia (Djurichkovic, 2011) covered an exhaustive literature review of art in prisons and found repeated thematic undercurrents that call for more quantitative data on art therapy within Australian prisons and a national program focus on consistent delivery and direction.[8] Notwithstanding these calls for change, there has been very little progress made in Australia toward holistic art program delivery during the last decade.

The J-Block art project at Darwin's Women's Correctional Centre began as a Domestic and Family Violence (DV&FV) initiative (Belton & Barclay, 2008). However, the program facilitators felt that the variable nature of prison life and the transient rotation of inmates made it challenging to remain focused on therapy assisting with DV or FV. Similar problematic themes arose in other therapy programs (Byrne et al., 2001; Dean & Field, 2003; Heseltine et al., 2011; Hopkins et al., 2019). According to the literature, data collection routinely runs into unanticipated problems regarding the maintenance of inmate participation numbers, obtaining follow-up interviews, verbal communication, cultural barriers, and environmental shifts (Day, 2020; Gussak, 2016; Hopkins et al., 2019). Furthermore, facilitators have unintentionally hindered report processes due to inconsistent methods of program delivery, and there is a need for "highly trained staff" who can engage with the prison culture without inmates "hijacking" the perceived privilege (Byrne et al., 2001; Djurichkovic, 2011; Gannon et al., 2019; Giles et al., 2016). In hindsight, informal program approaches have been questioned as potentially initiating unintentional harm by triggering traumas (Djurichkovic, 2011), thus motivating a

---

[8] Following Djurichkovic's (2011) case study and appeal from Arts Council Australia for more robust and quantitative data collation on art therapies in Australian prisons, no further piloting occurred since. Maragaret Burin (2014) in *The World Today* reports on an Indigenous Art program beginning in NSW prisons titled Arts Apology. Once again, despite its perceived success, there is no further information available.

recommendation to assess the effectiveness of appropriate interpersonal art psychotherapy in Australia (Hackett et al., 2020).

4.2 Prison Art Education: Quantitative Studies

Westwood (2015) documents an Indigenous art initiative with the external community, supported by Indigenous Arts in Prisons and Community (IAPC) and aided internally through Victorian prisons. The Torch externally engages Indigenous inmates toward rehabilitation while encouraging life skills. In 2018, an evaluation of The Torch program was published by IAPC (Westwood, 2015). Despite the lack of longitudinal data, this initiative highlighted reduced recidivism rates of art program participants and additionally noted a secondary benefit in that participants were able to sell their art within Victorian prisons, which created livelihood opportunities post-release (Westwood, 2015). Contrastingly, in 2008 Queensland prevented inmates from selling art from inside as it was legally viewed as proceeds of crime (Djurichkovic, 2011). In short, experiences in this area have been very different in the two Australian states of Victoria and Queensland.

Adding to the differences, Giles (2016) extensively cross-referenced quantitative data from Western Australian prison education databases and Government census records, highlighting the relevance of any form of art education as a step toward rehabilitation motivation. However, Giles et al. (2016) argue that the measurable outcomes used to report the successful or unsuccessful facilitation of art education within prisons are truncated due to the security protocols of the authorizing bodies, impeded by the lifestyle factors of prison populations (nomadic, socially excluded, etc.). Relatedly, they call for "better measures of all impacts of art studies in prisons … including qualitative and humanitarian aspects" (p. 690).

4.3 Prison Art Education: Qualitative Studies

Arts Council Australia funded $23,000 for a Risdon prison "Create" program, which employed external professional artists to work with eight prisoners over 6 months. Dean and Field (2003) found that such arts-based programs can target and redress offending behaviors while promoting self-discipline and healing. However, despite funding, facilitation became problematic as the external artists employed to work with inmates quickly found the prison population extraordinarily unique and challenging in that they were unlike any population the artists had previously worked with:

> They had very few emotional or social skills and almost without exception see the world through a narrow and fatalistic vision. Many had never started and completed anything in their lives … (Djurichkovic, 2011, p. 20)

Furthermore, Sydes et al. (2017) have evaluated the literature, emphasizing that prison art therapy

> offers a means of expression to those who lack education, literacy, or development, and promotes the disclosure of complex emotions and experiences without compulsion ... [Art therapy] is particularly relevant for inmates as incarceration can cause and exacerbate psychological distress. Further still, this population tends to experience poorer education outcomes as well as cognitive, and communicative difficulties. (Sydes et al., 2017, p. 30; attributed to Gussak, 2007)

In summary, this literary overview highlights the need for art programs to be facilitated by professionals who understand the prison inmate culture and the prison environment and who can engage with the prison culture without inmates "hijacking" the art therapy process (Djurichkovic, 2011). Despite some hopeful attempts to implement art programs in Queensland prisons, there is no longevity with any programs, and their success has been questioned (Heseltine et al., 2011).

4.4 Prison Art Exhibitions and Ethical Considerations

Securing ethics approval is pivotal for exhibiting and sharing inmate artwork. Soape and her colleagues (2022) underscore the ethical considerations surrounding the exhibition of prisoner artworks. Given the vulnerability of incarcerated individuals, there is a potential for exploitation, including for capital gain. At the same time, it is crucial to recognize the dual role of such exhibitions, acting as a bridge between society and those separated from it (AATA, 2013; Gussak, 2019; Jones, 2021; Moon & Nolan, 2019; Soape et al., 2022). This book emphasizes the need for prison art therapists to be vigilant against any forms of coercion, advocating for equal and dignified treatment of inmates. It also stresses the importance of considering victimology and the responsibility of safeguarding the broader public.

Exhibiting prisoner artwork involves acknowledging that all words and images hold personal meaning and constitute a visual form of privileged communication. The guiding principles of opportunity, safeguards, and empowerment shape the process of exhibiting the work of individuals with mental illness (Ling & Hauck, 2022). Offering a secure and ethical space for prisoners to showcase their creative expressions empowers them, challenging biases and stereotypes held by exhibitors and viewers. This may foster empathy and connection, reducing stigma and fostering social change (Ling & Hauck, 2022; Moon & Nolan, 2019).

Adhering to these principles means taking proactive and protective measures. For example, it may involve the scrutinous removal of artworks from public spaces at the conclusion of viewings to ensure that they are shared with discretion and consideration of community interests and associated issues of victimology (Cullen & Jonson, 2016, Gussak, 2019; Soape et al., 2022). Despite these and other logistical challenges, the benefits of facilitating prisoner art exhibitions outweigh the management demands involved. Art therapists must balance protecting clients and artworks from exploitation while recognizing the emotional gains of empowering public displays. Viewers and participants contribute to the exhibition's role as a bridge between those inside and outside (AATA, 2013; Gussak, 2019; Ling & Hauck, 2022; Soape et al., 2022).

All prisoner artists gave fully informed consent to participating in this research and having their artwork published. Correspondingly, given the above, it was paramount for the two authors to allow the prisoner's voices to be freely heard, wherefore an Open Access (OA) publication model was deemed essential. Crucially, it was established early on with the prisoners that their artwork would not be profited from. Therefore, honoring this commitment, including to publicize prisoner perspectives widely and freely for the benefit of other inmates and in support of enhancing rehabilitation outcomes, it was deemed vital to make this book fully open access so that it may be freely available to the widest possible readership and exert influence in Australia and beyond.

References

AATA—American Art Therapy Association. (2013). *Ethical principles for art therapists.* . Revised December 2013.

Aldington, C., Wallace, J., & Bilby, C. (2020). Out-casted/Re-casted: Towards a lexicon for restorative artmaking and co-creation. In G. Varona Martínez (Ed.), *Arte en prisión. Justicia restaurativa a través de proyectos artísticos y narrativos* (pp. 159–203). Editorial Tirant lo Blanch.

Auty, K. M., & Liebling, A. (2020). Exploring the relationship between prison social climate and reoffending. *Justice Quarterly, 37*(2), 358–381. https://doi.org/10.1080/07418825.2018.1538421

Belton, S., & Barclay, L. (2008). *J block women of art project report: Evaluating community education in a prison setting. Dawn House in association with Ruby Gaea*. Charles Darwin University. https://www.cdu.edu.au/sites/default/files/nursing/documents/JBlockWomenofArtProjectReport.pdf

Berman, H. (2019). Redressing social injustice: Transcending and transforming the borders of art therapy training in South Africa. In A. Di Maria (Ed.), *Exploring ethical dilemmas in art therapy* (pp. 68–75). Routledge.

Burin, M. (2014). *Art apology' aims to keep young aboriginal people out of prison: An Australian-first program on the New South Wales north coast is trying a different way of breaking the cycle of crime among indigenous youth—Young offenders are saying sorry to the victims of their crime in the form of a painting*. Australian Broadcasting Corporation.

Byrne, M. K., Byrne, S., Hillman, K., & Stanley, E. (2001). Offender risk and needs assessment: Some current issues and suggestions. *Behaviour Change, 18*, 18–27.

Cale, J., Day, A., Casey, S., Bright, D., Wodak, J., Giles, M., & Baldry, E. (2019). Australian prison vocational education and training and returns to custody among male and female ex-prisoners: A cross-jurisdictional study. *Australian and New Zealand Journal of Criminology, 52*(1), 129–147. https://doi.org/10.1177/0004865818779418

Cohen-Liebman, M. S. (2023). *Forensic art therapy: The art of investigating, interviewing and testifying*. Routledge.

Cohen-Liebman, M., & Gussak, D. (2001). Investigation vs intervention: Forensic art therapy and art therapy in forensic settings. *American Journal of Art Therapy, 40*, 123–135.

Craig, L. A., Gannon, T. A., & Dixon, L. (Eds.) (2013). *What works in offender rehabilitation: An evidence-based approach to assessment and treatment: An evidence-based approach to assessment and treatment*. ProQuest Ebook Central.

References

Cullen, F. T., & Jonson, C. L. (2016). *Correctional theory: Context and consequences.* Sage.

Dawe, S. (2007). *Vocational education and training for adult prisoners and offenders in Australia: Research readings.* National Vocational Education and Training Research. NCVER. Australian Government.

Day, A. (2020). At a crossroads? Offender rehabilitation in Australian prisons. *Psychiatry Psychology and Law, 27*(6), 939–949.

Day, A., Davey, L., Heseltine, K., Howells, K., & Sarre, R. (2004). *Correctional offender treatment programs: The national picture in Australia.* Report for the Criminology Research Council. crg.aic.gov/reports

Day, A., Casey, S., Vess, J., & Huisy, G. (2011). *Assessing the social climate of Australian prisons.* Australian Institute of Criminology.

Dean, C., & Field, J. (2003). *Building lives through an artistic community, IFECSA Conference 2003 Surfers Paradise (QLD).* Australasian Corrections Education Association Inc..

Djurichkovic, A. (2011). *Art in prisons: A literature review of the philosophies and impacts of visual arts programs for correctional populations.* Report for Arts Access Australia. UTS Shopfront Student Series no 3. UTSePress https://opus.lib.uts.edu.au/bitstream/10453/19836/7/Art%20in%20Prisons.pdf

Gannon, T. A., Olver, M. E., Mallion, J. S., & James, M. (2019). Does specialized psychological treatment for offending reduce recidivism? A meta-analysis examining staff and program variables as predictors of treatment effectiveness. *Clinical Psychology Review, 73,* 101752–101752. https://doi.org/10.1016/j.cpr.2019.101752

Giles, M., Paris, L., & Whale, J. (2016). The role of art education in adult prisons: The Western Australian experience. *International Review of Education, 62*(6), 689–709. https://doi.org/10.1007/s11159-016-9604-3

Gussak, D. (2004). Art therapy with prison inmates: A pilot study. *The Arts in Psychotherapy, 31*(4), 245–259.

Gussak, D. (2006). Effects of art therapy with prison inmates: A follow-up study. *The Arts in Psychotherapy, 33*(3), 188–198.

Gussak, D. (2007). The effectiveness of art therapy in reducing depression in prison populations. *International Journal of Offender Therapy and Comparative Criminology, 51*(4), 444–460.

Gussak, D. (2009a). Comparing the effectiveness of art therapy on depression and locus of control of male and female inmates. *The Arts in Psychotherapy, 36*(4), 202–207.

Gussak, D. (2009b). The effects of art therapy on male and female inmates: Advancing the research base. *The Arts in Psychotherapy, 36*(1), 5–12.

Gussak, D. (2013, October 22). Art behind bars: The trials of providing therapy in prison—is art the key? *Psychology Today* [blogpost]. https://www.psychologytoday.com/blog/arttrial/201310/art-behind-bars

Gussak, D. E. (2016). Art therapy in the prison milieu. Part V: Practicing art therapy in interdisciplinary settings. In D. E. Gussak & M. L. Rosal (Eds.), *The Wiley handbook of art therapy* (pp. 478–486). Wiley.

Gussak, D. (2019). *Art and art therapy with the imprisoned: Re-creating identity.* Routledge.

Gussak, D. E., & Rosal, M. L. (2016). *The Wiley handbook of art therapy.* Wiley.

Hackett, S. S., Zubala, A., Aafjes-van Doorn, K., Chadwick, T., Harrison, T. L., Bourne, J., Freeston, M., Jahoda, A., Taylor, J. L., Ariti, C., McNamara, R., Pennington, L., McColl, E., & Kaner, E. (2020). Correction to: A randomised controlled feasibility study of interpersonal art psychotherapy for the treatment of aggression in people with intellectual disabilities in secure care. *Pilot and Feasibility Studies, 6*(1), 195–195. https://doi.org/10.1186/s40814-020-00743-6

Hayman, G. W. (2012). *Turning prisons into learning communities: A new vision for corrections education* (Order No. 3541666). ProQuest One Academic (1115149061)

Heseltine, K., Sarre, R., & Day, A. (2011). Prison-based correctional rehabilitation: An overview of intensive interventions for moderate to high risk offenders. *Trends and Issues in Crime and Criminal Justice, 412,* 1–6. https://www.aic.gov.au/publications/tandi/tandi412

Hopkins, A., Bartels, L., & Oxman, L. (2019). Lessons in flexibility: Introducing a yoga program in an Australian prison. *International Journal for Crime Justice and Social Democracy, 8*(4), 47–61. https://doi.org/10.5204/ijcjsd.v8i4.1046

Howells, K., Watt, B., Hall, G., & Baldwin, S. (1997). Developing programmes for violent offenders. *Legal and Criminological Psychology, 2*, 117–128.

Howells, K., Heseltine, K., Sarre, R., Davey, L. & Day, A. (2004). *Correctional offender treatment programs: The national picture in Australia*. Report for the Criminology Research Council.

Jones, P. (2021). *The arts therapies: A revolution in healthcare* (2nd ed.). Routledge.

Junge, M. B. (2006). The art therapist as social activist: Reflections on a life (Ch, 2, 40, 58). In F. Kaplan (Ed.), *Art therapy and social action: Treating the world's wounds*. Jessica Kingsley Publishers.

Ling, T. J., & Hauck, J. M. (2022). *Navigating ethical dilemmas in creative arts therapies: A case-based approach*. Routledge. https://doi.org/10.4324/9781003175124

McMillan, A. (2003). *Creative arts vision for corrections education, IFECSA Conference 2003*. Australasian Corrections Education Association Inc. Retrieved October 20, 2010, from http://www.acea.org.au/Content/2003%20papers/Paper%20McMillan.pdf

Moon, B. L., & Nolan, E. G. (2019). *Ethical issues in art therapy*. Charles C Thomas Publisher.

Nahimas, A. (2021). Art and Krimes by Krimes. *Arja*. Paramount.

Newton, D., Day, A., Giles, M., Wodak, J., Graffam, J., & Baldry, E. (2018). The impact of vocational education and training programs on recidivism: A systematic review of current experimental evidence. *International Journal of Offender Therapy and Comparative Criminology, 62*(1), 187–207. https://doi.org/10.1177/0306624X16645083

Prison Arts Collective. (2020). *Prison Arts Collective expands access to the transformative power of the arts by providing programming in prisons and for communities impacted by incarceration*. https://www.prisonartscollective.com/

Prison Fellowship. (2018). *Queensland productivity commission inquiry into imprisonment and recidivism*. www.qpc.gov.au

Rothwell, K. (Ed.) (2016). *Forensic art therapies: Anthology of practice and research*. Free Association Books UK.

Russell, S., & Baldry, E. (2020). *The Booming Industry Continued: Australian Prisons. A report*. 22 p. University of New South Wales. https://www.cclj.unsw.edu.au/article/report-booming-industry-continued-australian-prisons-2020-update

Sarre, R. (2010). Prison-based correctional offender rehabilitation programs: The 2009 national picture in Australia. *Criminology Research Council: Consultancy, c05*, 08/09.

Seiter, R. (2017). *Corrections: An introduction* (5th ed.). LSC Communications, Pearson Education.

Soape, E., Barlow, C., Gussak, D. E., Brown, J., & Schubarth, A. (2022). Creative IDEA: Introducing a statewide art therapy in prisons program. *International Journal of Offender Therapy and Comparative Criminology, 66*(12), 1285–1302.

Sydes, M., Eggins, E., & Mazzerolle, L. (2017). *What works in corrections? A review of the evaluation literature*. University of Queensland, Queensland Government.

Varona Martínez, G. (Ed.) (2020). *Arte en prisión: Justicia restaurativa a través de proyectos artísticos y narrativos*. Editorial Tirant lo Blanch. https://editorial.tirant.com/es/ebook/arte-en-prision-justicia-restaurativa-a-traves-de-proyectos-artisticos-y-narrativos-gema-varona-martinez-9788413368269

Watson, R. (2013). *The cell was my canvas: Stories of artwork inspired by the experience of political conflict in Northern Ireland*. 179 p., Kindle Edition

Westwood, M. (2015, February 11). *Unlocking creativity in prisons* [Australian edition]. The Torch. https://thetorch.org.au/wp-content/uploads/1.-Torch_Summary_of_EvaluationV8.pdf

Wright, R. (2005). Going to teach in prisons: Culture shock. *Journal of Correctional Education, 56*(1), 19–38.

Open Access This chapter is licensed under the terms of the Creative Commons Attribution 4.0 International License (http://creativecommons.org/licenses/by/4.0/), which permits use, sharing, adaptation, distribution and reproduction in any medium or format, as long as you give appropriate credit to the original author(s) and the source, provide a link to the Creative Commons license and indicate if changes were made.

The images or other third party material in this chapter are included in the chapter's Creative Commons license, unless indicated otherwise in a credit line to the material. If material is not included in the chapter's Creative Commons license and your intended use is not permitted by statutory regulation or exceeds the permitted use, you will need to obtain permission directly from the copyright holder.

Chapter 5
Materials and Methods

5.1 Study Overview, Context, and Prospects

Incarceration rates have been increasing as above, and therefore overcrowding in Australian prisons is prevalent (ABS, 2022). Current models of rehabilitation, prison culture, and prison programs are not fulfilling the demand for breaking the cycle of recidivism (Baldry, 2010; Baldry & Cunneen, 2014; Schwartz et al., 2020). Due to the continued increase in prison populations coinciding with budget cuts, programs have been cut back in most Australian prisons, and program access is being restricted due to increasing violence resulting in lockdowns of centers, thus increasing the need for contemporary interventions of a more targeted and holistic nature (CCC, 2018a, 2018b; Wordsworth, 2018). Art is proven as a successful communication tool and therapeutic practice in prison environments while decreasing the risk of vicarious trauma for empathetic workers (Cohen-Liebman & Gussak, 2001).

Art is prevalent throughout history as a meaningful visual communication tool in holistic practices. Visual input can re-enforce learning. Using art in a meaningful manner can support self-actualization (Gardner, 2014). The "Change the Design of your Life" (CDL) program has been offered successfully at two Australian prisons (2018–2019). This pilot program has run four full-length iterations and has seen a high proportion of participants successfully complete the program and continue with their art. Preliminary evidence suggests that this cross-disciplinary program assists in regulating emotional reactions in highly stressful conditions (Tucker & Luetz, 2021). Based on this early apparent success, there is a case to explore how art therapy can be most helpfully utilized to support inmates in rehabilitation, including in Queensland (Borzycki & Baldry, 2003; Robinson, 2013).

The CDL program fits the requirements of the Women's Custodial Estate Review (WCER) and therefore represents a fitting context for this research (Robinson, 2013). Art therapy within this program requires low to moderate emotional input, which limits stress and ensures that program participation is comfortable. As emphasized by Howells et al. (2004), keeping program participation within a certain hourly range is considered to be an essential requisite for successful cognitive interventions.

For the purposes and duration of this empirical research, the CDL program benefited from the support and backing of the correctional agency. As described by Seiter (2017), pertinent processes, debriefings, and inmate assessments can significantly contribute to best practice for evidence-based programs.

5.2 Research Rationale, Study Aims, and Methodological Design Features

Art therapy in the prison context remains under-researched in Australia and represents a major knowledge gap even beyond its borders (Cohen-Liebman & Gussak, 2001; Cohen-Liebman, 2016; Djurichkovic, 2011; Giles et al., 2016; Hass-Cohen & Carr, 2008; King, 2016). By engaging with selected inmates over the course of an eight-session art therapy program, this research addresses this knowledge gap. According to Green (2019), "art therapy, and the art therapist, can be a tool for social change" (p. 17). This notion is forcefully underpinned by Kaplan (2007) and Hocoy (2006). A better understanding of the efficacy of art therapy in prisons is thus conjectured to support the welfare of prisoner populations and may benefit diverse stakeholder groups, including inmates, prison ministries, sentence management, parole services, voluntary facilitators, policymakers, criminologists, and taxpayers, among others.

Research Question This research explores how art therapy can contribute to prisoner welfare, including inmate emotional well-being. For the purposes of this research, the concept of "art" is comprehended in a broad and inclusive manner. As such, the art produced comprised paintings, drawings, experimental/abstract, craft, coloring-in, collages, card-making, script-writing, architectural drawings, illustrations, shadings, and sketches, among others. (According to each prison's security ratings, the availability of resources was subject to change and altered to suit each inmate's skills and interests.)

Study Design and Methodological Features This research follows a mixed-methods exploratory design of social inquiry, which is weighted in favor of qualitative data collection and analysis (Punch, 2014, pp. 308–326). Having arisen from 5 years of piloting and extensive prison volunteering experience, the study design is appropriate for answering the research question and addressing the knowledge gap (Spencer, 2011). The study also builds on prior prison art therapy experience in Australian prisons (Tucker & Luetz, 2021).

This research follows a mixed-methods approach set within an exploratory design paradigm that is weighted in favor of qualitative research and analysis rather than quantitative study (Creswell, 2013; Creswell & Plano Clark, 2011; Punch, 2014). Even so, the study does take into account the comparatively lower levels of educational attainment among prisoner populations (AIHW, 2018), as well as mental health disorders and cognitive disability and impairment, which tend to characterize contemporary prisoner communities (Baldry, 2011; Baldry et al., 2012, 2013; MacGillivray & Baldry, 2013). Hence the research design intentionally integrated selected Likert scale questions and qualitative ("visual") questions, which were more readily comprehended and completed by inmates from different educational backgrounds.

The multi-week art therapy program schedule made the design broadly reminiscent of Action Research, which Bryman (2016) describes as follows: "action researcher … work(s) on the diagnosis … and solution of a problem … the investigator becomes a part of the study" (p. 397). Furthermore, the study also involved active listening and reflexive practice (Creswell, 2014; Gardner, 2014).

Importantly, the methodological approach rests on a pretest–posttest quasi-experimental design, which can be "[u]seful in demonstrating certain relationships between variables and effects of treatments" (Kapitan, 2011, p. 60). This means that the same questionnaire was used both before and after the CDL program. It is acknowledged that due to the small size of the study, it may be difficult to conclusively establish cause-and-effect relationships (Punch, 2014). Nevertheless, despite this limitation, including multiple methods of data collection, analysis, and synthesis (next sections) reduced the possibility of bias and avoided blurring the lines between the art activity of the CDL program and the evaluation being conducted. This process is known as "methodological triangulation" (Kapitan, 2011, p. 111) and exempts data analysis from being affected by the personal bias of the CDL art program facilitator. For this reason, the study design incorporated assistance with data analysis from external researchers. Finally, the study also involved behavioral observations (as prisoners did artwork), which was immersive and unobtrusive (Sect. 6.7) (Kapitan, 2011; Liamputtong, 2010).

As noted, exploring the nexus between art therapy and prisoner welfare, the research leaned on a qualitative research paradigm of inquiry and focused on inductive approaches and theory generation (Creswell, 2013, 2014; Kapitan, 2011; Spencer, 2011). "If the research is conducted rigorously enough … and a significant correlation does exist, the researcher may add credence to the theory of projection in art therapy" (Deaver, 2002, p. 24). A rigorous scientific methodology thus supported the art therapist in interpreting the imagery that subconsciously emerged from the participants. The study duration was approximately 6 months, in addition to approximately 5 years of piloting and study preparation as noted above. Data collection commenced in 2023, having been delayed due to government-imposed restrictions arising from the global COVID-19 pandemic.

Participant Recruitment and Enrolment The study recruited research participants from two Australian correctional centers. Regrettably for this research, data collection could not be completed at the second prison. The prison centers will be introduced in Chap. 6.

All possible participants were screened and selected by the correctional agency based on security considerations, upon meeting the required security and sentence management criteria. Prisoners were made aware of the program through posters displayed within the prisons advertising the CDL program. The ultimate participant selection was made by psychology teams and intelligence within correctional facilities. Participation was voluntary.

Based on prior piloting experience (Tucker & Luetz, 2021), each program group initially enrolled 15 art therapy participants, with numbers expected to subsequently reduce to an average of 8–12 remaining participants per prison. Furthermore, to ensure that the study yields valid and reliable findings, the questionnaire was additionally completed by a matched sample/control group comprising the same number of inmates who were not completing the CDL program. Accordingly, this study recruited a total of 30 research participants from each prison. Assistance with supplies was provided by Uniting Care Prison Ministry.

5.3 Data Collection and Outcome Measures

Data collection involved three steps.

First, in agreement with the research question, the questionnaire asked inmates to reflect on areas where art may affect—or may have affected—their emotional well-being. The following sample questions give an idea of the kinds of questions that were asked:

- How do you feel when you do art?
- What have you learned about yourself/life/others through art?

Questions were peer reviewed by an unnamed ex-inmate for appropriateness and comprehension (see Sect. 5.5). The principal researcher collected the completed questionnaires from the inmate participants prior to the start of the art sessions in Week 1 and at the end of the CDL program in Week 8. The final week marked the conclusion of the CDL program, which recognized and celebrated the inmate artwork. Participants who completed the CDL program received a signed certificate of completion (Sect. 11; Appendix 3). Participants who dropped out were invited to share their reasons for discontinuing the CDL program (exit interview), in part to limit and manage self-selection bias (Olsen, 2011), support ethical engagement by honouring participant voice, and identify patterns of attrition that might enhance program equity and design.

The questionnaire tool asked questions in the following six areas. Section 1 asked demographic and background questions. Section 2 investigated areas of inmate self-awareness, Section 3 asked questions about the prison environment, and Section 4 asked questions about the past 8 weeks. Sections 2, 3, and 4 collected quantitative data, and Sections 5 and 6 collected qualitative data. Section 5 asked visual questions, which inmates were requested to answer as "visual responses" in their own artistic expression, and Section 6 comprised open-ended questions. The research instrument is available (Sect. 11; Appendix 1).

5.3 Data Collection and Outcome Measures

To ensure the validity of the data collection tool, several questions were used with adaptation from the 2010 Health and Wellbeing Survey (Annex C)[1] Mental Health Prevalence and Wellbeing Study conducted by the Australian Government (AG). The findings from this data collection process are considered to be both valid and reliable (Australian Defence Forces [ADF], 2010). All the questions included in Section 4 of the Questionnaire were adapted from this AG survey (Questions 2.8, 2.10, 2.11, 2.15, 2.16, 4.21, 4.31, 4.34); however, minor adjustments were accommodated to suit the prison environment more aptly. Relatedly, questions were loosely based upon the Composite International Diagnostic Interview (CIDI) process used for prisoner assessment (Heffernan et al., 2012).

Second, the principal researcher took note of group dynamics and behaviors through personal note taking, journaling, and prison staff input.

Third, an art exhibition (3-day duration), supported by Uniting Care Prison Ministry, was held at a public venue (see Sect. 6.6), featuring inmate artwork generated by prisoners during the 8-week CDL program. To avoid blurring the lines between the art activity of the CDL program and the evaluation being conducted, displayed artwork was evaluated separately and independently of the art program by members of the public using the Anonymous Art Research Tool (AART), which was specifically developed for this purpose by the principal investigator. The development and use of art therapy assessment tools is important for advancing the field of art therapy. This has been highlighted by Betts (2006), "creative investigation can be fruitful" (p. 77). Furthermore, Oster and Crone (2004) state,

> Art therapy assessments can be directed and/or non-directed, and can include drawings, paintings, and/or sculptures (Arrington, 1992). Referred to by some as projective techniques (Brooke, 1996), art therapy instruments are '… alluring with their ability to illustrate concrete markers of the inner psyche' (p. 1).

The AART instrument is based on existing art evaluation tools that are discussed in the literature, including the Ulman Personality Assessment Procedure (UPAP) (Agell, 1990); Diagnostic Drawing Series (DDS) (Cohen, 1986); and the Formal Elements Art Therapy Scale (FEATS)[2] (Gantt, 1990; Gussak, 2007). The AART tool represents a simplified measuring instrument for inexperienced viewers from which the major structural forms of art are line, shape, color, and emotive symbolism (Billingsley, 1998). The AART assessment tool does not follow the exact methodology of the UPAP, DDS, or FEATS, as these assessments require specific structure and art supplies, which cannot be confirmed in some prisons. Therefore, the proposed AART instrument was based on these well-researched and structured methodologies and then adapted to be suited to the Queensland prison environment (Gantt & Anderson, 2009; Gantt et al., 1997; Gussak, 2007).

---

[1] https://www.defence.gov.au/Health/DMH/Docs/10MHPWSreport-AnnexC.pdf.

[2] The FEATS art therapy scale was developed to measure 14 different global variables, including prominence of color, problem solving, space, color fit, developmental level, implied energy, details of objects and environment, logic, realism, line quality, perseveration, and personal identity (Carol et al., 2000).

While the FEATS scale was used as a basis for developing the AART tool, this tool is limited by its ratio intervals of 1–5. Furthermore, the FEATS scale is limited in that it does not incorporate baseline data in its analysis to assess cognitive progression (Latessa et al., 2002). The AART tool, on the other hand, is ratioed at intervals of 1–10, thus allowing for more complexity, nuance, and spread to be reflected in the evaluations. While Likert scales are viewed as dimensional, they can be limiting to a level of ordinance, creating reductionist data analysis, which can rob artwork of its unique meaning (Barron et al., 1973; Betts, 2006; Carol et al., 2000). Ensuring capacity to accommodate complexity is highlighted as important by Wiersma (2000): "A rating scale presents a statement or item with a corresponding scale of categories, and respondents are asked to make judgments that most clearly approximate their perceptions" (p. 311). The AART instrument is available (Sect. 11; Appendix 2).

During Week 1 of the CDL program, inmates were asked to complete a sketch of a "safe place" (e.g., home, house, and garden). Inmate artists were deidentified using a numerical coding system to identify securely and anonymously. This artwork formed the "initial" (baseline), against which their "final" artwork was compared. Both the "initial" and "final" artwork were evaluated by members of the public during the 3-day art exhibition (Sect. 6.6).

5.4 Data Analysis, Triangulation, and Synthesis

Analyses of the three above-named data sources were undertaken as follows:

First, questionnaires were analyzed both quantitatively and qualitatively (Punch, 2014). More specifically, Sections 2, 3, and 4 of the questionnaires were analyzed quantitatively, and Sections 5 and 6 were analyzed qualitatively. As mentioned, emphasis was given to qualitative data analysis. Notwithstanding, the quantitative data analysis was undertaken to support and confirm the qualitative data analysis. Quantitative data analysis was aided by SPSS25.

Qualitative data analysis followed the norms commonly used in qualitative research (Bryman, 2016) and used thematic analysis, which Bryman (2016) defines as a process "used in connection with the analysis of qualitative data to refer to the extraction of key themes" (p. 697). "Analysis in qualitative design tends toward inductive methods that move from the specifics of a situation to broader understandings plausibly revealed by the data" (Kapitan, 2011, p. 212).

In practical terms, it was necessary to separate out those respondents who did not complete the CDL program. While the views of these participants were not discounted entirely, their perspectives were analyzed separately from the other participants who did complete the program and submitted completed questionnaires in both Week 1 and Week 8. This process limited response bias (Creswell & Creswell, 2018, p. 157).

Second, the journaling process involved reflective considerations on the part of the researcher, taking into account possible sudden alterations in behaviors, which

5.4 Data Analysis, Triangulation, and Synthesis

can manifest in prison environments (Campbell, 2015; Gussak & Rosal, 2016; Seiter, 2017). In this context, reflective practice and keen observation can take note of "unconscious phenomena [which] manifest themselves in an individual's behaviour. An attentive observer can detect them without difficulty, while the observed person remains quite unaware…" (Jung, 1980, p. 276). This approach assisted in comprehending the overall collective of the prison and individual, which Spencer (2011) has characterized as follows:

> Identities and complex cultural meanings are the object of study, understanding is always positioned and subjective. Therefore, it can be seen that the knowledge produced by research, through the visual researcher's collection and interpretation of data is socially constructed. Hence only by pursuing a reflexive approach, in which a rigorous analysis of motives behind the interpretative path chosen, takes place, might a tentative sense of validity be achieved. (p. 141)

Furthermore, journaling (Sect. 6.7) recorded the observations empirically, including any relevant autobiographical conversations that took place throughout the 8-week CDL program. This ensured that analysis did not take on the researcher's personal biases or became "interpretations of interpretations or second-order stories" (Kapitan, 2011, p. 210). In this way, it was ensured that the inmate's artwork and story remained honest to the artist/inmate, which was the subject of data analysis conducted under step three (next).

Third, despite all collected artworks being meaningful in their own right, there is merit in a systematic process of analyzing the final exhibited artworks. This involved a process of "winnowing" data so as to extract key themes. The benefits of "winnowing" imagery data have been described by Creswell and Creswell (2018) as follows:

> Because text and image data are so dense and rich, all of the information cannot be used in a qualitative study. Thus, in the analysis of the data, researchers need to 'winnow' the data (Guest et al., 2012), a process of focusing in on some of the data and disregarding other parts of it. (p. 192)

The prominence of themes emerged in colors, imageries, symbolisms, and semiotics through visual analysis (Gussak, 2007; Gussak & Rosal, 2016). Each step leaned toward the "idiographic, which is concerned with what is unique and variable" (Kapitan, 2011, p. 212). The researcher incorporated an adaptation of a process used in piloting this research, previously called the Symbolic Repetition Scale (Tucker & Luetz, 2021). Importantly, the inmates were encouraged to write their own personal reflections and artwork meanings to complement their artworks. Participating in their own story-making and storytelling process has the capacity to transform and re-imagine lives (Maruna, 2001). These personal artist statements added weight to the final analysis of inmate artwork and thus contributed to ensuring that the interpretations were valid. This approach "implies a purposeful and constant process of steering toward validity, and negotiating the reefs of misinterpretation" (Spencer, 2011, p. 158).

5.5 Proposal Development: Pretesting, Retesting, and Calibrating

This multidimensional research design was developed through an iterative process that involved input and feedback from an interdisciplinary team of stakeholders. Proposal development incorporated several review, revision, and pretesting cycles. Development took approximately 5 years to complete and benefited from multiple rounds of input. Feedback was provided by former inmates, academics, three Human Research Ethics Committee (HREC) boards, the correctional agencies' Research and Evaluation Committee, a Senior Project Manager and voting member of the BioDesk Institutional Biosafety Committee (IBC), the State Coordinator State Chaplaincy Board (SCB) for prisons, a Uniting Care Community Engagement Officer, a Professor of Criminology at the University of New South Wales (UNSW), the former Coordinator of the Uniting Care First Peoples Prison Ministry, and an artist and academic with expertise and experience in the interpretation and analysis of visual art. Peer review and pretesting led to several improvements and ultimately confirmed the adequacy of the data collection instruments (Bryman, 2016, pp. 260–261).

References

Agell, G. (1990). *The Ulman personality assessment procedure: An analysis of protocols* [Unpublished paper; referenced in Betts 2006].

Arrington, D. (1992). Art-based assessment procedures and instruments used in research. In H. Wadeson (Ed.), *A guide to conducting art therapy research* (pp. 141–159). The American Art Therapy Association.

Australian Bureau of Statistics. (2022). *Prisoners in Australia, Reference period 2022.* https://www.abs.gov.au/statistics/people/crime-and-justice/prisoners-australia/2022

Australian Defence Forces. (2010). *Mental health in the Australian defence force. 2010 ADF Mental health prevalence and wellbeing study report.* https://www.defence.gov.au/Health/DMH/Docs/MHPWSReport-FullReport.pdf

Australian Institute of Health and Welfare. (2018). *Australia's health 2018: 5.7 Prisoners.* https://www.aihw.gov.au/getmedia/0f15de30-8575-4e80-ac9d-5560633635e0/aihw-aus-221-chapter-5-7.pdf.aspx

Baldry, E. (2010). Women in transition: From Prison to …. *Current Issues in Criminal Justice, 22*(2), 253–267. https://doi.org/10.1080/10345329.2010.12035885

Baldry, E. (2011). Navigating complex pathways: People with mental health disorders and cognitive disability in the criminal justice system in NSW. *HIV Australia, 9*(1), 44.

Baldry, E., & Cunneen, C. (2014). Imprisoned Indigenous women and the shadow of colonial patriarchy. *Australian and New Zealand Journal of Criminology, 47*(2), 276–298. https://doi.org/10.1177/0004865813503351

Baldry, E., Dowse, L., & Clarence, M. (2012). People with intellectual and other cognitive disability in the criminal justice system. University of New South Wales. https://www.facs.nsw.gov.au/__data/assets/pdf_file/0005/591368/189-Intellectual_and_cognitive_disability_in_criminal_justice_system-accessible.pdf

References

Baldry, E., Clarence, M., Dowse, L., & Trollor, J. (2013). Reducing vulnerability to harm in adults with cognitive disabilities in the Australian criminal justice system. *Journal of Policy and Practice in Intellectual Disabilities, 10*(3), 222–229. https://doi.org/10.1111/jppi.12039

Barron, F., Gaines, R., Lee, D., & Marlowe, C. (1973). Problems and pitfalls in the use of rating schemes to describe visual art. *Perceptual and Motor Skills, 37*(2), 523–530. https://doi.org/10.2466/pms.1973.37.2.523

Betts, D. J. (2006). Art therapy assessments and rating instruments: Do they measure up? *The Arts in Psychotherapy, 33*(5), 422–434. https://doi.org/10.1016/j.aip.2006.08.001

Billingsley, G. (1998). *The efficacy of the diagnostic drawing series with substance-related disordered clients*. Unpublished doctoral dissertation, Walden University (cited in Betts 2005).

Borzycki, M., & Baldry, E. (2003). Promoting integration: The provision of prisoner postrelease services. *Trends and Issues in Crime and Criminal Justice, 262*. https://www.aic.gov.au/publications/tandi/tandi262

Brooke, S. L. (1996). *A therapist's guide to art therapy assessments: Tools of the trade*. Charles. C. Thomas.

Bryman, A. (2016). *Social research methods* (5th ed.). Oxford University Press.

Campbell, L. (2015). *Queensland offenders. 'Once were prisoners'*. Dead Set Publishing.

Carol, T. C., Agell, G., Cohen, B. M., & Gantt, L. (2000). Are you assessing what I am assessing? Let's take a look! *American Journal of Art Therapy, 39*(2), 48.

CCC—Crime and Corruption Commission. (2018a). *Transcript of investigative hearing*. Taskforce Flaxton Transcripts. www.ccc.qld.gov.au/sites/default/files/Docs/Public-Hearings/Flaxton/Transcripts/Taskforce-Flaxton-Transcript-Day-2-15-May-2018-Sam-Zhouand QCS.pdf

CCC—Crime and Corruption Commission. (2018b). *Transcript of investigative hearing*. Taskforce Flaxton Transcripts. www.ccc.qld.gov.au/sites/default/files/Docs/Public-Hearings/Flaxton/Transcripts/Taskforce-Flaxton-Transcript-Day-11-28-May-2018-Scott-Collins-QCS.pdf

Cohen, B. M. (1986). *The diagnostic drawing series rating guide*. (Available from the DDS Project, P.O. Box 9853, Alexandria, VA 22304; referenced in Carol et al. 2000).

Cohen-Liebman, M. S. (2016). Forensic art therapy: Epistemological and ontological underpinnings. In D. E. Gussak & M. L. Rosal (Eds.), *The Wiley handbook of art therapy* (pp. 469–477). John Wiley & Sons.

Cohen-Liebman, M., & Gussak, D. (2001). Investigation vs intervention: Forensic art therapy and art therapy in forensic settings. *American Journal of Art Therapy, 40*, 123–135.

Creswell, J. W. (2013). *Qualitative inquiry and research design: Choosing among five approaches* (3rd ed.). Sage.

Creswell, J. W. (2014). *Research design: Qualitative, quantitative, and mixed methodsapproaches* (4th ed.).

Creswell, J. W., & Creswell, J. D. (Eds.). (2018). *Research design: Qualitative, quantitative and mixed methods approaches* (5th ed.). Sage.

Creswell, J. W., & Plano Clark, V. L. (2011). *Designing and conducting mixed methods research* (2nd ed.). Sage.

Deaver, S. P. (2002). What constitutes art therapy research? *Art Therapy: Journal of the American Art Therapy Association, 19*(1), 23–27.

Djurichkovic, A. (2011). *Art in prisons: A literature review of the philosophies and impacts of visual arts programs for correctional populations*. Report for Arts Access Australia. UTS Shopfront Student Series no 3. UTSePress https://opus.lib.uts.edu.au/bitstream/10453/19836/7/Art%20in%20Prisons.pdf

Gantt, L. M. (1990). *A validity study of the formal elements art therapy scale: The rating manual* [Unpublished dissertation, University of Pittsburgh].

Gantt, L. M., & Anderson, F. (2009). The formal elements art therapy scale: A measurement system for global variables in art. *Art Therapy, 26*(3), 124–129. https://doi.org/10.1080/07421656.2009.10129372

Gantt, L. M., Goodman, R., Williams, K., & Agell, G. (1997). Prescriptions for the future. *American Journal of Art Therapy, 36*(2), 31.

Gardner, F. (2014). *Being critically reflective: Engaging in holistic practice*. Bloomsbury Publishing.

Giles, M., Paris, L., & Whale, J. (2016). The role of art education in adult prisons: The Western Australian experience. *International Review of Education, 62*(6), 689–709. https://doi.org/10.1007/s11159-016-9604-3

Green, J. (2019). *Cultivating emotional wellbeing: Museums & art therapy* (Order No. 13900279). ProQuest One Academic (2295447226).

Guest, G., MacQueen, K. M., & Namey, E. E. (2012). *Applied thematic analysis*. Sage.

Gussak, D. (2007). The effectiveness of art therapy in reducing depression in prison populations. *International Journal of Offender Therapy and Comparative Criminology, 51*(4), 444–460.

Gussak, D. E., & Rosal, M. L. (2016). *The Wiley handbook of art therapy*. Wiley.

Hass-Cohen, N., & Carr, R. (2008). *Art therapy and clinical neuroscience*. Jessica Kingsley Publishers.

Heffernan, E. B., Andersen, K. C., Dev, A., & Kinner, S. (2012). Prevalence of mental illness among Aboriginal and Torres Strait Islander people in Queensland prisons. *Medical Journal of Australia, 197*(1), 37–41.

Hocoy, D. (2006). Art therapy as a tool for social change: A conceptual model (Ch, 1, 21, 39). In F. Kaplan (Ed.), *Art therapy and social action: Treating the world's wounds*. Jessica Kingsley Publishers.

Howells, K., Heseltine, K., Sarre, R., Davey, L. & Day, A. (2004). *Correctional offender treatment programs: The national picture in Australia*. Report for the Criminology Research Council.

Jung, C. G. (1980). *The archetypes and the collective unconscious*. Routledge.

Kapitan, L. (2011). *Introduction to art therapy research*. Routledge.

Kaplan, F. (2007). *Art Therapy and social action: Treating the world's wounds*. Jessica Kingsley Publishers.

King, J. (2016). *Art therapy, trauma and neuroscience. Theoretical and practical perspectives*. Routledge.

Latessa, E. J., Cullen, F. T., & Gendreau, P. (2002). *Beyond correctional quackery: Professionalism and the possibility of effective treatment* (pp. 43–49). Federal Probation.

Liamputtong, P. (2010). *Research methods in health*. Oxford University Press.

MacGillivray, P., & Baldry, E. (2013). Indigenous Australians, mental and cognitive impairment and the criminal justice system: A complex web. *Indigenous Law Bulletin, 8*(9), 22–26.

Maruna, S. (2001). *Making good: How ex-convicts reform and re-build their lives*. American Psychological Association.

Olsen, R. (2011). Self-selection bias. In P. J. Lavrakas (Ed.), *Sage research methods: Encyclopedia of survey research methods* (p. 4). Sage.

Oster, G. D., & Crone, P. G. (2004). *Using drawings in assessment and therapy: A guide for mental health professionals* (2nd ed.). Brunner-Routledge.

Punch, K. F. (2014). *Introduction to social research: Quantitative and qualitative approaches* (3rd ed.). Sage.

Robinson, C. (2013). *Women's custodial estate review (WCER)*. National Offender Management Service. https://assets.publishing.service.gov.uk/government/uploads/system/uploads/attachment_data/file/252851/womens-custodial-estate-review.pdf

Schwartz, M., Russell, S., Baldry, E., Brown, D., Cunneen, C., & Stubbs, J. (2020). *Obstacles to effective support of people released from prison: Wisdom from the field*. https://unswprimo.hosted.exlibrisgroup.com/permalink/f/a5fmj0/unsworks_modsunsworks_71832

Seiter, R. (2017). *Corrections: An introduction* (5th ed.). LSC Communications, Pearson Education.

Spencer, S. (2011). *Visual research methods in the social sciences: Awakening visions*. Routledge.

Tucker, S., & Luetz, J. M. (2021). Art therapy and prison chaplaincy—A review of contemporary practices considering New Testament teachings. In J. M. Luetz & B. Green (Eds.), *Innovating Christian education research—Multidisciplinary perspectives* (pp. 239–269). Springer. https://doi.org/10.1007/978-981-15-8856-3_15

References

Wiersma, W. (2000). *Research methods in education: An introduction* (7th ed.). Allyn and Bacon.

Wordsworth, M. (2018). *Prisoner violence at record levels, cell 'double ups' a major contributor, commissioner admits*. 7 Aug. *ABC*. https://www.abc.net.au/news/2018-08-07/prisoner-violence-record-levels-cell-double-ups-major-problem/10070216

Open Access This chapter is licensed under the terms of the Creative Commons Attribution 4.0 International License (http://creativecommons.org/licenses/by/4.0/), which permits use, sharing, adaptation, distribution and reproduction in any medium or format, as long as you give appropriate credit to the original author(s) and the source, provide a link to the Creative Commons license and indicate if changes were made.

The images or other third party material in this chapter are included in the chapter's Creative Commons license, unless indicated otherwise in a credit line to the material. If material is not included in the chapter's Creative Commons license and your intended use is not permitted by statutory regulation or exceeds the permitted use, you will need to obtain permission directly from the copyright holder.

Chapter 6
Results and Key Findings

This chapter discusses the research findings. The chapter will begin by introducing the data collection time frame and prison centers where data collection occurred. This includes a brief overview of the eight CDL sessions (Sect. 6.1). Next, it will give an overview of the prisoner demographics, covering both the CDL program participants and control group participants (Sect. 6.2). Thereafter, the chapter will present the findings from the questionnaires: quantitative data (Sect. 6.3), qualitative written data (Sect. 6.4), and visual data (Sect. 6.5). Next, the chapter will present the findings from the public art exhibition (Sect. 6.6) and feature a synthesis of researcher reflections derived from journaling (Sect. 6.7).

6.1 Introduction to Prison Centers

Data collection occurred at two Australian prisons. This section will succinctly introduce the two centers. Consistent with Australian urban design, the two prisons were located an average distance of approximately 60 kilometers from major city area/s. Prison 1 is a high-security men's prison with a capacity of approximately 500 beds. Like other Australian prison centers, Prison 1 also faces acute overcrowding, often significantly exceeding its limits. Prison 2 is a high-security women's prison. Both prisons face similar conditions and accommodate high-profile violent offenders and some remand inmates. Following local government productivity reviews, some centers shifted their focus from education to a more restrictive regime (CCC, 2018a, 2018b). This holds relevance for the volatile environment that this research was conducted within and which pertinaciously characterizes many contemporary prisons (ABC, 2015; Biles, 1997; Harding et al., 2019).

Gaining access to the prison involved multiple steps of police checks and security clearance. Data collection commenced on March 22, 2023, and concluded on May 5, 2023. The session dates are reflected in Table 6.1.

The sessions were facilitated by the principal investigator, who was joined on the first and last week by the co-investigator. This assisted in clearly communicating the program, explaining the informed consent procedures and requirements, and facilitating the structured data collection (completing pre- and posttest questionnaires). Due to low levels of education and literacy among prisoner populations (Tables 6.2 and 6.3), it was necessary to allocate a significant amount of time on the first and

Table 6.1 Data collection dates

Date attended	Content covered
22/3/2023	**Session 0.5:** Research introduction; informed consent; program overview; pretest questionnaire completed. CDL program introduction
24/3/2023	**Session 1.5:** Holding pencils, line work, shading, and tone
29/3/2023	**Session 2.5:** This session was delayed by a center lockdown AM—Re-discussed research purpose and consent, line work, and tonal recognition. Basic anatomy, brain function; reaction and action PM—Weekend homework explained and distributed
31/3/2023	**Session 3.5:** Color theory with primaries
19/4/2023	**Session 4.0:** Catch up, and revisit basics, including some literacy
21/4/2023	**Session 5.0:** Backgrounds configuration; telling "your authentic story"
26/4/2023	**Session 6.0:** Preliminary layout, background painting
3/5/2023	**Session 7.5:** Final work to complete final artworks
5 May 2023	**Session 8:** CDL program conclusion; posttest questionnaire completed; celebration/ceremony (certificates of completion distributed) (Appendix 3)

Table 6.2 Complete commencing cohort of CDL program participants (P)

Participant code	Declared age (YRS)	Declared gender	First time in prison?	Highest level of education (YRS)
P01	27	Male	No	10
P02	22	Male	Yes	10
P03	38	Male	Yes	9
P04	41	Male	No	9
P05	21	Male	No	10
P06	24	Male	No	9
P07	21	Male	No	10
P08	33	Male	No	10
P09	32	Male	No	12; TAFE (Voc Ed)
P10	32	Male	No	12
P11	39	Male	No	9
P12	23	Male	No	10
P13	44	Male	No	No information
P14	28	Male	Yes	12; Certificate IV in Fitness
P15	28	Male	No	9
Average numbers	**30.2 YRS**	**100% M**	**First time: 20%** **Repeated: 80%**	**School attendance:** **9.21 YRS**

last day of the program to ensure all inmates were fully informed, comfortable, and aware of all aspects of their involvement in this research. All participants consented to participating in this research and having their artwork published.

Each center visit required the investigator to arrive at 8 am and commence the program at 8:30 am. Program facilitation covered a structured agenda (Chap. 5), and typically finished at 3:30 pm unless there were unforeseen disruptions (e.g.,

6.1 Introduction to Prison Centers

Table 6.3 Complete commencing cohort of control group participants (C)

Participant code	Declared age (YRS)	Declared gender	First time in prison?	Highest level of education (YRS)
C01	47	Male	No	11
C02	33	Male	Yes	9
C03	26	Male	No	10
C04	22	No information	No	8
C05	29	Male	No	12
C06	31	Male	No	8
C07	31	Male	No	10
C08	27	Male	No	10
C09	26	Male	No	10
C10	28	Male	No	8
C11	32	Male	No	8 (2 weeks grade 9)
C12	39	Male	No	9
C13	46	Male	No	5
C14	35	Male	No	9
C15	42	Male	No	10
Average numbers	**32.9 YRS**	**93.3% M 6.7% not declared**	**First time: 6.7% Repeated: 93.3%**	**School attendance: 9.13 YRS**

lockdowns). The CDL program relied on art supplies that were specifically purchased for this research by the principal investigator using funds that she raised for this purpose.

Each inmate was allocated the same supplies throughout the program (Appendix 4). The first sessions focused on basic pencil work, followed by shape formation, tonal work, color theory, landscapes, design and format, planning, and structure with each day homework allocation before prisoners returned to units, and the principal researcher cleaned up, removed rubbish, took notes, and reported any incidents as required.

Data collection commenced with a thorough session on research introduction, informed consent, program overview, and the completion of the pretest questionnaires. The research in Prison 2 had completed six sessions (the last session was on June 23, 2023) when it was prematurely terminated on June 27, 2023. Given that data from Prison 2 participants are incomplete and do not have posttest responses, this research could not fully include and honor the women's perspectives; see above (Sect. 5.2) and below (Sect. 8.2).

6.2 Prisoner Demographics (CDL Program Participants and Control Group Participants)

Fifteen prisoners commenced the CDL program (Table 6.2) and were matched against a control group with the same number of participants who had no involvement with the CDL program (Table 6.3). Notably, given the overall low levels of school attendance, many participants struggled to read and write and requested assistance with the completion of the questionnaires. Difficulties with articulation are shown in an exemplary response (Fig. 6.1). Crucially, the demographic data in Tables 6.1 and 6.2 also highlight the very high proportion of recidivists.

6.3 Questionnaire Results (Quantitative Data)

Responses to Questions 2.1–2.6 are reflected below for CDL program participants (Tables 6.4 and 6.5) and matched control group participants (Tables 6.6 and 6.7). Despite the research commencing with fifteen participants in both groups, several inmates did not complete the CDL program, were relocated to a different prison center, or were released back into the community and, therefore, were not present for the posttest data collection. Therefore, only those inmates who completed both pre- and posttests were counted in the results presented in this section. Eight CDL program participants completed pretest and posttest questionnaires, as did six control group participants. Question 2.5 was answered by seven CDL participants.

Notably, comparing pre- and posttest data from the art program participants shows an increase in interest and perhaps even passion in artwork (Tables 6.4 and 6.5). This is perhaps unsurprising given that few prisoners had any prior art skills and/or access to art education. Interestingly, the data reflect a clearly perceptible increase in the appreciation of art in times of personal distress (Question 2.3) and the ability to instill peace (Question 2.4). It also emerged that while artwork minimally reduced inmate feelings of loneliness (Questions 2.6 and 3.4), it is no panacea (Sect. 7.3).

Naturally, the conjectures made in this section are limited by a very small sample as already acknowledged. Nevertheless, some hypotheses are carefully deduced from the data. These hypotheses may be useful to test and confirm in future studies.

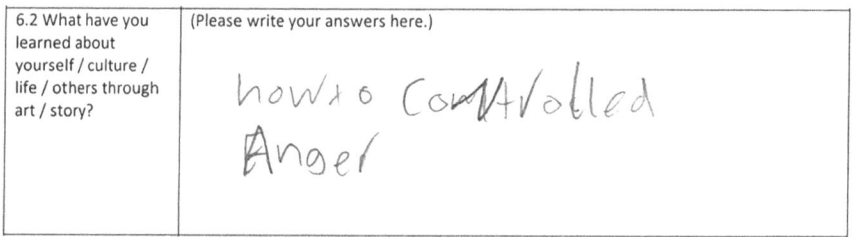

Fig. 6.1 Participant P15 responding to Question 6.2

6.3 Questionnaire Results (Quantitative Data)

Table 6.4 CDL program participants (**pretest**)

2. Questions about self-awareness							
Please tick how much you agree with each sentence.☑	Strongly agree (5)	Agree (4)	Neither (3)	Disagree (2)	Strongly disagree (1)	Total (n =?)	Average
2.1. I enjoy art	4	3	1	0	0	8	4.375
2.2. I feel good about myself when I am creative	3	4	1	0	0	8	4.25
2.3. I think beautiful art can be calming for people when upset or in distress	3	2	2	1	0	8	3.875
2.4. Creative hobbies like coloring in or writing letters help me to feel peaceful	3	5	0	0	0	8	4.375
2.5. I think art and being creative can lift my emotional well-being	4	3	0	0	0	7	4.571
2.6. Learning art and craft skills can stop me from feeling lonely	4	1	2	1	0	8	4

Table 6.5 CDL program participants (**posttest**)

2. QUESTIONS ABOUT SELF-AWARENESS							
Please tick how much you agree with each sentence. ☑	Strongly Agree (5)	Agree (4)	Neither (3)	Disagree (2)	Strongly Disagree (1)	Total (n =?)	Average
2.1 I enjoy art.	5	3	0	0	0	8	4.625
2.2 I feel good about myself when I am creative.	6	2	0	0	0	8	4.75
2.3 I think beautiful art can be calming for people when upset or in distress.	7	1	0	0	0	8	4.875
2.4 Creative hobbies like colouring in or writing letters help me to feel peaceful.	8	0	0	0	0	8	5
2.5. I think art and being creative can lift my emotional wellbeing.	6	2	0	0	0	8	4.75
2.6. Learning art and craft skills can stop me from feeling lonely.	4	3	1	0	0	8	4.375

Interestingly, the control group (Tables 6.6 and 6.7) also reflected an increase in data averages (green shading) for four questions (2.1, 2.3, 2.4, 2.5), one decrease (red shading) in average value (Question 2.6), and one question reflected the same average (yellow shading) for both pretest and posttest responses (Question 2.2). Overall, it seemed, the control group experienced some vicarious overflow effect within the

Table 6.6 Control group **(pretest)**

2. Questions about self-awareness							
Please tick how much you agree with each sentence.☑	Strongly agree (5)	Agree (4)	Neither (3)	Disagree (2)	Strongly disagree (1)	Total (n =?)	Average
2.1. I enjoy art	2	4	0	0	0	6	4.333
2.2. I feel good about myself when I am creative	2	4	0	0	0	6	4.333
2.3. I think beautiful art can be calming for people when upset or in distress	1	5	0	0	0	6	4.166
2.4. Creative hobbies like coloring in or writing letters help me to feel peaceful	1	5	0	0	0	6	4.166
2.5. I think art and being creative can lift my emotional well-being	1	5	0	0	0	6	4.166
2.6. Learning art and craft skills can stop me from feeling lonely	2	4	0	0	0	6	4.333

Table 6.7 Control group **(posttest)**

2. QUESTIONS ABOUT SELF-AWARENESS							
Please tick how much you agree with each sentence. ☑	Strongly Agree (5)	Agree (4)	Neither (3)	Disagree (2)	Strongly Disagree (1)	Total (n =?)	Average
2.1 I enjoy art.	5	1	0	0	0	6	4.833
2.2 I feel good about myself when I am creative.	2	4	0	0	0	6	4.333
2.3 I think beautiful art can be calming for people when upset or in distress.	2	4	0	0	0	6	4.333
2.4 Creative hobbies like colouring in or writing letters help me to feel peaceful.	2	4	0	0	0	6	4.333
2.5. I think art and being creative can lift my emotional wellbeing.	3	3	0	0	0	6	4.5
2.6. Learning art and craft skills can stop me from feeling lonely.	1	5	0	0	0	6	4.166

prison units, also engaging/sharing in some of the homework activities given to the CDL participants within the prison units, thus seemingly also benefiting in well-being as a result. The drop in numerical average value for Question 2.6 may be explained by a range of factors, including the pervasive loneliness in prisons

6.3 Questionnaire Results (Quantitative Data)

Table 6.8 CDL program participants (**pretest**)

3. Questions about the prison environment							
Please tick how much you agree with each sentence. ☑	Strongly agree (5)	Agree (4)	Neither (3)	Disagree (2)	Strongly disagree (1)	Total (n =?)	Average
3.1. I would like to use art for my parole application	1	3	2	1	0	7	3.571
3.2. I would be interested to learn more about art while I am in prison	5	2	1	0	0	8	4.5
3.3. Creative activities can help to reduce anger in prison	3	4	1	0	0	8	4.25
3.4. I would feel less lonely during lockdowns if I could do art	4	3	1	0	0	8	4.375

Table 6.9 CDL program participants (**posttest**)

3. QUESTIONS ABOUT THE PRISON ENVIRONMENT							
Please tick how much you agree with each sentence. ☑	Strongly Agree (5)	Agree (4)	Neither (3)	Disagree (2)	Strongly Disagree (1)	Total (n = ?)	Average
3.1 I would like to use art for my parole application.	1	4	2	0	0	7	3.857
3.2 I would be interested to learn more about art while I am in prison.	6	2	0	0	0	8	4.75
3.3 Creative activities can help to reduce anger in prison.	8	0	0	0	0	0	5
3.4 I would feel less lonely during lock downs if I could do art.	7	1	0	0	0	8	4.875

discussed above, and a sense of having been excluded from actively participating in the CDL program.

As with Tables 6.4, 6.5, 6.6, and 6.7, Tables 6.8, 6.9, 6.10, and 6.11 reflect a similar trend: improvements (green shaded data) were noted in all categories, both for the CDL program participants and the control group participants. The largest increase is most notable in Question 3.3 (Creative activities can help to reduce anger in prisons). This again supports the emergent hypothesis that art can help to reduce violence within the prison milieu. As above, this trend is replicated by the control group, which is hypothesized to be a result of the program participants communicating and collaborating with control group participants and the larger inmate population (Tables 6.12, 6.13, 6.14, and 6.15).

As anticipated, CDL participants experienced an overall decrease in worries, feelings of discouragement, restlessness, inability to remain still, and an increased ability to smile (Tables 6.12, 6.13). Interestingly, both art program participants (Tables 6.12, 6.13) and control group subjects (Tables 6.14, and 6.15) reflected a

Table 6.10 Control group (**pretest**)

3. Questions about the prison environment							
Please tick how much you agree with each sentence.☑	Strongly agree (5)	Agree (4)	Neither (3)	Disagree (2)	Strongly disagree (1)	Total (*n* =?)	Average
3.1. I would like to use art for my parole application	3	0	2	1	0	6	3.833
3.2. I would be interested to learn more about art while I am in prison	2	4	0	0	0	6	4.333
3.3. Creative activities can help to reduce anger in prison	2	3	1	0	0	6	4.166
3.4. I would feel less lonely during lockdowns if I could do art	2	3	0	1	0	6	4

Table 6.11 Control group (**posttest**)

3. QUESTIONS ABOUT THE PRISON ENVIRONMENT							
Please tick how much you agree with each sentence. ☑	Strongly Agree (5)	Agree (4)	Neither (3)	Disagree (2)	Strongly Disagree (1)	Total (n = ?)	Average
3.1 I would like to use art for my parole application.	3	1	2	0	0	6	4.166
3.2 I would be interested to learn more about art while I am in prison.	3	2	1	0	0	6	4.333
3.3 Creative activities can help to reduce anger in prison.	3	3	0	0	0	6	4.5
3.4 I would feel less lonely during lock downs if I could do art.	3	3	0	0	0	6	4.5

decrease in feeling positive and happy about the future. This could be related to the prison environment, including matters of accommodation, deaths in custody, and incidences of removal of contraband that occurred toward the end of the of the CDL program conclusion (Sect. 7.1). Once again, the trends were similar across program participants and control group members.

6.4 Questionnaire Results (Qualitative Data)

This research also invited qualitative responses from CDL program participants (P1–P15) and control group participants (C1–C15), who responded during pretesting (PRE) and posttesting (POST). The findings discussed in this section are organized in the order of the questionnaire: Responses to Question 6.1 (How do you feel when you do art?) reflected some significant changes, eliciting interesting perspectives. While responses between program participants and control group members

6.4 Questionnaire Results (Qualitative Data)

Table 6.12 CDL program participants (**pretest**)

4. Questions about the past 8 weeks							
Please tick how much you agree with each sentence.☑	All of the time (5)	Most of the time (4)	Some of the time (3)	A little of the time (2)	None of the time (1)	Total (n =?)	Average
4.1. In the past eight (8) weeks, about how often did you feel worried?	0	3	2	2	1	8	2.875
4.2. In the past eight (8) weeks, about how often did you feel discouraged/put down?	0	2	1	3	1	7	2.571
4.3. In the past eight (8) weeks, about how often did you feel restless/fidgety?	1	3	3	0	1	8	3.375
4.4. In the past eight (8) weeks, how often did you smile?	0	2	3	2	1	8	2.75
4.5. In the past eight (8) weeks, about how often did you feel idle/useless?	0	2	3	2	1	8	2.75
4.6. In the past eight (8) weeks, about how often did you have happy dreams?	1	1	1	3	2	8	2.5
4.7. In the past eight (8) weeks, about how often did you find it easy to focus?	1	0	5	1	0	7	3.142
4.8. In the past eight (8) weeks, about how often did you feel that your future could be more positive/happier?	2	4	2	0	0	8	4

completing the pretest questionnaire similarly highlighted an appreciation for art in general, posttest responses clearly showed a growth in self-awareness through communication. For example, one participant (P1-PRE) said, "dumb, I don't understand it." Following the completion of the CDL program, the same participant responded as follows to the same question: "I have mixed emotions when doing art. I feel calm but a little upset. I'm still not that good" (P1-POST).

Responses to Question 6.2 (What have you learned about yourself/culture/life/others through art/story?) similarly raised interesting perspectives. For example, one participant (P12-PRE) left the question unanswered initially, but later commented, "You can show where you come from and who you are" (P12-POST). Similarly, one participant (P4-PRE) also left the question unanswered initially, but later commented, "about addiction; that I can do things when I focus; things I would normally not think I could" (P4-POST).

Responses to Question 6.3 (What other creative activities do you enjoy? For example, writing, sculpting, building, sewing, designing, gardening, making music, mechanics, etc.? Please list the first five that come to mind) did not really change much (in pre- and posttest comparison) because the hobbies referred to life on the outside. The repetition of creative hobbies highlighted the lack of meaningful activities available on the inside.

Table 6.13 CDL program participants (**posttest**)

4. QUESTIONS ABOUT THE PAST EIGHT WEEKS							
Please tick how much you agree with each sentence. ☑	All of the time (5)	Most of the time (4)	Some of the time (3)	A little of the time (2)	None of the time (1)	Total (n = ?)	Average
4.1 In the past eight (8) weeks, about how often did you feel worried?	1	1	2	2	2	8	2.625
4.2 In the past eight (8) weeks, about how often did you feel discouraged / put down?	0	0	3	2	2	7	2.142
4.3 In the past eight (8) weeks, about how often did you feel restless / fidgety?	0	2	2	4	0	8	2.75
4.4 In the past eight (8) weeks, how often did you smile?	1	3	3	1	0	8	3.5
4.5 In the past eight (8) weeks, about how often did you feel idle / useless?	0	3	3	2	0	8	3.125
4.6 In the past eight (8) weeks, about how often did you have happy dreams?	0	1	1	3	2	7	2.142
4.7 In the past eight (8) weeks, about how often did you find it easy to focus?	0	2	4	0	1	7	3
4.8 In the past eight (8) weeks, about how often did you feel that your future could be more positive / happier?	0	5	1	1	1	8	3.25

Table 6.14 Control group (**pretest**)

4. Questions about the past 8 weeks							
Please tick how much you agree with each sentence.☑	All of the time (5)	Most of the time (4)	Some of the time (3)	A little of the time (2)	None of the time (1)	Total (n =?)	Average
4.1. In the past eight (8) weeks, about how often did you feel worried?	0	2	3	0	1	6	3
4.2. In the past eight (8) weeks, about how often did you feel discouraged/put down?	0	2	2	1	1	6	2.833
4.3. In the past eight (8) weeks, about how often did you feel restless/fidgety?	2	1	1	2	0	6	3.5
4.4. In the past eight (8) weeks, how often did you smile?	1	0	3	0	1	5	3
4.5. In the past eight (8) weeks, about how often did you feel idle/useless?	0	1	2	2	1	6	2.5
4.6. In the past eight (8) weeks, about how often did you have happy dreams?	1	1	0	0	4	6	2.166
4.7. In the past eight (8) weeks, about how often did you find it easy to focus?	0	2	2	1	1	6	2.833
4.8. In the past eight (8) weeks, about how often did you feel that your future could be more positive/happier?	0	3	1	0	2	6	2.833

6.4 Questionnaire Results (Qualitative Data)

Table 6.15 Control group **(posttest)**

4. QUESTIONS ABOUT THE PAST EIGHT WEEKS							
Please tick how much you agree with each sentence. ☑	All of the time (5)	Most of the time (4)	Some of the time (3)	A little of the time (2)	None of the time (1)	Total (n = ?)	Average
4.1 In the past eight (8) weeks, about how often did you feel worried?	0	2	3	0	1	6	3
4.2 In the past eight (8) weeks, about how often did you feel discouraged / put down?	0	0	4	0	2	6	2.333
4.3 In the past eight (8) weeks, about how often did you feel restless / fidgety?	1	0	3	1	1	6	2.833
4.4 In the past eight (8) weeks, how often did you smile?	1	2	1	1	1	6	3.166
4.5 In the past eight (8) weeks, about how often did you feel idle / useless?	0	0	3	2	1	6	2.333
4.6 In the past eight (8) weeks, about how often did you have happy dreams?	1	0	2	0	3	6	2.333
4.7 In the past eight (8) weeks, about how often did you find it easy to focus?	0	3	1	1	1	6	3
4.8 In the past eight (8) weeks, about how often did you feel that your future could be more positive / happier?	1	0	2	2	1	6	2.666

Responses to Question 6.4 (If you had an opportunity to speak to the Minister for Corrections about art, what would you say?) reflected considerable nuance. Notably, one participant (P1-PRE) answered initially, "Art is fun," and subsequently responded, "I believe art can help prisoners destress in lockdowns; it helps in many different ways. It personally helped me through a dark headspace where I normally would have taken that out on other prisoners" (P1-POST). Two control group members stated: "Get some consistence your system is flawed lack of program availability excess wait times to get on programs." (C2-POST); "We haven't got anything else to do. Not all of us are fitness people so we need something more accesible (sic) now for all demorgraphics (sic)" (C2-PRE).

The final qualitative Question 6.5 gave an opportunity for inmates to comment on other matters of significance (Is there anything else you would like to say?). At the end of the CDL program, several inmates took advantage of responding to this question, previously left blank. Selected responses include: "I personally witnessed art bring prisoners together. I've watched others encourage people to do art. Please bring more art to prison" (P1-POST). Similarly, "I am grateful having the chance to be in this art course and been (sic) given supplies and being taught different things" (P4-POST). "Whether it is run by prisoners or staff there are so many prisoners who would appreciate having the ability to create art and would like more opportunity to do so" (P14-POST).

It is worth noting that several control group subjects were visibly disappointed when they discovered that they were not participating in the CDL program but were merely responding to questionnaires: "It makes us fell (sic) better, I'm Desappointed (sic) that we only had to do the survey – we should have all got to do the art program" (C6-PRE). Another control group member expressed: "next program can I actually be part of the art side" (C2-POST).

A final note about qualitative responses is in order: Most respondents seemed somewhat reticent and often gave only one-word responses, for example, "happy" (C15-POST), "good" (P15-PRE), "calm" (P9-POST), "focused" (P4-POST), "strong" (C2-POST), "no" (P11-PRE), "confused" (P1-PRE), "sad" (P2-PRE), and "dumb" (P1-PRE), among others. This may be unsurprising in light of the prevalent levels of education among respondents (Tables 6.2 and 6.3). Limited levels of education underscore the meaningfulness of the visual responses, covered in the next two sections.

6.5 Questionnaire Findings (Visual Responses)

The questionnaire gave respondents several opportunities to answer questions expressively, such as Questions 5.1 (Please picture your biggest dream) and 5.2 (This is how I feel right now). While there were no perceptible changes in the answers of the control group members (Fig. 6.2), CDL participants exhibited considerable improvements in artistic skill and engagement (Figs. 6.3, 6.4, 6.5, 6.6, and 6.7). Themes of note include images of families, houses, footballs, Indigenous flags, and freedom, among others. Selected examples are depicted in Figs. 6.3, 6.4, 6.5, 6.6, and 6.7.

Although the women's prison research was discontinued prematurely, it is worth noting the distinct nuances between female and male expressive ability and desire for art, reflected in preliminary artwork (e.g., Fig. 6.8). This is an area conceptualized for future research (Sect. 8.2).

6.6 Findings from the Public Art Exhibition

As outlined in Chap. 5, the study's methodology, data collection, and analysis also comprised and drew on a public art exhibition, which enlisted input from members of the public who were invited to rate the prisoner artwork. The rating process encompassed each CDL program participant's baseline illustration (from Week 1) and their final art project, prepared during the final weeks (Table 6.1). This section will first introduce the art exhibition context and then showcase the prisoner artwork alongside commentary from the researchers. The section will close with quantitative data analysis derived from AART instrument (Appendix 2) questionnaire analysis.

6.6 Findings from the Public Art Exhibition

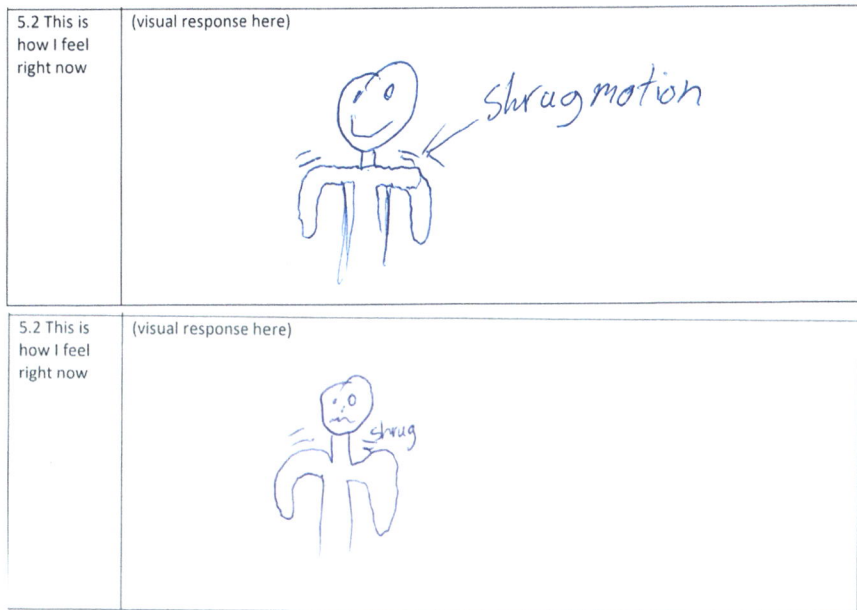

Fig. 6.2 Control group participant C2 responding to Question 5.2 (pretest above, posttest below); no significant change in expression is observed

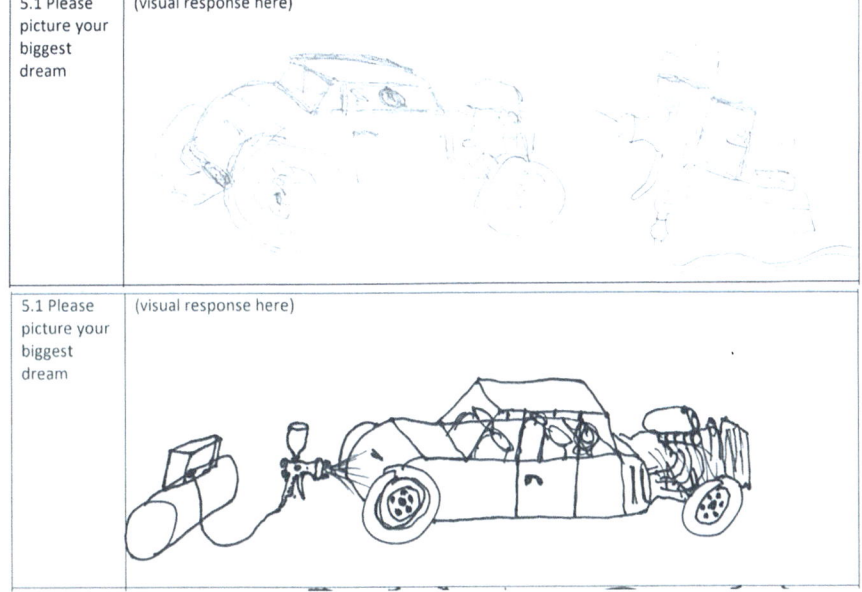

Fig. 6.3 Participant P2 responding to Question 5.1 (pretest above, posttest below)

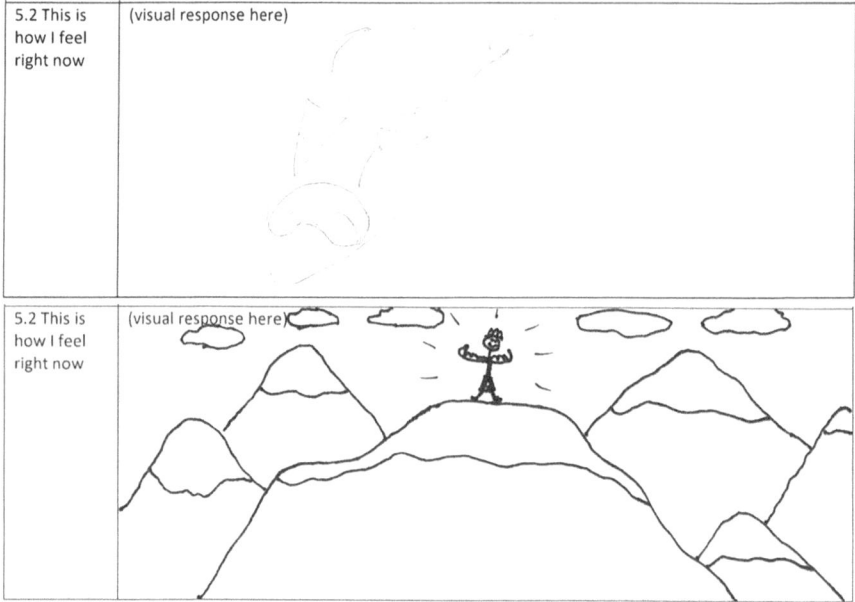

Fig. 6.4 Participant P2 responding to Question 5.2 (pretest above, posttest below)

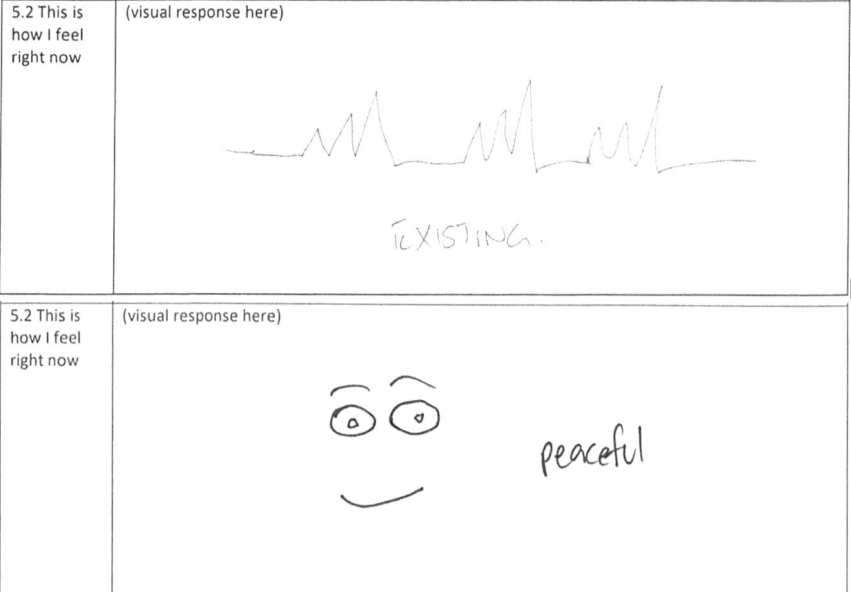

Fig. 6.5 Participant P9 responding to Question 5.2 (pretest above, posttest below)

6.6 Findings from the Public Art Exhibition

Fig. 6.6 Participant P14 responding to Question 5.1 (pretest above, posttest below)

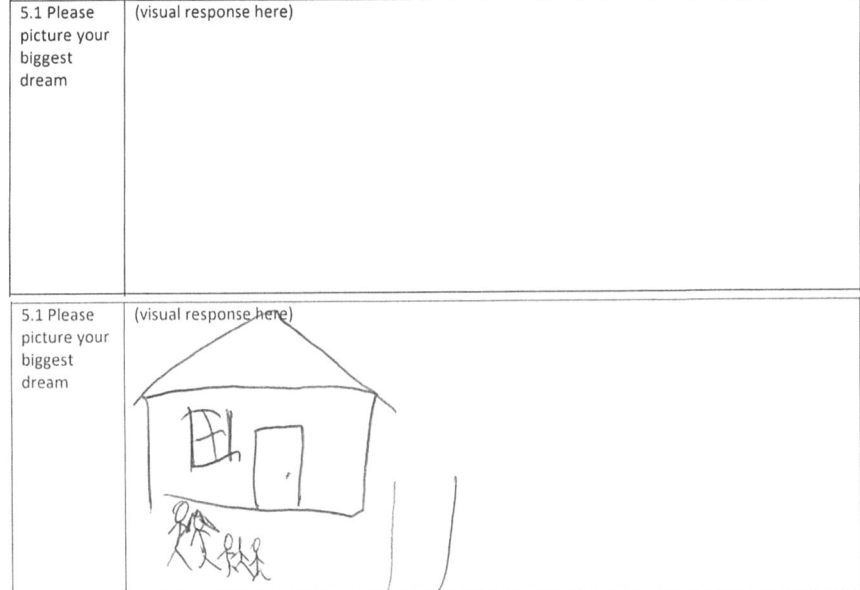

Fig. 6.7 Participant P12 responding to Question 5.1 (pretest above, posttest below)

Fig. 6.8 Participant F14: Week 2 progress illustrates unique expression of female art

The art exhibition was arranged by the principal investigator through negotiations with a Uniting Care facility. Given that only eight CDL participants completed the program in Week 8, with only seven presenting a final project piece, data collection during the exhibition was limited to seven final artworks. Due to the limited number of artworks available for external assessment by members of the public, the exhibition additionally hosted artwork of recently released inmates who wished to showcase their art. This additional artwork was on display but was not assessed by the public as part of this research. However, showcasing a broad range of prisoner art offered a meaningful opportunity for the broader public to witness the artistic progress of the prison art program and helped recently released prisoners to establish themselves as artists on the outside, contributing positively to society and the community.

The exhibition was held from Monday to Wednesday, September 11–13, 2023 (9 am–4 pm). The art exhibition was advertised to members of the public via social media, local cafés and art galleries, a homeless shelter, church and neighborhood community centers, and community radio stations, in addition to several music venues (Fig. 6.9 depicts a poster at a local radio station).

A total of 68 visitors attended the art exhibition (28 on Monday, 25 on Tuesday, and 15 on Wednesday). In addition, several street kids came inside daily, prompted by the cold weather, to hang out and paint with the researcher. In total, 28 AART instrument surveys were completed and informed the art exhibition data analysis presented below (see also Sect. 5.4 and Appendix 2). Ten AART instrument surveys remained incomplete and were thus excluded from the final analysis.

This section is organized as follows. First, the research will present the seven final artworks.exhibited and rated by the public. This discussion features reflections on the participants' backgrounds and experiences during the program. Second, this section will present the data collected when members of the public rated the artworks using the AART instrument (Figs. 6.10, 6.11). The seven artworks featured in the art exhibition are depicted in Figs. 6.12, 6.14, 6.15, 6.16, 6.17, 6.19, 6.20. Each figure is divided into two parts. The baseline illustration (created on the first

6.6 Findings from the Public Art Exhibition

Fig. 6.9 Poster advertising the research art exhibition at a community radio (Photo: Sarah Tucker)

day) is shown on the left; the final art project (prepared during the final weeks) is shown on the right. The artworks reflect the prisoner artists' personal progress, emotional investment, and active involvement in the therapeutic art program.

Context P1, initially skeptical about how art could help him navigate social situations in prison, displayed remarkable progress throughout the course. Confronting difficulties, such as struggles in communication with staff and experiencing the theft of his art supplies, he persevered in participating through in-cell tasks and class

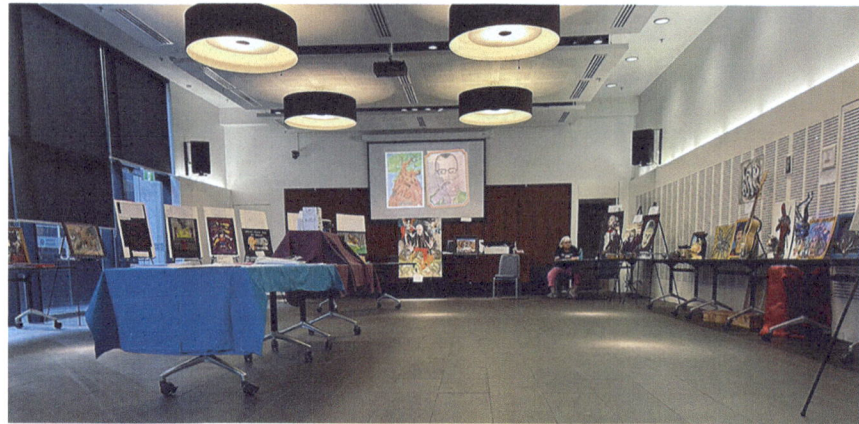

Fig. 6.10 Art exhibition, September 11–13, 2023 (Photo: Sarah Tucker)

Fig. 6.11 Members of the public completing the AART instruments used in this research (Photo: Johannes M. Luetz)

interactions despite facing challenges typical of his autism spectrum disorder. A component of the CDL program on "the art of reading people" focuses on illustrating micro-expressions (Fig. 6.13). This was conducive to assisting his understanding of social interactions and dynamics.

His developing artistic skills were challenged by cognitive and motor skill difficulties and hindered his ability to recognize facial expressions, symmetry, and layout (see baseline artwork above). His overall relational understanding improved through his dedicated efforts. The final artwork, a therapeutic piece, reflects his growth in self-reflection and addresses painful memories (Fig. 6.12). The artwork

6.6 Findings from the Public Art Exhibition

Artist: P1 Fig. 12	
Baseline Artwork	Final Artwork

	Title: Words Hurt **Mediums:** Gouache paint, paint pens, acrylic, pencils **Description:** Growing up on the spectrum & also having ADHD, I've always struggled with "fitting in" & "behaving". I've been called many names wether by people who don't know me or even friends & family. Every time I feel like I'm doing good, these names come back to haunt me & I self-sabotage.

Fig. 6.12 Artist: P1

Fig. 6.13 The art of reading people is a key focus of the art program (workbook pp. 13–15)

portrays a face emerging from a dark, blood-red background, symbolizing the negative inner self-talk and words he grapples with. The title card prominently features the word "DUMB," which also appears across the forehead, with vertical lines representing bars through the eye sockets. The circumference of the face features the words "Special needs, Ugly, Silly, Weird, Criminal, Liar, Thief, Useless, Scum, Menace to society, Drugdealer, Gronk, Dickhead, Loser, Bad, Stupid, Idiot, Retard, Terrible, Awful." This powerful image encapsulates his journey and his challenges, reflecting his resilience and showcasing his progress.

Context Despite a family history tied to prison, this 22-year-old inmate, while not prison-savvy, openly acknowledged his lack of "street smarts." Grappling with a lack of "unit respect" and frequent theft of his art supplies, P2 exhibited a genuine interest in art. Despite challenges, he dedicated extra time to complete homework, even sacrificing restroom breaks. His artwork, though skillful, was only restricted by a lack of art education. Throughout the program, he absorbed advice and honed observational skills, evidenced by his pretest and posttest questionnaire responses (see Sects. 6.3 and 6.4). His final artwork, portraying a symbolic theater-courtroom-prison (as he awaited sentencing), depicted a soulless scene with a puppet master manipulating the main character. The inscription "Mi Vida Loca—My Crazy Life" at the bottom encapsulates the complexity of his life and experiences (Fig. 6.14).

Context Inmate P4 exhibited clear signs of cognitive atrophy early on in the program, which he attributed to excessive methamphetamine use (Researcher Journal, 24 March 2023, p. 6). He could not remain focused and follow instructions without

6.6 Findings from the Public Art Exhibition 57

Artist: P2 Fig. 14	
Baseline Artwork	Final Artwork
This is my representation of how I see my life.. I am the puppet trying to break free of control	**Title:** My Crazy Life **Mediums:** Acrylic, pencil, & markers on card **Description:** This is my representation of how I see my life… I am the puppet trying to break free of control

Fig. 6.14 Artist: P2

repeating or interjecting his interpretation. Due to relocation in the center he could take on instruction and further his learning from basic prison art style and form. His journey is reflected in his answer to Question 6.2 (What have you learnt about yourself/culture/life/others through art/story?). In the posttest, he responded: "About addiction, that I can do things when I focus, things I would not normally think I could." In his final piece, P4 depicts an eagle breaking through bars over clear fields. Not only does he show a willingness to use layers in this part, but he has also experimented with different mediums that he reportedly found pleasing and recognized a significant symbolic representation within the eagle, which has long been a symbol of strength and freedom in both Indigenous and Western cultures (Fig. 6.15).

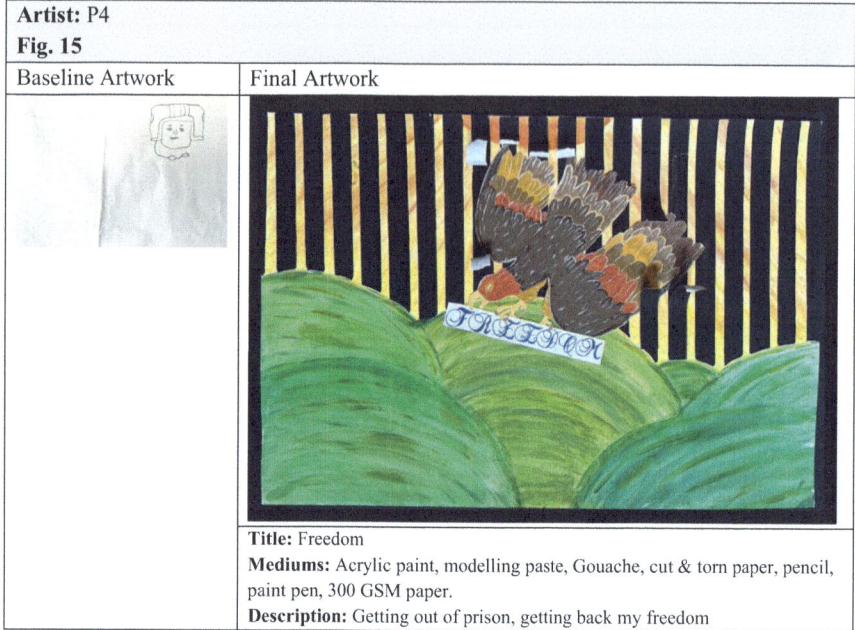

Fig. 6.15 Artist: P4

Context Initially doubtful about the ability of inmate P9 to complete the course due to his considerably distracted nature, it emerged that his struggles were rooted in excessive drug abuse that ultimately led to his imprisonment. As the program progressed, he became more engaged in the work. Subsequent art sessions witnessed the emergence of an expressive and organized art form involving experimentation. Notably, he delved into a geometric style, leading to the suggestion of creating a three-dimensional final piece. Overcoming initial skepticism, inmate P9 created a 6-sided box, a symbolic prison art representation reflecting the confinement of self and separation from the external world (Fig. 6.16). The final piece depicts a colorful, messy exterior representing the moments leading up to his crime. The interior is painted in prison green, featuring a grid pattern reminiscent of the caged prison exercise yards. Throughout this project, inmate P9 not only enhanced his problem-solving skills for complex dimensional tasks but also experienced a significant improvement in his overall mental capacity, a noteworthy transformation. This is powerfully illustrated in his answers to Question 5.2 (This is how I feel right now), which reflect a considerable shift from his pretest to posttest responses, from simply "existing" to being "peaceful" (see Fig. 6.5).

Context Inmate P12 showed minimal engagement in the course, prioritizing gaining personal access to art supplies and interactions with other inmates. Being influenced by Islamic practices, he attended relevant spiritual gatherings, which are often utilized for drug distribution. His vulnerability lay in the paradox of his

6.6 Findings from the Public Art Exhibition

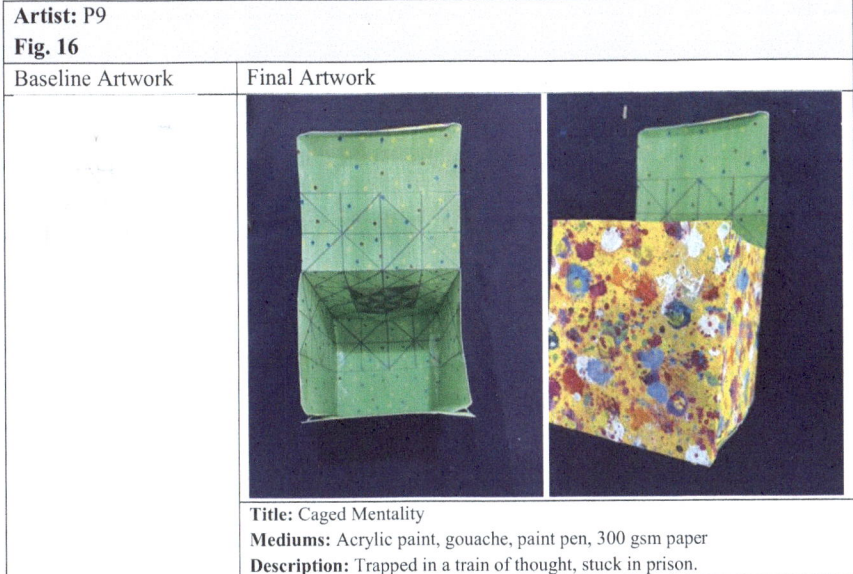

Artist: P9 Fig. 16	
Baseline Artwork	Final Artwork

Title: Caged Mentality
Mediums: Acrylic paint, gouache, paint pen, 300 gsm paper
Description: Trapped in a train of thought, stuck in prison.

Fig. 6.16 Artist: P9

Indigenous background and affiliation with Islam. He reflected his connection to spirituality and culture (Sect. 7.4) through his pre- and posttest responses to Question 6.1 (What have you learnt about yourself/culture/life/others through art/story?) While he left the pretest question unanswered, his posttest response was: "You can show where you come from and who you are…" Although he did work on his final piece (Fig. 6.17), it remained incomplete, and he did not finish all the homework requirements. As reflected in his preliminary draft work (Fig. 6.18), P12 intended to outwork his final art piece in the image of an Islamic prayer mat intersecting with his cultural flag (Sect. 7.4). He benefited from assistance in spelling the words in the final piece (Fig. 6.17).

Context Inmate P14 was very invested in the course from the beginning. His purpose was to use art to stay connected with his young son from inside the prison through letters and written correspondence. He demonstrated resourcefulness by securing a kitchen job for access to art supplies. For example, he created detailed drawings for his son using greaseproof paper from the kitchen for tracing (kitchen access provided natural colors, e.g., beetroot, coffee, and other kitchen resources to mix pigment). From the start, P14 struggled with contrast colors, and the color-mixing session proved challenging. Although his color use was initially limited, he gained valuable knowledge over time and persevered through color theory. Despite his kitchen commitments, he attended all program sessions and learnt composition, which enhanced the design layout. His final artwork conveyed a powerful message: "Addiction destroys lives, not criminals" (Fig. 6.19).

Artist: P12 Fig. 17	
Baseline Artwork	Final Artwork
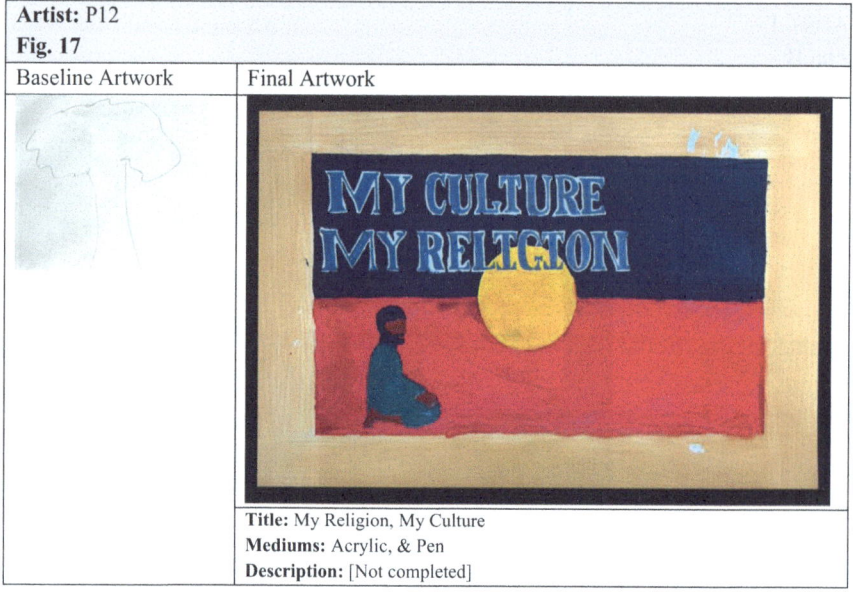	
	Title: My Religion, My Culture Mediums: Acrylic, & Pen Description: [Not completed]

Fig. 6.17 Artist: P12

Fig. 6.18 Draft of final (intended) artwork

Context Inmate P15 initially faced distractions and revealed his heavy medication use, yet he managed to actively participate in the program. He was repeatedly observed taking art supplies, and he later admitted to pilfering materials from the facilitator's art supplies trolley. His sexual abuse as a child emerged prolifically in

6.6 Findings from the Public Art Exhibition

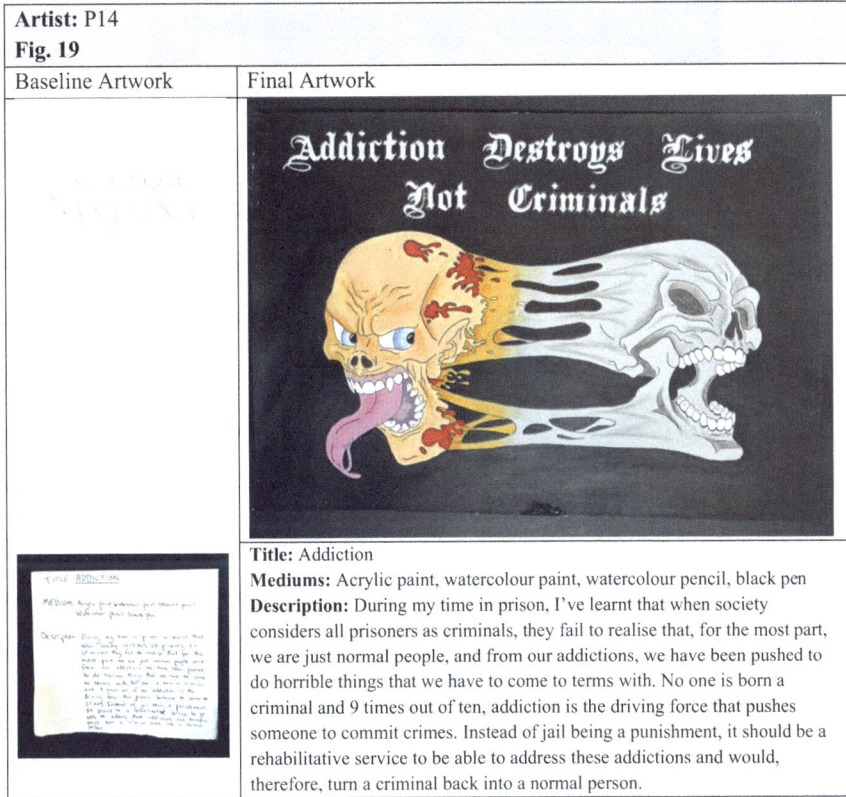

Fig. 6.19 Artist: P14

his language regarding his bisexuality in prison. Showing signs of anxious attachment, his need for attention and approval made him competitive in group dynamics. Although intentional in his art focus, he consistently disrupted the class dynamics. Notwithstanding, when other inmates left during muster breaks, he absorbed information and produced significant work while confiding in the art program facilitator about his life experiences.

Despite the participant disclosing sustained brain damage from childhood drug use, he showed flashes of genius with slow guidance (Researcher Journal, 19 April 2023, pp. 19–21). In one-on-one sessions, he disclosed painful childhood memories of extreme abuse. By the third or fourth session, he displayed self-motivation, excelling in homework, especially during lockdowns. His art style emerged during one of the experimental painting sessions. In this unconventional exercise, inmates relinquish control over paper and paint, using various tools and materials to splash, "damage," and "attack" memories from the past, using broad arm strokes to reclaim their agency. During these sessions with experimental art in the program, some resist, reverting to illustration, while others experiment with the unpredictable process, revealing alternate color preferences and fresh styles. During the session, P15 expressed anger and frustration about his troubled childhood, violently covering

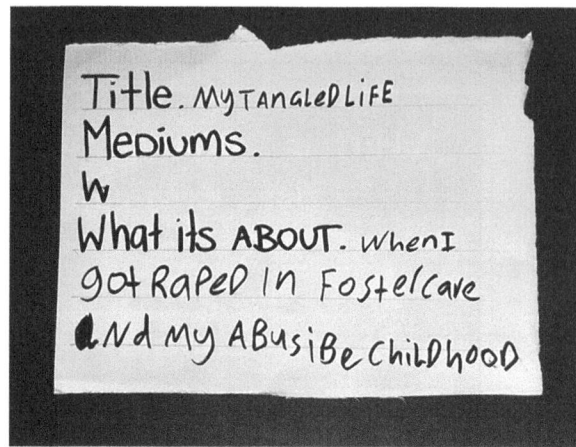

Fig. 6.20 The final artwork placard reflects considerable self- and life awareness

and obliterating the paper for his final piece. Encouraged by the facilitator, he found a powerful moment of control amidst life's chaos, forming the basis for his final piece. Notably, in response to Question 6.2 (What have you learnt about yourself/culture/life/art/others through art/story?), P15 responded: "How to control Anger" (see Fig. 6.1).

The experiences of P15 offer insight into some of the consequences of abuse and institutionalization that an individual may sustain over time (Fig. 6.20). This is also reflected in his baseline artwork, which depicts two circles representing the very small eyes of a vulnerable child. His final piece was prominent in the final art exhibition in its ability to connect the public to the vulnerabilities and experiences of prisoners. This was commented on by an art exhibition research participant as a comment scribbled at the bottom of the AART instrument (Appendix 2): "The messages in this piece could be so helpful to form the basis of further therapy. I want to tell the stories of this person, their pain is so captured in this piece" (E5). Specific to the final piece is the happy childhood experience of fishing, which connects painful and tragic memories assisting the therapeutic art process (Fig. 6.21). The fishhooks in the artwork reflect how entangled his life became once fostered out from his original family.

This final section discusses the findings from the external art exhibition participants (E), who rated the final artworks using the AART instrument (Appendix 2). The findings are shown in Table 6.16 and are accompanied by relevant quantitative analysis.

It was nice to see robust positive changes in several categories, including "Words/text in artwork," "Perspective/Dimension," and "Mediums/art supplies used." This signifies an increase in the participants' literacy, referring to verbal and artistic expression. As discussed in relation to Fig. 6.17, all participants appreciated help from the facilitator in "spelling" to prepare their artworks and placards. Furthermore, it was encouraging to perceive a positive change in the confidence of the prisoners

6.6 Findings from the Public Art Exhibition

Artist: P15	
Fig. 20	
Baseline Artwork	Final Artwork
	Title: My Tangled Life
	Mediums: Acrylic Paint, collage, paint pen, oil pastels
	Description: When I got raped in foster care, and my abusive childhood.

Fig. 6.21 Artist: P15

to understand composition and design, reflecting growth in cognitive awareness. Importantly, one art exhibition participant observed and reflected on the ability of program participants to understand and utilize the available space on paper or canvas: "With the exception of one or two baseline images (including the intriguing portrait crammed into the top right-hand corner of the page, as if the participant didn't feel they had the right to own the whole page)" (E5).

Interestingly, there were decreases in the categories "Color variety" and "Use of space on canvas/paper." This may be attributed to two factors. First, it could signify that the baseline exercise consisted of line work only (pencil), meaning the baseline artwork was incomparable to the final pieces. Furthermore, it is noted as a limitation of the AART instrument, which should have been designed to be simpler and feature

Table 6.16 Data analysis derived from the AART Instrument ($n = 28$)

Therapy	Median (Md) [before]	Median (Md) [after]	Standardised Test Statistic (z)	p-value	*r (effect size)
Realism/expression	41.00	46.50	1.299	.194	0.17
Colour usage	38.50	32.50	-0.694	.486	-0.09
Colour variety	60.50	26.00	-3.222	.001	-0.42[1]
Subject matter	36.50	40.00	1.347	.178	0.18
Themes	36.00	24.00	-1.686	.092	-0.22
Use of space on canvas/paper	43.00	14.50	-2.494	.013	-0.33[2]
Symbolism (if any)	34.00	41.00	1.310	.190	0.17
Words/text in artwork	8.00	28.00	4.624	.001	0.61[3]
Perspective/dimension	7.50	40.50	4.623	.001	0.61[4]
Mediums/art supplies used	7.00	43.50	4.623	.001	0.61[5]
Overall score	34.50	32.00	-0.057	.955	-0.01

The Wilcoxon Signed-Rank Test is a non-parametric statistical test used to compare two related samples—such as before-and-after measurements on the same subjects. It is often used as an alternative to the paired t-test when the data does not follow a normal distribution. The test evaluates whether the **median difference** between the paired observations is significantly different from zero.

[1] A Wilcoxon signed rank test revealed that the participant scores were significantly lower after the therapy on colour variety ($Md = 26.00$, $n = 28$), compared to before ($Md = 60.50$, $n = 28$), $z = -3.222$, $p = .001$, with high effect size, $r = -0.42$

[2] A Wilcoxon signed rank test revealed that the participant scores were significantly lower after the therapy on use of space on canvas/paper ($Md = 14.50$, $n = 28$), compared to before ($Md = 43.00$, $n = 28$), $z = -2.494$, $p = .013$, with medium effect size, $r = -0.33$

[3] A Wilcoxon signed rank test revealed that the participant scores were significantly higher after the therapy on words/text in artwork ($Md = 28.00$, $n = 28$), compared to before ($Md = 8.00$, $n = 28$), $z = 4.624$, $p = .001$, with high effect size, $r = 0.61$

[4] A Wilcoxon signed rank test revealed that the participant scores were significantly higher after the therapy on perspective/Dimension ($Md = 40.50$, $n = 28$), compared to before ($Md = 7.50$, $n = 28$), $z = 4.623$, $p = .001$, with high effect size, $r = 0.61$

[5] A Wilcoxon signed rank test revealed that the participant scores were significantly higher after the therapy on mediums/art supplies used ($Md = 43.50$, $n = 28$), compared to before ($Md = 7.00$, $n = 28$), $z = 4.623$, $p = .001$, with high effect size, $r = 0.61$

*Effect size r, is a standardised measure to know how large the effect of the change was between the before and after

some categories on opposing sides. This similarly applies to the "use of space on canvas/paper" and is acknowledged in the research limitations section (Chap. 8).

Qualitative commentary made by several exhibition participants complements the quantitative analysis. Notably, comments highlighted the powerful emotional response that the art elicited from members of the public. Exhibition participants commented:

> The description of this piece is powerful and shows the self-reflection that took place during creating this piece. Before, pic shows this person focussed on being trapped in walls, after is trapped in self (E5 commenting on artwork produced by P14).

Furthermore, the public also expressed that the artworks exhibited a kind a basis for future intervention and research:

> The messages in this piece could be so helpful to form the basis of further therapy. I want to tell the stories of this person, their pain is so captured in this piece (E5 commenting on artwork produced by P15).

As noted below (Sect. 8.3), a resounding wish was noted from several members of the public to hear more of the prisoners' voices through visual art via public art exhibitions of this kind.

6.7 Researcher Reflections on Journaling

This section describes how researcher journaling was used to capture and report important data and support the analyses and findings of this research. First, it is important to understand that preapproval is always required to supply any programs with any required external resources and that many tools that are customary to use in qualitative research are expressly prohibited, including computers, phones, and recording equipment, among other electronic devices. Importantly, given that electronic recording devices come under "prohibited things," it implied that all information needed to be documented in a "hard copy" format within the prison (Chap. 5). For this reason, the principal researcher used a preapproved journal with a deterring locking mechanism to support her on-site observations while preventing prisoners from gaining access to other inmate information (Fig. 6.22).

It was important to reassure the inmates that the diary was solely a research documentation tool, not an intelligence-gathering device. This clarification was reiterated multiple times, and concerned inmates regularly questioned the facilitator about what she was writing down. Prisoners are well known to be suspicious (Gussak, 2019; Sapolsky, 2017; Ursprung, 1997). Prisoners are notorious for utilizing information for their survival, and in light of this, written information regarding persons inside or outside of prison can be advantageous to them, as documented in the well-known prisoner's dilemma.[1] As such, the journal served as an effective strategy against inmate manipulation (Tulloch, 2010). Therefore, keeping the journal close at hand had a high priority.

Prisons are densely populated by both inmates and staff. Inmates are often isolated from each other and lack social connections for extended periods of time. Isolation can result in a hunger for conversation and interaction. High levels of inmate enthusiasm were anticipated by the program facilitator, as highlighted in her journal entry: "The night before commencing, my mind is in overdrive as how to best negotiate the class dynamics whilst keeping the inmates at optimum engagement" (Researcher Journal, March 21, 2023, p. 1).

In an environment of heightened emotions, documenting every detail can prove difficult. The required solitude was discovered only during lunch breaks, typically between 12 and 1 pm. The lead researcher often skipped lunch breaks to maximize the time for reflection, journaling, and recovery. On some occasions, the 1.5-hour journey home allowed the researcher opportune breaks, providing moments to

---

[1] The prisoner's dilemma is a thought exercise that models many real-world situations involving behaviors used by the incarcerated (Kuhn, 2019; see also Sapolsky, 2017).

Fig. 6.22 Researcher journal with locking mechanism (Photo: Sarah Tucker)

process, reflect, and journal. Finding such moments of intentional journal writing proved beneficial in exploring and synthesizing emergent key themes (Chap. 7). For confidentiality reasons, journal notes cannot be extensively shared. A few selected quotes have been judiciously selected and exemplify the kind of self-reflection that occurred:

> [Afternoon]: It's only after an hour or two of silent reflection afterwards that I can re-assess my own exhaustion and then imagine the exhaustion the inmates are suffering through stress and interrupted sleep. Trying to articulate to the inmates the benefits of the research with limited resources is difficult. (Researcher Journal, April 26, 2023, p. 9)

While journaling may be limited in its ability to capture "verbatim quotes" (as is customary in qualitative research that typically relies on audio recordings), journal notes can also offer some distinct advantages in promoting self-reflection, self-care, and mitigating self-biases (Gardner, 2014; Jones, 2021). Despite the potential therapeutic benefits of journaling for self-reflective awareness, prisoners lack the privilege of privacy. This was reflected in a pretest response from one female inmate, highlighting the risk of keeping pictures of family members in their cells:

my paintings and drawings that I've given away in here have made people really happy ... I do not want to put pictures of my kids on the wall, I want to put art. My kids are somewhere else. (Female Participant P2)

Consequently, anything within the confines of the prison walls may become susceptible to exploitation by fellow inmates. As a result, prisoners tend to refrain from documenting personal information that might be construed as vulnerable or could be wielded as a tool for manipulation by the broader inmate community (Tucker & Luetz, 2021). Crucially, this supports the inmates' admiration for art and illustration as a secure means of self-expression. During lockdowns that heighten stress, the human mind can become disturbed (Haney, 2020). Hence, expressing one's distress through artistic means can provide solace and "catharsis," as elaborated in Sect. 7.2. In summary, considering corrections policies and procedures, journaling proved fruitful in capturing key information, rekindling memories of interactions, and synthesizing and supporting key emergent themes that might otherwise have remained under recognized.

References

ABC—Australian Broadcasting Corporation. (2015). *Queensland government will be liable for Borallon prison deaths on hanging points: Sisters Inside*. Thu 9 Jul. https://www.abc.net.au/news/2015-07-09/borallon-prisondeaths-in-custody-hanging-points-qld-govt/6606498

Biles, D. (1997). Private Prisons-Welcome or Not? *Australian Journal of Forensic Sciences, 29*(1), 3–8. https://doi.org/10.1080/00450619709411361

CCC—Crime and Corruption Commission. (2018a). *Transcript of investigative hearing*. Taskforce Flaxton Transcripts. www.ccc.qld.gov.au/sites/default/files/Docs/Public-Hearings/Flaxton/Transcripts/Taskforce-Flaxton-Transcript-Day-2-15-May-2018-Sam-Zhouand QCS.pdf

CCC—Crime and Corruption Commission. (2018b). *Transcript of investigative hearing*. Taskforce Flaxton Transcripts. www.ccc.qld.gov.au/sites/default/files/Docs/Public-Hearings/Flaxton/Transcripts/Taskforce-Flaxton-Transcript-Day-11-28-May-2018-Scott-Collins-QCS.pdf

Gardner, F. (2014). *Being critically reflective: Engaging in holistic practice*. Bloomsbury Publishing.

Gussak, D. (2019). *Art and art therapy with the imprisoned: Re-creating identity*. Routledge.

Haney, C. (2020). The science of solitary: Expanding the harmfulness narrative. *Northwestern University Law Review, 115*(1), 211–256.

Harding, R. W., Rynne, J., & Thomsen, L. (2019). History of privatized corrections. *Criminology & Public Policy, 18*(2), 241–267. https://doi.org/10.1111/1745-9133.12426

Jones, P. (2021). *The arts therapies: A revolution in healthcare* (2nd ed.). Routledge.

Kuhn, S. (2019). Prisoner's dilemma. In E. N. Zalta (Ed.). *The Stanford encyclopedia of philosophy*. https://plato.stanford.edu/archives/win2019/entries/prisoner-dilemma/

Sapolsky, R. M. (2017). *Behave: The biology of humans at our best and worst*. Penguin.

Tucker, S., & Luetz, J. M. (2021). Art therapy and prison chaplaincy—A review of contemporary practices considering New Testament teachings. In J. M. Luetz & B. Green (Eds.), *Innovating Christian education research—Multidisciplinary perspectives* (pp. 239–269). Springer. https://doi.org/10.1007/978-981-15-8856-3_15

Tulloch, B. (2010). Guarding against manipulation by criminal offenders. *Australasian Journal of Correctional Staff Development*. https://hdl.handle.net/10627/456.

Ursprung, W. (1997). Insider art: The creative ingeniuty of the incarcerated artist. In D. Gussak & E. Virshup (Eds.), *Drawing time: Art therapy in prisons and other correctional settings* (pp. 13–24). Magnolia Street Pub.

Open Access This chapter is licensed under the terms of the Creative Commons Attribution 4.0 International License (http://creativecommons.org/licenses/by/4.0/), which permits use, sharing, adaptation, distribution and reproduction in any medium or format, as long as you give appropriate credit to the original author(s) and the source, provide a link to the Creative Commons license and indicate if changes were made.

The images or other third party material in this chapter are included in the chapter's Creative Commons license, unless indicated otherwise in a credit line to the material. If material is not included in the chapter's Creative Commons license and your intended use is not permitted by statutory regulation or exceeds the permitted use, you will need to obtain permission directly from the copyright holder.

Chapter 7
Discussion

This experience-informed empirical research has raised a plethora of issues, challenges, emotions, complexities, and opportunities. It is impossible to do justice to all the issues and themes impacting the incarceration of prisoners in relation to this research. This Discussion chapter has identified four key themes that will be examined in the context of the available body of literature. The discussion begins by looking at Australian prison environments that are impacted by a myriad of influences (Sect. 7.1). Thereafter, it explores prisoner perceptions of art as calming and conducive to reducing violence (Sect. 7.2). Next, it examines the effects of art programs on non-art therapy program participants or control group members (Sect. 7.3). Finally, the chapter closes by exploring Indigenous identity as being intricately connected to Country and Kinship (Sect. 7.4).

7.1 Australian Prison Environments Are Impacted by a Plethora of Influences (External and Internal) and Agendas that Impinge on Daily Art Program Delivery (Theme 1)

Program and control group participation dropped from an initial starting cohort of 15 each to a completing participant group of seven for both CDL research participants and control group members. This reduction rate in research participants was noted during 5 years of piloting (Tucker & Luetz, 2021) and was anticipated (Sect. 5.5). The reasons for this contraction in research and program participation are explored in this themed section.

Prison systems are a nexus where conflicting forms of governance intersect, shaped by social dynamics that impact policies, judgments, and rehabilitative strategies. These external influences are consistently at play in the daily routine, collectively creating an environment marked by instability (Braithwaite, 1989; Cullen &

Jonson, 2016; Gussak, 2019; Innes, 2015). In contrast to the Guiding Principles for Corrections in Australia (CSAC, 2018), which advocate for a comprehensive federal strategy to ensure community safety through corrective services, each State/Territory maintains its distinct operational standards. Adding to this lack of uniformity is the independent management of each prison or correctional center, where varying approaches to justice mirror the leadership style of the general prison manager (Griffin & Woodward, 2017; Seiter, 2017). Furthermore, external vendors compete for service contracts, offering a range of provisions. Services may encompass chaplaincy, ecumenical spiritual guidance, health services, Indigenous mental health services, programs addressing issues like drug and alcohol abuse, sex-offender rehabilitation and domestic violence (these services are crucial for parole approval), and TAFE trade certifications, coffee barista, and hairdressing, among others (Day et al., 2004; Heseltine et al., 2011). These services also vie for attention alongside daily operational functions such as community corrections, legal representation, court appearances, external visits, video-linked funeral services, facilitated inter-institutional phone calls, drug tests, drug detection dog operations, muster counts, and potential emergency responses ("codes") at any given moment (Cunneen et al., 2013; Day, 2020; Queensland Productivity Commission, 2020; Russell & Baldry, 2020; Sarre, 2010; Tucker & Luetz, 2021; Wright, 2005).

Throughout the art program, there was a sense that each day could present a new and unanticipated issue or problem. For instance, the lack of shared required information among prison center staff teams created challenges. This manifested in constant alterations to research support, which saw the CDL program liaise with different prison team members on different days, including prison psychologists, education officers, and the cultural liaison officers, who willingly assisted, albeit having limited knowledge of the research. Notably, during the time frame of data collection, there were three changes in the position of the manager responsible for offender rehabilitative programs and activities (MOD). This lack of continuity created a lingering sense of instability within the center, which emerged as frustration noted by several inmate responses, exemplified by Fig. 7.1.

These systemic challenges are not unique to Australia but have been amply documented in other international art therapy research. For example, Gussak (2019) has noted:

> the institutions see the entire population as one to be controlled and secured for overall safety. Thus, given the nature and primary focus of the setting, rights and privileges are often suspended and denied, usually outside of the control of the clinician. Groups and sessions are delayed or cancelled without preamble, inmates are moved to another unit or prison without warning, or the facility is "locked down", thus making treatment impossible. (p. 148)

The research was also impacted by the limited and varying availability of basic spaces and facilities (Gussak, 2019), which Grenfell et al. (2023) have attributed to the increasing prisoner populations in Australia (see Chap. 3). Inconsistencies impacted program delivery, including unpredictable provision of room allocations, sinks, tables, seating, whiteboards, and toilet facilities. The consequences of inconsistent access to basic CDL program requirements impeded its delivery. For

7.1 Australian Prison Environments Are Impacted by a Plethora of Influences… 71

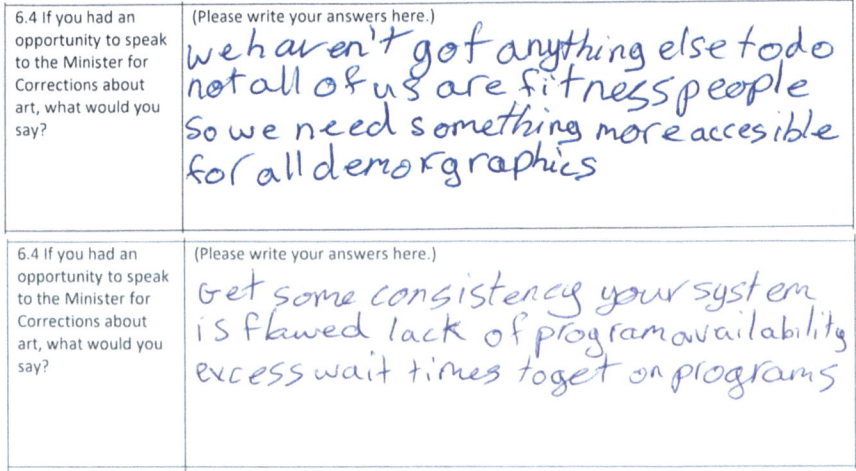

Fig. 7.1 Participant CONT-02 responding to Question 6.4 (pretest above, posttest below)

example, "One inmate had to urinate in a cup and throw it" (Researcher Journal, 29 March, p. 10). This detail highlights the need for more attention to basic facilities and shows an unanticipated incident that this prison research navigated. Research has shown that unpredictability is conducive to creating conditions in which manipulative prisoners may take advantage of human and/or systemic weaknesses (Banks et al., 1971; Gussak, 2019; Innes, 2015; Cohen-Liebman, 2016; Sapolsky, 2017; Seiter, 2017).

The resultant situation explains, at least in part, why some participants did not return or had to be removed from the program at the request of the facilitator and principal researcher. For example, the primary researcher excluded one inmate (P7) from the CDL program after he attempted to bribe her. Another inmate (P13) was caught with contraband and thus was removed from the program. A third prisoner (P6) could not deal with authenticity, accountability, and identity and, after expressing this very vocally to the researcher/facilitator, did not return after Session 5.0 (see Table 6.1), which addresses these areas and is an important aspect of self-development, as highlighted by Cohen-Liebman (2016): "To survive the correctional environment, where the weak are prey, the inmate may develop sociopathic behaviours. To hide vulnerability or weakness, 'masked identity' is assumed." (p. 128). Haney has also documented that "Prisoners struggle to preserve a viable sense of self in an environment that subordinates and diminishes them" (Haney, 2012, p. 6). The analysis highlights that center inconsistencies, volatilities, and associated dynamics can adversely affect prisoner rehabilitation (Maguire & Raynor, 2017).

Notably, although only seven participants in both the CDL program and control group cohorts formally completed the program (as captured in pre- and posttest questionnaires and reported in quantitative results; see Sects. 6.3 and 6.4), other non-completing inmates nevertheless regularly attended the art program and consistently produced art. For example, Participant 8 did not complete the program but

Fig. 7.2 Nearly completed final artwork produced by non-completing P8

nevertheless engaged in many hours of focused and relaxed drawing and coloring, exemplified here by Fig. 7.2.

In summary, Australia's prison environments continue to face logistic challenges of overcrowding, which implies that program delivery was impacted by a plethora of forces, influences, and agendas. Set within this context of inconsistency and flux, the CDL program participation reduced as anticipated (Sect. 5.5). This reduction in participant numbers should not be misconceived as signifying that non-completing participants did not benefit from the program, as exemplified by Fig. 7.2, and further elaborated below (Sects. 7.2 and 7.3). Finally, this research was conducted as a provision of an external service and hence may not have benefitted from full organizational-level buy-in.

7.2 Prisoners Consider Therapeutic Art Programs Calming and Conducive to Reducing Violence Within Their Prison Environment (Theme 2)

As discussed in Chaps. 3–5, Australian prisons face intense strain due to rising inmate numbers, resulting in a volatile environment (Russell & Baldry, 2020). Over time, this heightened frustration can build up, seeking release in a state of catharsis (Gussak, 2004, 2006, 2007, 2009a, b, 2013, 2016, 2019).

This study extends previous research by focusing on therapeutic art within the Australian prison milieu (Djurichkovic 2011). Many subjects, themes, and formulas from previous international research were replicated in this study (Deaver, 2002). Notably, although the study was conducted in a different continent, context, culture, and era, the research reproduced many identical findings from Gussak's work conducted over decades, both in the United Kingdom and in the United States (e.g., Gussak, 2004, 2006, 2007): "art therapy catharses and sublimates aggression and violence, by-products of this [prison] environment, simultaneously allowing [inmates] to escape from their boring, restrictive and constraining environment" (Gussak, 2017, p. 73).

The program, pilot, and research consistently highlighted the positive effects of incorporating art in prison (Giles et al., 2016; Tucker & Luetz, 2021, 2023). After the initial session, one participant reportedly faced violence and intimidation from other inmates in his unit, thus preventing his return to the CDL program. Notwithstanding other challenges, over subsequent weeks, the CDL group's initially "standoffish" and unapproachable dynamics progressively transformed into a small yet supportive art community. By the program's end, all participants had formed a cohesive group, noted by their communal approach to supporting each other's artistic achievements and united in a calmer manner. There were hints of this noticed even in the control group (see Theme 3).

Throughout this research and over many years of piloting, it was noticeable that art commands considerable respect within the prison community, fostering a peaceful atmosphere for facilitated sessions and individual, self-taught practices (Tucker & Luetz, 2021). Consistent with the literature, this reputation promotes nonviolent interactions among inmates, as evidenced by numerous conversations where inmates expressed a desire for art due to its calming nature (Howells et al., 1997; Latessa et al., 2002). One participant commented, "I've personally witnessed art bring prisoners together. I've watched others encourage people who do art. Please bring more art to prison" (P1-POST; Question 6.5). Similarly, another participant observed that art has a positive effect on prisoner well-being, saying, "Doing art and having it accessible to prisoners helps the mood & outlook of the mind" (P9-POST; Question 6.4).

The calming qualities of art were recurrently highlighted throughout the questionnaire results (Sects. 6.3–6.4) and most clearly noted in responses to Questions 2.3 (I think beautiful art can be calming for people when upset or in distress) and 3.3 (Creative activities can help to reduce anger in prison) (Tables 6.4, 6.5, 6.8, and 6.9). Furthermore, inmates habitually queried why art has become so restrictive. The most common questions were, "Why don't they let us have art? It's good for us; It was good when we had art, there were less fights and boredom … and stuff" (pers. comm. with anonymous inmate; Researcher Journal, 24 March, p. 4). This again supports the hypothesis that art can help reduce violence within the prison milieu (Gussak, 2019; King, 2016; Ursprung, 1997).

In summary, and as depicted in Fig. 6.1, the quantitative findings and inmates' questionnaire responses underscore the widespread agreement among inmates that art and creative interventions can serve as an outlet for cathartic experiences in the prison setting. Despite the geographical distance between Australia and research done in the United States, there was strong concurrence that inmates noticeably experienced art as having a calming effect when facilitated therapeutically (Arjona & Van Lith, 2024; Gussak, 2019; Rothwell, 2016). This finding also underscores the positive influence of personalized creative interventions in prisons where art has been shown to effectively redirect behaviors from *re*active to *inter*active (Moschini, 2005; Needs, 2012). Crucially, art in prison can promote tranquility amidst heightened arousal, thus fostering a calmer environment. Moreover, conjoining therapeutic art interventions with psychoanalytic insights can lay the foundation for future research on the enduring impact of artistic therapy in the prison setting (Rothwell, 2016; Tucker & Luetz, 2023).

7.3 Art Programs Appropriate to the Prison Culture Offer Cascading Benefits to the Prison Milieu and Can Exert a Positive Influence Even on Non-Art Therapy Program Participants (Theme 3)

As discussed in Sects. 6.3 and 6.4, it was observed that the control group, though not formally involved in the CDL program facilitation, exhibited a rise in mean scores from pretesting to posttesting (Tables 6.6 and 6.7). Interestingly, this phenomenon was observed in several questions: Question 2.1 response scores (I enjoy art) increased from 4.333 (pretest) to 4.833 (posttest); Question 2.3 scores (I think beautiful art can be calming for people when upset or in distress) increased from 4.166 (pretest) to 4.333 (posttest); Question 2.4 scores (Creative hobbies like coloring in or writing letters help me to feel peaceful) rose from 4.166 (pretest) to 4.333 (posttest); Question 2.5 responses (I think art and being creative can lift my emotional well-being) rose from 4.166 (pretest) to 4.5 (posttest). This correlation was unanticipated. Given that control group members were not involved in the art therapy facilitation, the numbers were expected to remain unchanged.

This phenomenon (of increased scores) is hypothesized here to result from the shared living arrangements of control group prisoners, many of whom were housed together with CDL participants dispersed across high-security prison units (CCC, 2018). During designated "out-of-cell" times, when the CDL program was not in session, inmates in both groups often engaged in communal activities, such as drawing at stainless steel tables in common areas (Tucker & Luetz, 2021). This shared action fosters social interaction and social exchange. CDL participants, motivated by their program experiences, willingly assisted fellow prisoners in active teaching and participatory learning during such times and admitted doing so in conversations with the principal researcher (see Sects. 6.6 and 6.7). This interaction created a ripple effect resembling snowballing and the Fibonacci sequence (Gleick, 2008; Sapolsky, 2017). As prisoners moved within the facilities, they continued teaching others and sharing their skills. In some instances, these acquired skills were utilized

7.3 Art Programs Appropriate to the Prison Culture Offer Cascading Benefits…

in transactions within the environment's economy, where prisoner goods and services are exchanged (Gussak, 2019). It is hypothesized here that the increased posttest responses from the control group can be attributed to this social dynamic (Braithwaite, 1989; Cullen & Jonson, 2016).

Notably, there was a reduction shown in responses to Question 2.6 (Learning art and craft skills can stop me from feeling lonely), which reduced from 4.333 (pretest) to 4.166 (posttest). The decrease in these figures may be linked to the control group inmates not fully benefiting from the art skills taught to CDL participants. While there was some influence from other CDL participants in common areas, the control group lacked the comprehensive experience of full immersion and learning from the program, leaving them without the necessary artistic skills to alleviate solitude during lockdowns (Wener, 2012).

This observation may highlight the interdependence between the prison institutions' environment, their social and industrialized nature, and the individuals who are subject to incarceration. In responding to the environment for survival, mirroring occurs, leading to the development of a microculture characterized by interdependence in function, action, and reaction (King, 2016; Hass-Cohen & Carr, 2008; Sapolsky, 2017). Figure 7.3 reflects a clear shift from pretesting to posttesting in the control group participant's request for a more active engagement with therapeutic art facilitation. As noted in desistance theory (Maruna, 2001), inmates aim for success and purpose within their peer group. Art is viewed as embodying character and authenticity within a microculture that is desperate to express personal identity and individuality.

Interestingly, in contrast to the discussion above (Tables 6.6 and 6.7), responses to questions about the prison environment (Tables 6.10 and 6.11) highlight a shift in thinking by control group members regarding the benefits of full program participation. This was noted especially in terms of the propensity of art to reduce solitude

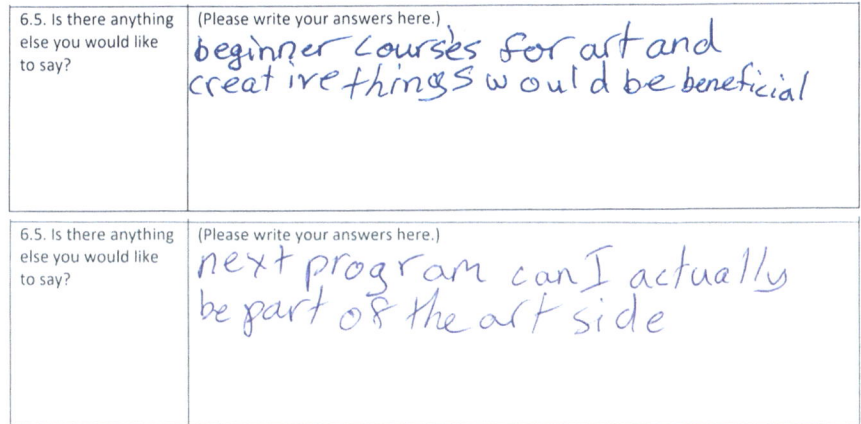

Fig. 7.3 Control group participant C2 responding to Question 6.5 (pretest above, posttest below). The responses signify a clear request to be included in the full CDL art program

during lockdowns and potentially improve communication skills with the parole board, particularly for low-literate participants (see Sect. 3.1). Participant responses to selected items indicated positive shifts in perception over the course of the program. The mean score for Question 3.4 (I would feel less lonely during lockdowns if I could do art) increased from 4 (pretest) to 4.5 (posttest). Similarly, scores for Question 3.1 (I would like to use art for my parole application) increased from 3.833 (pretest) to 4.166 (posttest), and for Question 3.3 (Creative activities can help to reduce anger) from 4.166 (pretest) to 4.5 (posttest). These research results support international findings, highlighting art as a fundamental human right. Creative skill development offers prisoners a vital outlet through which they can mentally and emotionally transcend the harsh conditions of the prison environment (Wener, 2012; Foucault, 2020).

In summary, art programs appropriate to the prison culture seemingly offer several cascading benefits to the prison milieu. They can exert a positive influence even on non-art therapy program participants. This apparent correlation would be highly relevant for future research to explore and confirm.

7.4 Indigenous Identity Is Bound to Artistic Expression and Remains Visually and Viscerally Connected to Country and Kinship—Despite the Injustices of Incarceration (Theme 4)

This research discovered important aspects of Indigenous culture and identity through art. Unanticipated insights emerged through interactions with Indigenous research participants observed in the CDL program and control group cohorts. This discussion covers selected consequences of Australia's hyper-incarceration of the Indigenous and how relevant impacts were observed during this research.

As discussed in Chap. 3, as of June 30, 2024, Aboriginal and Torres Strait Islander prisoners accounted for 36% of all prisoners incarcerated in Australia (ABS, 2025). While the demographic section of the questionnaires did not specifically ask participants to identify as Indigenous or non-Indigenous (Appendix 1), it can be inferred from these national statistics that approximately five CDL participants and control group members identified as Indigenous. This was also confirmed by program participants in conversations with the facilitator, especially during the program section that covers background, personal histories, and identity (Table 6.1). Therefore, the links between art and Indigenous identity are worth exploring.

The hyper-incarceration of Indigenous Australians is concomitant with the trauma of historical and contemporary colonization (McCausland & Baldry, 2023). Research has not sufficiently considered the long-lasting effects of ongoing colonization on Indigenous epistemology, axiology, and ontology (Kearney et al., 2023). Captive to their own land and yet persistently overruled by a foreign force, Australian Indigenous prisoners remain connected through art to their Law, Kinship, and Country, which constitute an integral component of the Indigenous knowledge system (Kearney et al., 2023; Morphy, 2009). The visual arts provide a fundamental means for Indigenous prisoners to remain connected to their own truth and story despite the walls that segregate the Indigenous from their Kinships and bloodlines (Gibson, 2019). Access to visual arts for prisoners permits culturally attuned and appropriate space to critique the colonial present and redefine a personal sense of autonomy (Van Styvendale et al., 2021).

As discussed in Chaps. 2 and 3, the contemporary over-representation of Indigenous inmates in Australia is interconnected historically with colonial methods of regulation to dispossess the original inhabitants of their land and freedom (ALRC, 2018). Importantly, Australia's history points to Indigenous people being conceived and violated as "property" by colonial bodies of authority and governance. For instance, Queensland records from 1935 highlight the use of the word "inmate" to signify authoritarian control and "ownership" over Indigenous Australians (Watson, 2005). Moreover, Rowse (2017) reports that "Queensland's legislation and institutional network enabled it to remove whole families from their country of origin to an institution" (p. 50). Further, Blake (1998) points out that this form of abuse extended well beyond notions of "justice":

> The removals program fulfilled a variety of objectives: removing the old and unemployable from station and fringe camps; controlling behaviour in fringe camps, on settlements and labour relations; as means of extending prison sentences and punishment over and beyond the legal system (p. 52)

Set against this background, prisons have been utilized as an additional tool for asserting dominance and control, exerting a legacy of authority over the Indigenous. Hyper-incarceration of Indigenous communities further led to increased dispossession from their own Law, Country, Kinship, and Culture (Kearney et al., 2023; McCausland & Baldry, 2023; Morphy, 2009). The deprivation of an entire culture is accentuated by the failed efforts to reduce Indigenous deaths in custody, as observed by the Royal Commission into Aboriginal Deaths in Custody (RCIADIC, 1991). Tragically, Indigenous deaths in custody have risen over recent decades: "In 2022–23, there were 21 Aboriginal and Torres Strait Islander deaths in prison custody…, the highest number of Indigenous deaths in prison custody since 1979–80" (McAlister et al., 2023, p. 10).

The above context is relevant to the experience of inmates, as exemplified by CDL Participant 11. This Indigenous inmate immediately displayed traditional knowledge of the arts and categorized his Indigenous culture as "his biggest dream" (see Fig. 7.4).

Using elements of action research (Chap. 5) and "yarning,"[1] Participant 11 discussed notions of Kinship, Country, and Law and how they remained consistently revered throughout his nearly 25 years of institutionalization. Opportunities for "yarning" arose whenever his mind was focused and not side-tracked by mourning

---

[1] Yarning "reflects a formal process of sharing knowledge that is reliant upon relationships, expected outcomes, responsibility and accountability between the participants, country and culture …" (Rynne & Cassematis, 2015, p. 105).

and "sorry business."[2] Notably, he frequently mentioned his own fears of becoming a death-in-custody statistic. He had aimed to prepare his final piece on the theme: "no more deaths in custody." It was unfortunate that despite his best efforts to complete the CDL program, the overwhelming impact of recurrent video-link funerals connected to deaths in his "Mob"[3] manifested in problematic behaviors that ultimately prevented him from achieving his final art piece. Notably, Participant 11 could easily paint the Australian landscape, as seen below (Fig. 7.5a–d), despite only spending approximately 15 years (of his 39 years) outside of institution or prison walls and living in urban settings only (Researcher Journal, March, pp. 13–16).

Crucially, without ever having experienced the visceral space of being "on Country" with its smells, sounds, wildlife, and colors, his imprinted knowledge and ability to apply brushwork to express cultural symbolism and tell "Story" was remarkable. Curiously, sentiments of attachment to Country and Dreaming were shared by CDL and control group participants alike (Fig. 7.6), signifying a high affinity between the Indigenous flag and Country being associated with Dreaming.[4]

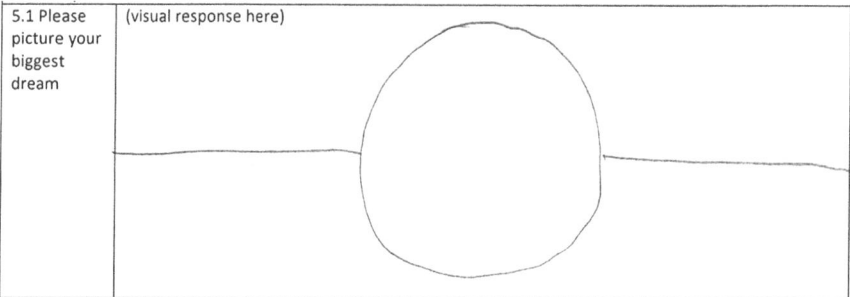

Fig. 7.4 CDL Participant 11 responding to Question 5.1 (pretest), outlining the Australian Indigenous flag, which symbolizes the Indigenous People, the sun under which they live, and their Country—his "biggest dream". The outline represents the significant collective desire for independence, recognition, and treaty

---

[2] "Sorry business" is a term within the Australian Indigenous context that delineates the mourning period following a death or acknowledges profound injustices within the community. It becomes particularly poignant when, for instance, a Native Title application is abandoned, resulting in the unrecognized severance of Indigenous ties to Country. In certain communities, the anguish of losing connection to culture or land resonates as profoundly as the grief experienced for a departed individual. This underscores the profound and intrinsic bond Indigenous communities share with the land (Kearney et al., 2023).

[3] The word "Mob" in Australian Indigenous context is a colloquial term used to identify a community of Indigenous members with a particular place, Country. Mob can represent the immediate family group, clan group, or wider Indigenous community, as in the Indigenous prisoners "us mob inside" (based on Researcher Journal, p. 14; see also Gibson, 2019).

[4] Dreaming in the Australian Indigenous Culture refers to a timeless connection to the spirit world (Gibson, 2019).

7.4 Indigenous Identity Is Bound to Artistic Expression and Remains Visually...   79

Fig. 7.5 (**a, b, c, d**) Images created by CDL Participant 11 reflect his ancestral connection to Indigenous Australian themes and/or colors. Top left: A rudimentary color wheel showcases skill in color mixing methods. Top right: An incomplete but accurately brush-lined image of an Australian native plant sacred to smoking ceremonies known as "Saltbush" (Atriplex nummularia) shown in its natural habitat, the Australian scrub. To the top left of the "Saltbush" is a swatch of painted color, which is impressionistic of the weather changing in the Australian outback. Bottom left: A pencil sketch of a turtle with Australian Indigenous tribal markings on its shell. Bottom right: A black silhouette fine-lined brushed painting of a native Australian plant known as a "Black Boy" (Xanthorrhoea preissii) or in some Aboriginal Australian dialects as "Wardnu". This silhouette is set against the outline of the Australian central outback landscape in a similar style to famous Indigenous artist Albert (Elea) Namatjira

In summary, Indigenous identity and autonomy are bound to artistic expression. The amazing ability to visually communicate Kinship and Country through art has been repeatedly observed by the art facilitator and principal researcher working alongside other Indigenous inmates, including across other centers; crucially, its significance in relation to notions of Indigeneity has not yet been adequately documented in other research. The preservation of Indigenous prisoner culture

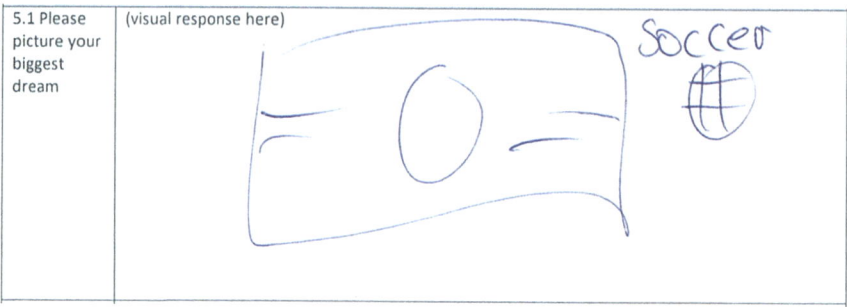

Fig. 7.6 Control group participant P10 responding to Question 5.1 (posttest), "the biggest dream." A line drawing of the Aboriginal Australian flag is stylized to mimic movement in the wind. To the right, there's a stylized pen outline of a soccer ball. These two images significance for Indigenous males. The images symbolize the dream of many to emulate their hero, Wiradjuri man Harry Williams, the first Indigenous member of the Australian national soccer team to play in a FIFA World Cup in 1974

expressing itself through art remains unscathed despite Australian society underappreciating its meaningfulness in the prison context (Gibson, 2019; Kearney et al., 2023).

Supported by knowledge sharing, which may include storytelling, ceremonies, painting, and "yarning," Indigenous Culture transcends geographical, ecological, ancestral, and socially shaped perspectives. Furthermore, the observations of this research support the view that Indigenous inmates—removed "from Country"—remain visually and viscerally connected to their heritage despite incarceration (Morphy, 2009; Rynne & Cassematis, 2015). This reaffirms Indigenous identity by retelling traditional stories through artwork that are contemporarily relevant to the prison context. As discussed in Themes 1 and 3, prisoners struggle with issues of authenticity and identity. This is even more prevalent for Indigenous survivors of assimilation practices. Art assists in sharing and rebounding from a history of exclusion. Artistic expression may strengthen identity, autonomy, and self-determination—far more so than currently recognized (Morphy, 2009), which is a key contribution of this research.

References

ALRC—Australian Law Reform Commission. (2018). *Pathways to justice—An inquiry into the incarceration rate of Aboriginal and Torres Strait Islander Peoples*. Australian Government. https://www.alrc.gov.au/wp-content/uploads/2019/08/final_report_133_amended1.pdf

Arjona, H., & Van Lith, T. (2024). Transformative connections: Exploring relational art therapy in a women's prison. *Art Therapy*, 1–7. https://doi.org/10.1080/07421656.2024.2354630

Australian Bureau of Statistics. (2025). *Prisoners in Australia*. ABS. Reference period 2024. Released 19/12/2024. https://www.abs.gov.au/statistics/people/crime-and-justice/prisoners-australia/latest-release

References

Banks, C. W., Haney, C., Jaffe, D., & Zimbardo, P. (1971). *The Stanford prison experiment. A simulation study of the psychology of imprisonment.* web.stanford.edu/dept/spec_coll/uarch/exhibits/Narration.pdf

Blake, T. (1998). Deported ... at the sweet will of the government: The removal of Aborigines to reserves in Queensland 1897–1939. *Aboriginal History, 22*, 51–61.

Braithwaite, J. (1989). *Crime, shame and reintegration.* Cambridge University Press.

CCC—Crime and Corruption Commission. (2018). *Transcript of investigative hearing.* Taskforce Flaxton Transcripts. www.ccc.qld.gov.au/sites/default/files/Docs/Public-Hearings/Flaxton/Transcripts/Taskforce-Flaxton-Transcript-Day-2-15-May-2018-Sam-ZhouandQCS.pdf

Cohen-Liebman, M. S. (2016). Forensic art therapy: Epistemological and ontological underpinnings. In D. E. Gussak & M. L. Rosal (Eds.), *The Wiley handbook of art therapy* (pp. 469–477). John Wiley & Sons.

CSAC—Corrective Services Administrators' Council. (2018). *Guiding principles for Corrections in Australia.* State Government of Victoria. https://www.corrections.vic.gov.au/guiding-principles-for-corrections-in-australia

Cullen, F. T., & Jonson, C. L. (2016). *Correctional theory: Context and consequences.* Sage.

Cunneen, C., Baldry, E., Brown, D., Brown, M., Schwartz, M., & Steel, A. (2013). *Penal culture and hyperincarceration: The revival of the prison.* Routledge.

Day, A. (2020). At a crossroads? Offender rehabilitation in Australian prisons. *Psychiatry Psychology and Law, 27*(6), 939–949.

Day, A., Davey, L., Heseltine, K., Howells, K., & Sarre, R. (2004). *Correctional offender treatment programs: The national picture in Australia.* Report for the Criminology Research Council. crg.aic.gov/reports

Deaver, S. P. (2002). What constitutes art therapy research? *Art Therapy: Journal of the American Art Therapy Association, 19*(1), 23–27.

Djurichkovic, A. (2011). *Art in prisons: A literature review of the philosophies and impacts of visual arts programs for correctional populations.* Report for Arts Access Australia. UTS Shopfront Student Series no 3. UTSePress https://opus.lib.uts.edu.au/bitstream/10453/19836/7/Art%20in%20Prisons.pdf

Foucault, M. (2020). *Discipline and punish.* Penguin Books.

Gibson, S. (2019). The pulse of history: In my blood it runs and Indigenous identity. *Screen Education, 96*, 72–77.

Giles, M., Paris, L., & Whale, J. (2016). The role of art education in adult prisons: The Western Australian experience. *International Review of Education, 62*(6), 689–709. https://doi.org/10.1007/s11159-016-9604-3

Gleick, J. (2008). *Chaos: Making a new science.* Penguin.

Grenfell, L., Mackay, A., & Rose, M. (2023). A human right to daily access to fresh air beyond prisons in Australia? *Australian Journal of Human Rights*, 1–18.

Griffin, O. H., III, & Woodward, V. H. (2017). *Routledge handbook of corrections in the United States.* Routledge.

Gussak, D. (2004). Art therapy with prison inmates: A pilot study. *The Arts in Psychotherapy, 31*(4), 245–259.

Gussak, D. (2006). Effects of art therapy with prison inmates: A follow-up study. *The Arts in Psychotherapy, 33*(3), 188–198.

Gussak, D. (2007). The effectiveness of art therapy in reducing depression in prison populations. *International Journal of Offender Therapy and Comparative Criminology, 51*(4), 444–460.

Gussak, D. (2009a). Comparing the effectiveness of art therapy on depression and locus of control of male and female inmates. *The Arts in Psychotherapy, 36*(4), 202–207.

Gussak, D. (2009b). The effects of art therapy on male and female inmates: Advancing the research base. *The Arts in Psychotherapy, 36*(1), 5–12.

Gussak, D. (2013, October 22). Art behind bars: The trials of providing therapy in prison—is art the key? *Psychology Today* [blogpost]. https://www.psychologytoday.com/blog/arttrial/201310/art-behind-bars

Gussak, D. E. (2016). Art therapy in the prison milieu. Part V: Practicing art therapy in interdisciplinary settings. In D. E. Gussak & M. L. Rosal (Eds.), *The Wiley handbook of art therapy* (pp. 478–486). Wiley.

Gussak, D. E. (2017). The continuing emergence of art therapy in prisons. In B. Elger, C. Ritter, & H. Stöver (Eds.), *Emerging issues in prison health*. Springer. https://doi.org/10.1007/978-94-017-7558-8_5

Gussak, D. (2019). *Art and art therapy with the imprisoned: Re-creating identity*. Routledge.

Haney, C. (2012). Prison effects in the era of mass incarceration. *The Prison Journal*. https://doi.org/10.1177/0032885512448604

Hass-Cohen, N., & Carr, R. (2008). *Art therapy and clinical neuroscience*. Jessica Kingsley Publishers.

Heseltine, K., Sarre, R., & Day, A. (2011). Prison-based correctional rehabilitation: An overview of intensive interventions for moderate to high risk offenders. *Trends and Issues in Crime and Criminal Justice, 412*, 1–6. https://www.aic.gov.au/publications/tandi/tandi412

Howells, K., Watt, B., Hall, G., & Baldwin, S. (1997). Developing programmes for violent offenders. *Legal and Criminological Psychology, 2*, 117–128.

Innes, C. (2015). *Healing corrections: The future of imprisonment*. Northeastern University Press.

Kearney, A., Bradley, J., Dodd, V., Norman a-Marrngawi, D., Timothy a-Muluwamara, M., Dimanyurru, G. F., & Karrakayny-a, A. (2023). *Indigenous law and the politics of kincentricity and orality*. Springer Nature. https://doi.org/10.1007/978-3-031-19239-5

King, J. (2016). *Art therapy, trauma and neuroscience. Theoretical and practical perspectives*. Routledge.

Latessa, E. J., Cullen, F. T., & Gendreau, P. (2002). *Beyond correctional quackery: Professionalism and the possibility of effective treatment* (pp. 43–49). Federal Probation.

Maguire, M., & Raynor, P. (2017). Offender management in and after prison: The end of 'end to end'? *Criminology and Criminal Justice, 17*(2), 138–157. https://doi.org/10.1177/1748895816665435

Maruna, S. (2001). *Making good: How ex-convicts reform and re-build their lives*. American Psychological Association.

McAlister, M., Miles, H., & Bricknell, S. (2023). *Deaths in custody in Australia 2022-23*. Statistical Report no. 44. Canberra: Australian Institute of Criminology. 10.52922/sr77222

McCausland, R., & Baldry, E. (2023). Who does Australia lock up? The social determinants of justice. *International Journal for Crime, Justice and Social Democracy, 12*(3), 37–53. https://doi.org/10.5204/ijcjsd.2504

Morphy, H. (2009). Art and social cohesion in Indigenous Australia. *Humanities Research, 15*(2), 115–131. https://doi.org/10.22459/HR.XV.02.2009.08

Moschini, L. B. (2005). *Drawing the line: Art therapy with the difficult client*. Wiley.

Needs, G. (2012). *Art therapy: Foundation and form*. InsideArts.

Queensland Productivity Commission. (2020). *Inquiry into imprisonment and recidivism*. https://s3.treasury.qld.gov.au/files/Imprisonment-Volume-2-final-report.pdf

RCIADIC—Australian Royal Commission. (1991). *Royal Commission into Aboriginal deaths in custody*. National Report, Vol. 2 (A Pp 1991 no 127) [1991] AURoyalC 2 (9 May 1991).

Rothwell, K. (Ed.) (2016). *Forensic art therapies: Anthology of practice and research*. Free Association Books UK.

Rowse, T. (2017). *Indigenous and other Australians since 1901*. UNSW Press.

Russell, S., & Baldry, E. (2020). *The Booming Industry Continued: Australian Prisons. A report*. 22 p. University of New South Wales. https://www.cclj.unsw.edu.au/article/report-booming-industry-continued-australian-prisons-2020-update

Rynne, J., & Cassematis, P. (2015). Assessing the Prison Experience for Australian First Peoples: A Prospective Research Approach. *International Journal for Crime, Justice and Social Democracy, 4*(1), 96–112. https://doi.org/10.5204/ijcjsd.v4i1.208

Sapolsky, R. M. (2017). *Behave: The biology of humans at our best and worst*. Penguin.

Sarre, R. (2010). Prison-based correctional offender rehabilitation programs: The 2009 national picture in Australia. *Criminology Research Council: Consultancy, c05*, 08/09.

References

Seiter, R. (2017). *Corrections: An introduction* (5th ed.). LSC Communications, Pearson Education.

Tucker, S., & Luetz, J. M. (2021). Art therapy and prison chaplaincy—A review of contemporary practices considering New Testament teachings. In J. M. Luetz & B. Green (Eds.), *Innovating Christian education research—Multidisciplinary perspectives* (pp. 239–269). Springer. https://doi.org/10.1007/978-981-15-8856-3_15

Tucker, S., & Luetz, J. M. (2023). Art therapy in Australian prisons—A research agenda. *International Journal of Offender Therapy and Comparative Criminology*. https://doi.org/10.1177/0306624X231165350

Ursprung, W. (1997). Insider art: The creative ingenuity of the incarcerated artist. In D. Gussak & E. Virshup (Eds.), *Drawing time: Art therapy in prisons and other correctional settings* (pp. 13–24). Magnolia Street Pub.

Van Styvendale, N., McDougall, J. D., Henry, R., & Innes, R. A. (2021). *The arts of Indigenous health and well-being*. University of Manitoba Press.

Watson, J. (2005). *A preponderance of Aboriginal blood*. Numero Uno Publications.

Wener, R. (2012). *The environmental psychology of prisons and jails: Creating humane spaces in secure settings*. Cambridge University Press.

Wright, R. (2005). Going to teach in prisons: Culture shock. *Journal of Correctional Education*, 56(1), 19–38.

Open Access This chapter is licensed under the terms of the Creative Commons Attribution 4.0 International License (http://creativecommons.org/licenses/by/4.0/), which permits use, sharing, adaptation, distribution and reproduction in any medium or format, as long as you give appropriate credit to the original author(s) and the source, provide a link to the Creative Commons license and indicate if changes were made.

The images or other third party material in this chapter are included in the chapter's Creative Commons license, unless indicated otherwise in a credit line to the material. If material is not included in the chapter's Creative Commons license and your intended use is not permitted by statutory regulation or exceeds the permitted use, you will need to obtain permission directly from the copyright holder.

Chapter 8
Concluding Synthesis

Set within an empirical mixed-methods research framework and experimental practice paradigm, this research has presented empirical data exploring the effects of therapeutic art programs on prisoner well-being. The conceptual blueprint design has benefited from 5 years of piloting and may be implemented in prisons both within and beyond the borders of Australia. Supported by creative and experience-informed practice, the multidimensional program and its methodological design proposition to interlace scientific and empirical discovery in support of a more humane criminological theory generation. By combining divergent methodologies to foster new knowledge and insights, the research presented in this book embodies a prototype that promises to overcome the limitations of previous research approaches (Richards & Ross, 2001). Importantly, by facilitating creative interventions through sensitively attuned art therapy delivery, this cross-disciplinary research promises benefits for diverse prison stakeholder groups, including inmates, chaplaincy and parole services, sentence management, voluntary facilitators, policymakers, criminologists, prisoner advocacy groups, and taxpayers, among others. In the age of AI, prison privatization, and algorithm-driven data mining and analysis, human-centric prison art therapy may play a far more prominent role in facilitating community, rehabilitation, healing, and reconciliation while breaking the cycle of recidivism to benefit both offenders and society (Baldry, 2010; Baldry et al., 2018; Baldry & Cunneen, 2014; Bolwerk et al., 2014; Hayman, 2012; Maruna, 2001; Peck, 1998; Schwartz et al., 2020; Sydes et al., 2017; Westwood, 2015).

This concluding chapter summarizes key research findings. It will first discuss the contribution of this research to the field (Sect. 8.1), then cover limitations and opportunities for future research (Sect. 8.2), and lastly close with selected recommendations for research, policy, and practice (Sect. 8.3).

8.1 Key Findings from This Research

The immensity of the current project makes a comprehensive coverage of all discoveries virtually impossible. The following five points are advanced as a modest and condensed synthesis of the key research findings.

First, prison art therapy demonstrates measurable benefits and warrants broader implementation, guided by the expertise of trained and experienced facilitators. Prisons are complex environments for inmates, facilitators, and staff. Notwithstanding, it is appropriate and transformative for therapeutic art programs to be implemented that match the security requirements of the prison/s (Soape et al., 2022). Given the environmental complexity of prison systems, it is appropriate, if not essential, that facilitators have a level of "lived" and "living experience" coupled with social competence. This will assist in integrating and implementing effective therapeutic strategies that foster prisoner engagement and improve rehabilitation outcomes (Baldry et al., 2018; Day, 2020; Doyle et al., 2021; Howells et al., 2004; Sydes et al., 2017).

Second, the findings underscore the widespread agreement among inmates that art and creative interventions can be a meaningful outlet for cathartic experiences in the prison setting (see Sects. 6.3–6.5, and 7.2). Crucially, art in prison can promote tranquility amidst heightened arousal, thus fostering a calmer environment, in addition to alleviating loneliness and reinforcing well-being while contributing to a heightened sense of self and authentic identity (Gussak, 2019; Rothwell, 2016). The benefits of a calmer environment will accrue not only to therapeutic art program participants but will be felt by the wider inmate population, prison officers, and prison management teams. In short, art in prison is not a luxury—it is a low-cost, high-impact intervention that enhances individual well-being and cultivates systemic benefits across the carceral environment.

Third, the impact of art therapy appears to extend beyond direct participants, suggesting a wider communal effect. Therapeutic art programs, in this regard, seemingly offer cascading benefits to the wider prison community. They can exert a positive influence even on non-art therapy program participants and invigorate a prison micro-community of artists who engage in comradery through art (see Sects. 6.3–6.5, and 7.3). This correlation was unanticipated and expressed itself in the surprising control group data (Sects. 6.3 and 6.4). Notably, the control group demonstrated modest but consistent increases in self-reported appreciation for art and its emotional benefits, with improvements noted in six of eight measured question categories. These gains, though limited, suggest a potential vicarious or spillover effect from the CDL art therapy program within the prison environment. In short, the emerging evidence points to a previously overlooked ripple effect of art therapy within the broader prison population. This apparent correlation is newly discovered and would be highly relevant for future independent research to explore and confirm (Gussak, 2019).

Fourth, art serves as a powerful conduit for sustaining and expressing Indigenous identity within the prison system. Indigenous identity and autonomy are bound to artistic expression. Strikingly, Indigenous identity stays visually linked to Country and Kinship. Despite the high incarceration of Indigenous inmates and ongoing deaths in custody, culturally integrated art education can reaffirm Indigenous identity. Significantly, Indigenous inmates—although removed "from Country"—remain visually and viscerally connected to their heritage despite incarceration (Morphy, 2009; Rynne & Cassematis, 2015). Art can assist in sharing and rebounding from a history of exclusion, which may strengthen identity, autonomy, and self-determination—far more so than currently recognized (Morphy, 2009). This is another key contribution of this research.

Fifth, this research broke new ground by incorporating visual methodologies to elicit inmate perspectives in culturally relevant ways. Accordingly, the research design effectively captured inmate perspectives through questions that asked for visual responses (Appendix 1). This innovative approach has not previously been documented in the literature and represents a significant contribution to prison-based research methods. Using immersive and culturally appropriate methods of collecting quantitative and qualitative data, including innovative visual responses (Questions 5.1 and 5.2; see Chap. 5), yielded fresh perspectives and enabled prisoners to reveal aspects of their hidden selves when given alternate opportunities for communication. This was reflected through overwhelming evidence of additional artwork that could not be formally included and analyzed in the above discussion. Some additional artwork is featured in Supplementary Chaps. 9 and 10. In short, by integrating visual responses into its design, this study advanced a more inclusive method of capturing inmate voices, revealing that art constitutes valuable research data and holds enormous promise for future research and practice. Giving prisoners alternate methods of communication through art provides opportunities to communicate in alternate ways and points to fertile opportunities to innovate rehabilitation practice (Sect. 8.2).

8.2 Limitations and Opportunities for Future Research

This research is subject to some limitations.

First, the principal researcher performed the two roles of being both the program facilitator and lead investigator. This dual role may be conceived as a limitation, given that her focus rested simultaneously on both program delivery and data collection and analysis. This has been described by Kapitan (2011) in relation to the so-called espouse theory, which has been theorized as follows: "how art therapists *think* they act as compared to the *actual* behaviours that reflect their 'theories in use'" (p. 100; emphasis original). As noted in Chap. 5, several mitigating strategies were embedded in the research design and implemented to limit the propensity of researcher bias, including but not limited to (1) data analyses by multiple and external researchers and (2) the integration of a public art exhibition inviting independent analyses and perspectives, among others.

Second, as noted in Sect. 7.1, prisons are challenging environments. Prisoner cohorts are complex populations and can pose a range of challenges to facilitators of prison programs. This is due, in part, to the burgeoning growth of prisoner populations, which outpaces provision and planning, as noted in the *Guiding Principles for Corrections in Australia*: "It is critical that agencies consider this growth to avoid overcrowding" (CSAC, 2018, p. 29). Ethical requirements heightened the complexities inherent in the research. Although the Information Sheet and Consent Form benefited from the helpful input of multiple ethics review boards, which simplified the language used in the forms, there remained a residual complexity in the forms that required considerable time and explanation to convey. On two occasions, the principal researcher was accompanied by the co-investigator, who was present in prison in the first and final week to observe and support the informed consent and data collection process. During the life of the CDL program, the co-investigator became increasingly convinced of the challenges involved and the resilience required by the primary researcher who facilitated most of the program alone. Importantly, the low literacy and education levels of the prisoners (Table 6.1) implied the need for a comprehensive and appropriate explanation of the research project in relatable language that the prisoners could readily understand. It is highly recommended that future therapeutic prison art programs involve at least one dedicated assistant who can offer the principal facilitator consistent support. Furthermore, it would be useful to modify and simplify the AART instrument, as discussed in Sect. 6.6.

Third, unfortunately, the study was impacted by a range of factors beyond the researchers' control. Disruptions arose from a range of directions, including the COVID-19 global pandemic, which led to the prolonged closure of prisons to all research and delayed the project completion by approximately 2 years. Additionally, changes in job positions throughout the project establishment altered communication channels significantly, which also impacted the continuity and planning reliability of different aspects of the program.

Regrettably, the research presented in the chapters above covers mostly male perspectives. This is a reflection of the currently higher male prisoner population, although female incarceration rates are increasing, both in Australia (ABS, 2022) and around the world (Walmsley, 2017). As of 2017, 714,000 women and girls are in prison globally (Walmsley, 2017). In Australia, despite a 3% increase in the total number of prisoners across the country, the female prisoner population has risen by 6% (ABS, 2022). Unfortunately, posttest data could not be collected at the women's prison, wherefore this research is limited to predominantly male perspectives.

Notwithstanding, the collected pretest research at the women's prison holds significant value for ongoing and future studies focusing on the desires and needs of female inmates (Baldry, 2010, 2011; Baldry & Cunneen, 2014). Here again, the finding discussed above (Sects. 7.2 and 7.3) was reproduced, namely that art is perceived as conducive to prisoner well-being: "Art has improved my depression is very enjoyable and helps with well-being" (Female Participant P7, pretest). Beneficially, utilizing visual and verbal open-ended questioning was very effective in gathering relevant information; however, the data were incomplete and incomparable, and the researchers (with a heavy heart) ultimately discounted it and did not include it in Chap. 6. Notably, the process of confirming informed consent was significantly smoother with women inmates, as the women demonstrated good comprehension when reading the information out loud and discussing the

8.2 Limitations and Opportunities for Future Research

implications with each other. The interesting difference in male and female responses in similar programs has been hypothesized by Gussak (2009a, b). His later research confirms that despite women having different and more complex issues to manage, their ability to problem-solve creatively is unquestioned:

> Although both male and female inmates will exhibit marked improvement, the male inmates will exhibit different responses to the art therapy services in mood and locus of control than female inmates within their respective correctional environments ... something striking emerged ... the numbers revealed that while the men and women displayed positive change, the women had more of a deficit to overcome than men (Gussak, 2019, pp. 123–124).

The implications of premature program termination are straightforward. The women's perspectives, which are just as valid as the men's experience, are mostly missing. Consequently, the sample size is smaller than anticipated and desired. The point bears repeating that the circumstances that led to this outcome were beyond the control of the principal researcher and co-investigator and reflect the changeable conditions that prison research is commonly subject to (Baldry, 2010, 2011; Baldry & Cunneen, 2014; Haney, 2012; Gussak, 2019; Ursprung, 1997).

Fourth, numerous factors, including agendas and directives from multiple stakeholders, who were involved in this study, contributed to the challenges faced by the researchers. The disparity in the program stakeholdership involves a large faith-based charity, government-run management, prisoner advocacy groups, and universities, in addition to the ethics review boards associated with each of these organizations. This led to challenges wherein the researchers felt pulled in different and sometimes incompatible directions, requiring significant diplomatic effort to satisfy all the different interests.

Despite the many challenges that extended the project timeline, the research discovered and synthesized meaningful findings that contribute to knowledge in the field. It remains that historical recognition of art therapy as a psychotherapeutic tool and its full benefits, when well-implemented, remain underappreciated, undervalued, and underleveraged by prisons. Much work remains to be done, as observed in other similar research:

> The session ended with a call to arms for increased research .... It is more important that more research be conducted and more theoretical papers be published that explore the benefits and challenges that art therapists have in these environments. Please encourage others to heed the call to publish their much needed work. (Gussak, 2016, p. 484)

Art therapy deserves respect and acknowledgment from government bodies for its considerable potential as a rehabilitative tool that brings with it minimal cost (Gussak, 2016). Set against the background of the above-documented limitations, experiences, and opportunities, future implementation should prioritise co-facilitation models, gender inclusivity, and simplified tools to strengthen participation and data quality. Given the consistent evidence of benefit, further investment in culturally responsive, creative programming is not only justified but long overdue. More specifically, future research might consider making more contact with control group members, expanding visual answers, and/or including longitudinal studies of Indigenous art and symbolism across multiple centers and incarcerated families ("Mob").

8.3 Recommendations for Research, Policy, and Practice

This final section presents a shortlist of recommendations for selected stakeholders, including program facilitators, policymakers, prison centers, prisoner advocacy groups, universities/researchers, funders/philanthropists, and external prison service providers.

- *Program facilitators:* Ensure programs are accessible by adapting delivery to typical group contexts characterized by low levels of participant literacy. Helpful adjustments may include using printed materials with larger fonts and simplified language, as well as incorporating basic literacy support—such as writing skills and alphabet familiarity—into the program design. Moreover, future therapeutic prison art programs are likely to be more effective and enduring when facilitators are supported by at least one dedicated assistant who can provide consistent operational, interpersonal, and educational support.
- *Policymakers:* Support the development of enabling policies that embed therapeutic art as a standard feature of prison rehabilitation services. This includes allocating dedicated funding to ensure the sustainable delivery of art programs and facilitating prisoner art exhibitions to foster public understanding of victimology, recidivism, rehabilitation, and the lived realities of imprisonment. In doing so, policymakers can help normalise, mainstream, and leverage art therapy as a legitimate and impactful element of standard correctional rehabilitative practice.
- *Prison centers:* Employ and provide institutional support for qualified art therapists trained to navigate the complexities of correctional environments. Doing so will enable the safe, effective, and sustainable facilitation of therapeutic art programs as part of standard rehabilitative programming.
- *Prisoner advocacy groups:* Strengthen rights-based collaboration across sectors by working in alignment with correctional policy and institutional partners to promote access to art therapy and other creative rehabilitative initiatives. Doing so will enhance the effectiveness of therapeutic programming, amplify advocacy impact, and foster broader community well-being—outcomes that serve the shared interests of all stakeholders.
- *Universities/Researchers:* Provide proactive support to prospective research students with lived experience who wish to build on the findings and methodologies developed in this study. Doing so will advance inclusive research practices and creative methodologies, fostering innovation in the emerging field of rehabilitative prison art therapy, and deepening epistemic diversity within criminology and correctional research.
- *Funders/Philanthropists:* Identify and release targeted funding streams to proactively support independent researchers and facilitators pioneering new directions in therapeutic prison art. Doing so will raise the profile of an underdeveloped field and drive sustained investment and innovation in creative, evidence-based approaches to rehabilitation within prison settings. As a low-cost, high-impact intervention, therapeutic prison art presents an excellent funding opportunity with strong potential for social and systemic return on investment.

- *External prison service providers:* Adopt culturally holistic approaches—such as "yarning"—to better understand and meet the needs of Indigenous inmates through art-based programming. Doing so can foster culturally safe engagement, sustain ethnocultural identity, and enhance the therapeutic effectiveness of creative interventions. Cultivating culturally respectful practices also encourages greater participant engagement and acknowledges the systemic imperative to respond decisively to the over-incarceration of Indigenous people.

References

Australian Bureau of Statistics. (2022). *Prisoners in Australia, Reference period 2022*. https://www.abs.gov.au/statistics/people/crime-and-justice/prisoners-australia/2022

Baldry, E. (2010). Women in transition: From Prison to …. *Current Issues in Criminal Justice, 22*(2), 253–267. https://doi.org/10.1080/10345329.2010.12035885

Baldry, E. (2011). Navigating complex pathways: People with mental health disorders and cognitive disability in the criminal justice system in NSW. *HIV Australia, 9*(1), 44.

Baldry, E., & Cunneen, C. (2014). Imprisoned Indigenous women and the shadow of colonial patriarchy. *Australian and New Zealand Journal of Criminology, 47*(2), 276–298. https://doi.org/10.1177/0004865813503351

Baldry, E., Bright, D., Cale, J., Day, A., Dowse, L., Giles, M., Hardcastle, L., Graffam, J., McGillivray, J., Newton, D., Rowe, S., & Wodak, J. (2018). A future beyond the wall: Improving post-release employment outcomes for people leaving prison final report. *UNSW Sydney*. https://doi.org/10.26190/5b4fd2de5cfb4

Bolwerk, A., Mack-Andrick, J., Lang, F. R., Dörfler, A., & Maihöfner, C. (2014). How art changes your brain: Differential effects of visual art production and cognitive art evaluation on functional brain connectivity. *PLoS One, 9*(7), e101035. https://doi.org/10.1371/journal.pone.0101035

CSAC—Corrective Services Administrators' Council. (2018). *Guiding principles for Corrections in Australia*. State Government of Victoria. https://www.corrections.vic.gov.au/guiding-principles-for-corrections-in-australia

Day, A. (2020). At a crossroads? Offender rehabilitation in Australian prisons. *Psychiatry Psychology and Law, 27*(6), 939–949.

Doyle, C., Gardner, K., & Wells, K. (2021). The importance of incorporating lived experience in efforts to reduce Australian reincarceration rates. *International Journal for Crime, Justice and Social Democracy, 10*(2), 83–98.

Gussak, D. (2009a). Comparing the effectiveness of art therapy on depression and locus of control of male and female inmates. *The Arts in Psychotherapy, 36*(4), 202–207.

Gussak, D. (2009b). The effects of art therapy on male and female inmates: Advancing the research base. *The Arts in Psychotherapy, 36*(1), 5–12.

Gussak, D. E. (2016). Art therapy in the prison milieu. Part V: Practicing art therapy in interdisciplinary settings. In D. E. Gussak & M. L. Rosal (Eds.), *The Wiley handbook of art therapy* (pp. 478–486). Wiley.

Gussak, D. (2019). *Art and art therapy with the imprisoned: Re-creating identity*. Routledge.

Haney, C. (2012). Prison effects in the era of mass incarceration. *The Prison Journal*. https://doi.org/10.1177/0032885512448604

Hayman, G. W. (2012). *Turning prisons into learning communities: A new vision for corrections education* (Order No. 3541666). ProQuest One Academic (1115149061).

Howells, K., Heseltine, K., Sarre, R., Davey, L. & Day, A. (2004). *Correctional offender treatment programs: The national picture in Australia*. Report for the Criminology Research Council.

Kapitan, L. (2011). *Introduction to art therapy research*. Routledge.
Maruna, S. (2001). *Making good: How ex-convicts reform and re-build their lives*. American Psychological Association.
Morphy, H. (2009). Art and social cohesion in Indigenous Australia. *Humanities Research, 15*(2), 115–131. https://doi.org/10.22459/HR.XV.02.2009.08
Peck, M. S. (1998). *The different drum: Community making and peace* (2nd ed.). Touchstone.
Richards, S. C., & Ross, J. I. (2001). Introducing the new school of convict criminology. *Social Justice, 28*(1), 177–190. https://www.jstor.org/stable/29768063
Rothwell, K. (2016) (Ed.). *Forensic art therapies: Anthology of practice and research*. Free Association Books UK.
Rynne, J., & Cassematis, P. (2015). Assessing the Prison Experience for Australian First Peoples: A Prospective Research Approach. *International Journal for Crime, Justice and Social Democracy, 4*(1), 96–112. https://doi.org/10.5204/ijcjsd.v4i1.208
Schwartz, M., Russell, S., Baldry, E., Brown, D., Cunneen, C., & Stubbs, J. (2020). *Obstacles to effective support of people released from prison: Wisdom from the field*. https://unswprimo.hosted.exlibrisgroup.com/permalink/f/a5fmj0/unsworks_modsunsworks_71832
Soape, E., Barlow, C., Gussak, D. E., Brown, J., & Schubarth, A. (2022). Creative IDEA: Introducing a statewide art therapy in prisons program. *International Journal of Offender Therapy and Comparative Criminology, 66*(12), 1285–1302.
Sydes, M., Eggins, E., & Mazzerolle, L. (2017). *What works in corrections? A review of the evaluation literature*. University of Queensland, Queensland Government.
Ursprung, W. (1997). Insider art: The creative ingenuity of the incarcerated artist. In D. Gussak & E. Virshup (Eds.), *Drawing time: Art therapy in prisons and other correctional settings* (pp. 13–24). Magnolia Street Pub.
Walmsley, R. (2017). *Women and girls in penal institutions, including pre-trial detainees/remand prisoners. World female imprisonment list*. https://www.prisonstudies.org/sites/default/files/resources/downloads/world_female_prison_4th_edn_v4_web.pdf
Westwood, M. (2015, February 11). *Unlocking creativity in prisons* [Australian edition]. The Torch. https://thetorch.org.au/wp-content/uploads/1.-Torch_Summary_of_EvaluationV8.pdf

Open Access This chapter is licensed under the terms of the Creative Commons Attribution 4.0 International License (http://creativecommons.org/licenses/by/4.0/), which permits use, sharing, adaptation, distribution and reproduction in any medium or format, as long as you give appropriate credit to the original author(s) and the source, provide a link to the Creative Commons license and indicate if changes were made.

The images or other third party material in this chapter are included in the chapter's Creative Commons license, unless indicated otherwise in a credit line to the material. If material is not included in the chapter's Creative Commons license and your intended use is not permitted by statutory regulation or exceeds the permitted use, you will need to obtain permission directly from the copyright holder.

Chapter 9
Supplementary Chapter 1: Visual Vignette (A): Group Artwork

This visual vignette documents group artwork. Numerous inmates discarded valuable work due to shame or restrictions on keeping items in their cells. Some of these pieces were salvaged and are included in this supplementary chapter with the participants' consent. Other artworks were retrieved by the inmates from the rubbish bin with the encouragement of other group members and/or the facilitator. This vignette provides a snapshot of some of the salvaged artworks and the context surrounding their creation.

Due to the extensive scope of the project, not all the valuable visual data could be included in the preceding chapters. It is noteworthy to observe the evolution of the participating artists' work as they grappled with intricate and challenging aspects of the CDL program; some of this context is alluded to in this supplementary chapter. Program immersion proved to be highly beneficial for many program participants and had a wider effect that reached well beyond the participants themselves, as reflected by the nonparticipating control group (see Sect. 7.3). This supplementary chapter provides a glimpse into some of the group work.

Figure 9.1 shows how the program utilizes the prison environment for reference. Inmates are encouraged to draw the insides of their prison cells to gain a basic understanding of dimensions and structures (see bottom of the image).

Figure 9.2 reflects developmental struggles in comprehending basic dimensions. However, once achieved, the inmate gained a considerable sense of accomplishment from this exercise that he was able to continue inside his cell.

This sketch (Fig. 9.3) reflects symmetry, the Fibonacci sequence, organic structures, patterns, and design. This session potentially re-engages previously disrupted neural connections within the left and right hemispheres of the brain (Sects. 3.1 and 3.2).

The upcoming set of additional images depicts the advancement of participants during Session 3.5 (Table 6.1) on color theory. Adhering to the correctional services prisoner personal purchase supply lists (Fig. 11.1), this session exclusively utilizes primary colors. Participants engage in an intensive learning experience, mastering the art of mixing all necessary colors, hues, and tones for in-cell painting with

© The Author(s) 2025
S. Tucker, J. M. Luetz, *Therapeutic Prison Art Interventions*, SpringerBriefs in Criminology, https://doi.org/10.1007/978-3-031-85991-5_9

94   9 Supplementary Chapter 1: Visual Vignette (A): Group Artwork

Fig. 9.1 P9 Progress work from Session 1.5 (see Table 6.1)

Fig. 9.2 P14 Progress work from Session 1.5 (Table 6.1)

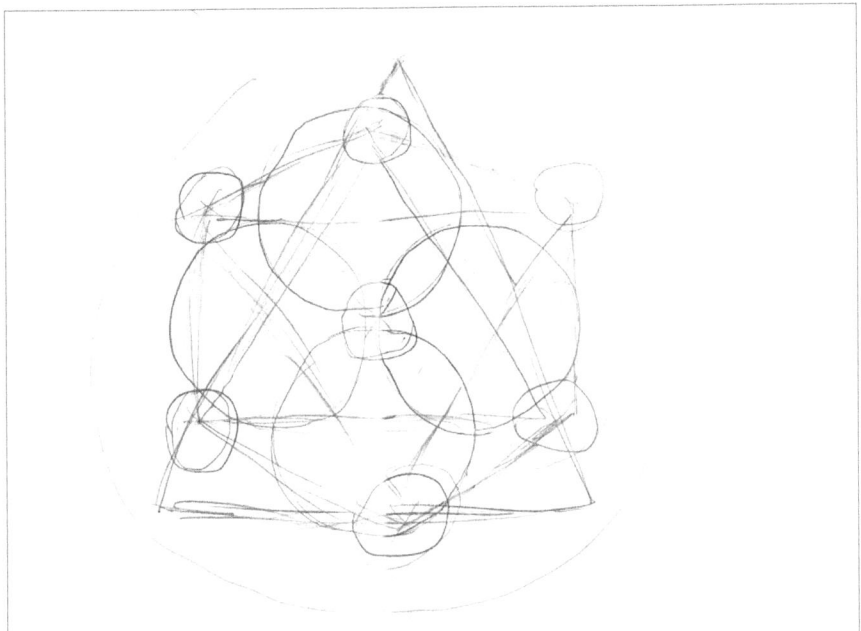

Fig. 9.3 P15 Progress work from Session 2.5 (Table 6.1)

limited resources. Despite being a challenging session, many inmates find it very rewarding. The supplementary images underscore some of the intricacies inmates faced in completing this course component.

Figure 9.4 shows paint swatches (brush strokes) that the inmate experimented with learning to mix colors.

The succession of images (Figs. 9.5, 9.6, 9.7, and 9.8) reflects an exercise in creating the inmates' own color wheels. Many inmates made multiple attempts to master this exercise and its theory. The facilitator used paper plates and shared a ruler to teach the inmates how to divide the sphere equally for the creation of a color wheel they could keep for future reference.

This color theory exercise enabled P11 to use the rudimentary art supplies available in prison (Appendix 4) and further his artwork in his cell, mixing the needed colors to express his Indigenous connection to Country using the unique colors of the Australian landscape, which are significant to his Kinship (Fig. 9.6). This highlights a considerable effort by P11 (Sect. 7.4).

Although inmates could keep the color wheels (Fig. 9.7), some chose to donate them willingly to the art facilitator out of concern for the limited quantity of personal items allowed in the cells.

Figure 9.8 reflects some of the complexity for inmates to grasp color theory, especially in view of their limited level of education (see Sect. 3.1).

Figure 9.9, created in Session 4.0 (Table 6.1), highlights P9 processing the program's information on neuropsychology and using it to illustrate his own thoughts

Fig. 9.4 Participants' color theory progress work

and reflections on his pre-arrest behavior. The gray and hazy paints at the top of the page symbolize his struggle with the weight of taking responsibility and being accountable for his actions. These insights arose from the group discussions and were captured by the facilitator in her journal (Researcher Journal, April 19, 2023, pp. 18–19; see Sect. 6.7).

These two exemplars (see Figs. 9.10 and 9.11) show the extensive preliminary work inmates put into the composition of their final piece. This is a difficult session for the inmates because their future goals and planning skills are limited. Understanding composition assists them in future goal-setting skills that assist in being able to create and picture an attainable life.

Continuing from Figs. 9.10 and 9.11, although the final piece (Fig. 6.14) reflects P2 as the puppet, in these preliminary sketches, the hand pictured below is his own, showing him as the puppet master—as opposed to the passive "victim." This perspective highlights a consciousness of assuming and expressing agency.

Figure 9.12 exemplifies social perceptions of inmates' experiences using words as "labels."

Figure 9.13 highlights self-identity work and the introspective awareness of P1 exploring alternative personas and masks of identity that inmates often use to survive the prison environment.

In Fig. 9.14 and using only words, P1 consolidates some of the social labels that have been placed upon him through his experiences. Outside (Face): Weird, Criminal, Liar, Stealer, Thief, Drugdealer, Useless, Scum, Menace to society,

9 Supplementary Chapter 1: Visual Vignette (A): Group Artwork

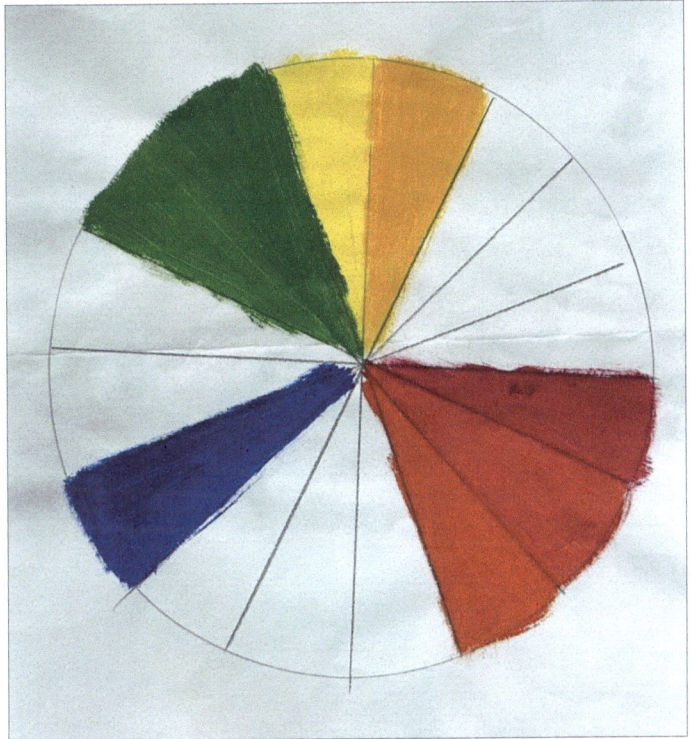

Fig. 9.5 P2 Preliminary understanding of primary and secondary colors

Gronk, Fuckwit, Loser, Dickhead, Bad, Angry, Stupid, Idiot, Retard, Terrible, Awful, Special needs, Ugly, Silly. Inside (Eyes): Gangster, Hothead, Outgoing, Bad, Thief, Cheat, Gronk, Loser, Stupid, Liar. Inside (Mouth): Doesn't shut up, Way too loud. Inmate P1 expressed his special needs, alluding to his attention-deficit/hyperactivity disorder (ADHD) and the difficulties associated with authentic communication. The words and narrative shifted from these original ideas to the final piece (Fig.6.12). Notably, the title of his final piece reflects more vulnerability ("DUMB"; "words hurt").

Visual analysis and winnowing of the data involved scanning, photocopying, printing, cutting, organizing, and pasting visual answers into categories for visual analysis and reflection, through which some of the poignant key themes emerged (Sects. 7.1–7.4). Visual analysis was time-consuming yet beneficial for synthesis. The photo (Fig. 9.15) shows A3-size pages reflecting some of the enormity of what was involved, showcasing the extensive scope of this research, and extending an invitation to future researchers to explore the fruitful possibilities using a comparable methodology.

Fig. 9.6 P11 Final attempt

Fig. 9.7 P9 Final color wheel

9 Supplementary Chapter 1: Visual Vignette (A): Group Artwork

Fig. 9.8 P1 Final color wheel

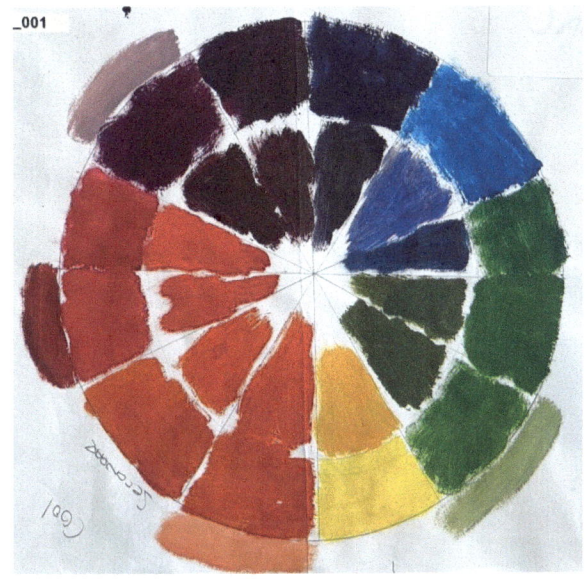

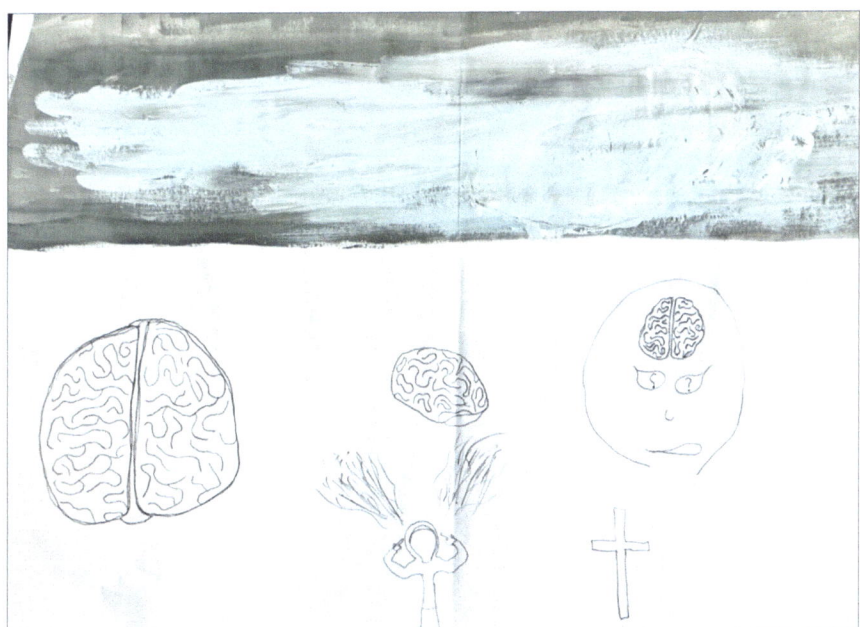

Fig. 9.9 Inmate responses to discussion on fight and flight processes (see Table 6.1)

Fig. 9.10 P2 Preliminary sketches for final piece

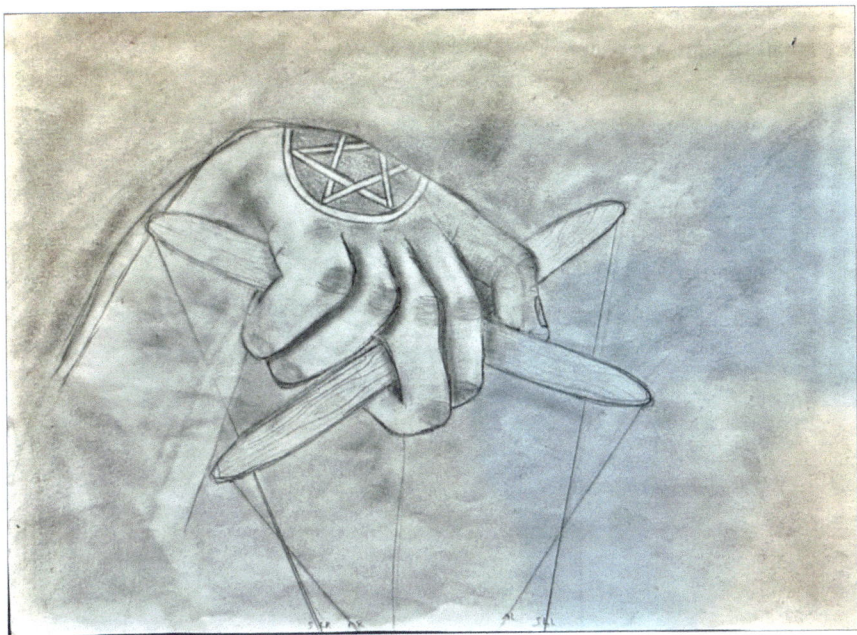

Fig. 9.11 P2 Preliminary sketches for final piece

Fig. 9.12 P1 Preliminary ideas manifesting during Sessions 4.0–6.0 (Table 6.1)

Fig. 9.13 P1 Preliminary ideas manifesting during Sessions 4.0–6.0 (Table 6.1)

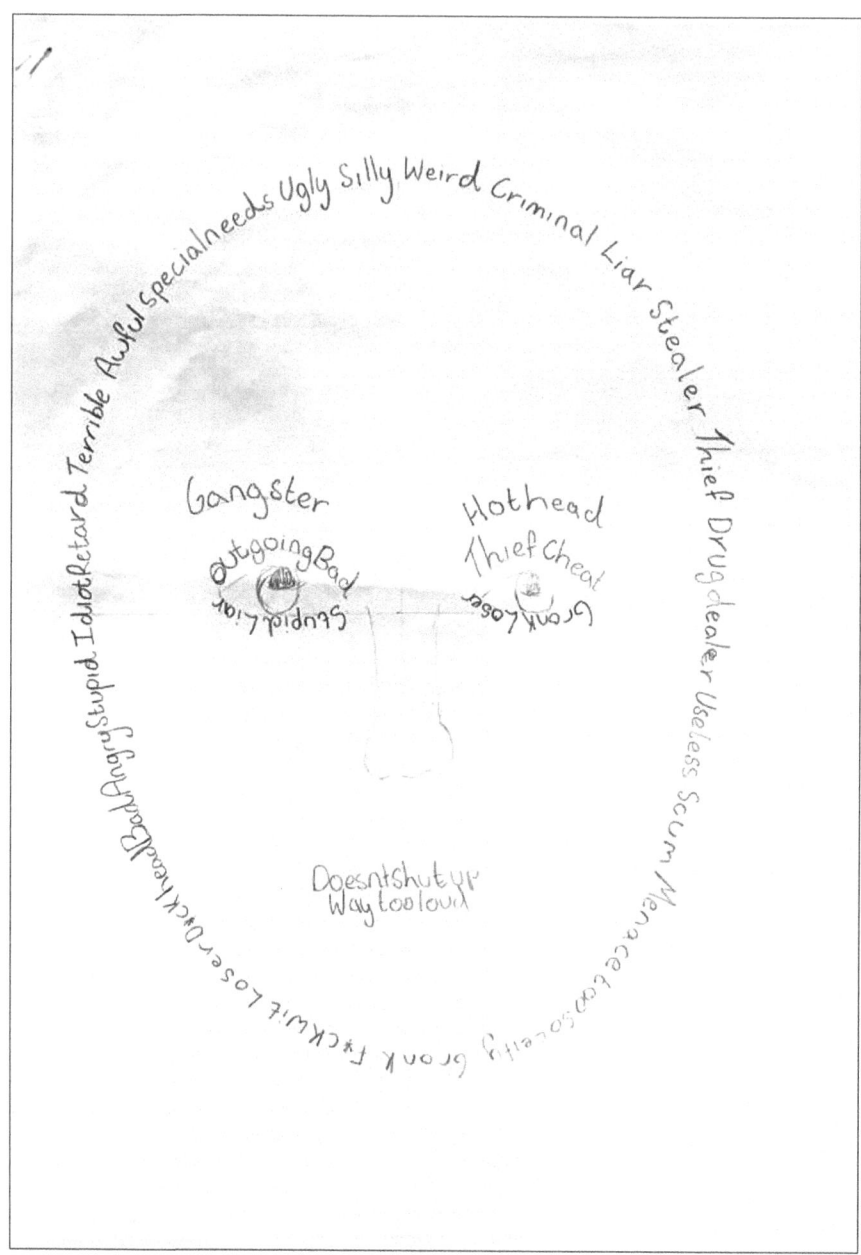

Fig. 9.14 P1 Preliminary sketch for final piece

9 Supplementary Chapter 1: Visual Vignette (A): Group Artwork

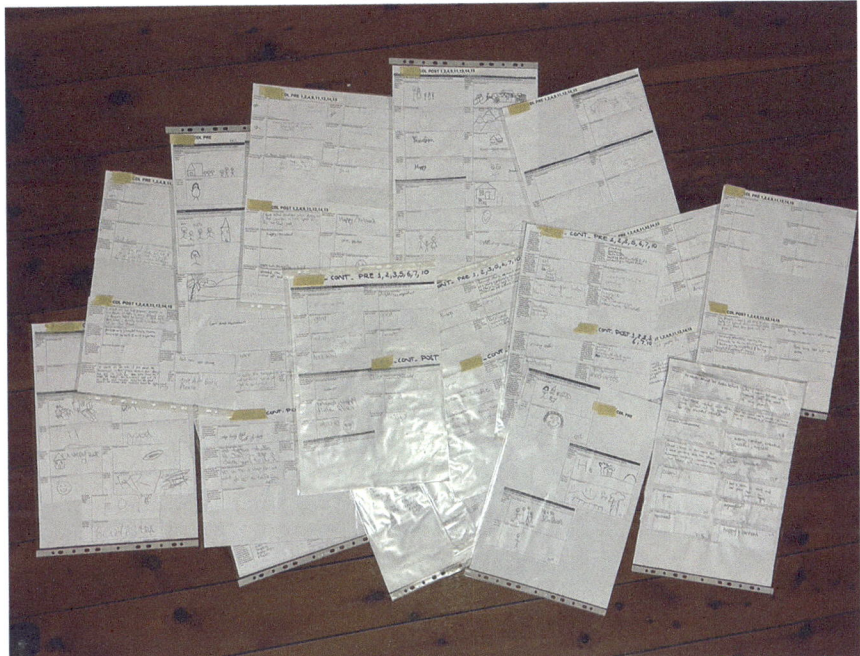

Fig. 9.15 Qualitative data analysis

Open Access This chapter is licensed under the terms of the Creative Commons Attribution 4.0 International License (http://creativecommons.org/licenses/by/4.0/), which permits use, sharing, adaptation, distribution and reproduction in any medium or format, as long as you give appropriate credit to the original author(s) and the source, provide a link to the Creative Commons license and indicate if changes were made.

The images or other third party material in this chapter are included in the chapter's Creative Commons license, unless indicated otherwise in a credit line to the material. If material is not included in the chapter's Creative Commons license and your intended use is not permitted by statutory regulation or exceeds the permitted use, you will need to obtain permission directly from the copyright holder.

Chapter 10
Supplementary Chapter 2: Visual Vignette (B): Single Case Study

This visual vignette documents a single case study. In contrast to Supplementary Chapter 1 (Chap. 9), which features the work of multiple inmates, this chapter traces the unique journey of a single inmate who successfully participated in the "Change the Design of Your Life" (CDL) program. It features selected art exercises from the CDL workbook that was specifically created by the first author for this research. Aligning with the program design, the participant responded to input and artwork, reflecting consistent improvements.

10.1 Vignette: Case Study of an Inmate's Progress in Therapeutic Art

The CDL program follows a gradually paced increase of skillsets that, through developing a client-led and safe "therapeutic alliance,"[1] can be implemented at the pace of the individual while adhering to the scheduled group timeline.

One inmate's work is featured here to highlight the potential prisoners can achieve when supported and actively involved in the program. It offers unique insights into the progress an inmate may make in a short period of time, leveraging art as a tool for healing and communication.

This case study is composed of a series of illustrations, presented in a consistent pattern throughout the chapter. First, the task is shown as it appears in the CDL workbook—typically a sample image produced by the facilitator that serves as the instructional prompt. Second, the participant's artwork created in response to the

---

[1] In a professional counseling context, the term "therapeutic alliance" describes the unique connection between a patient and therapist, including their mutual agreement to work together, and their joint sense of mission, collaboration, trust in each other, and the hope for a better future (Muran & Safran, 1998; Siegel, 2020).

© The Author(s) 2025
S. Tucker, J. M. Luetz, *Therapeutic Prison Art Interventions*, SpringerBriefs in Criminology, https://doi.org/10.1007/978-3-031-85991-5_10

task is displayed. Third, a brief commentary is provided on the participant's progress and the significance of their artistic contribution.

This case study is presented here with the inmate's full consent to publish their associated artwork. The case study demonstrates the progress of a "naïve"[2] artist from the inside who had no prior formal art training or experience. The case study is also supplemented with their responses from the pretest questionnaire, thus providing more in-depth insights into relevant thought processes and experiences during the program.

During the first session, inmates are given their personal copy of the CDL workbook (Tucker, 2021). This printed workbook is structured into a multi-session format that typically extends the program over a period of several weeks. The opening session includes a set of pencil exercises to establish three-dimensional form and function in shapes (Figs. 10.1 and 10.2).

An important focus of the first session is to foster group cohesion, safety, and mutual respect and set expectations that invite the prisoners to be active participants in the therapeutic art program regardless of their artistic skillset and prior experience. Prisoners are usually very excitable in the first session. It is an important focus

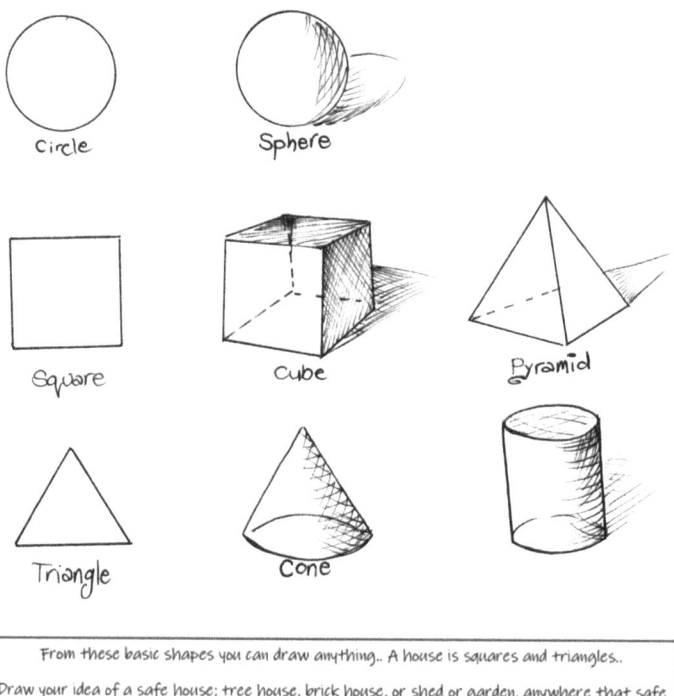

Fig. 10.1 Drawing basic shapes: Pencil example exercises from Session 1

---

[2] So-called naïve art is conventionally understood as visual art by a person who lacks the formal training that a professional artist undergoes in their development (Burger, 2023).

10.1 Vignette: Case Study of an Inmate's Progress in Therapeutic Art

Fig. 10.2 First page of inmate's sketchbook: Pencil exercises drawing basic shapes

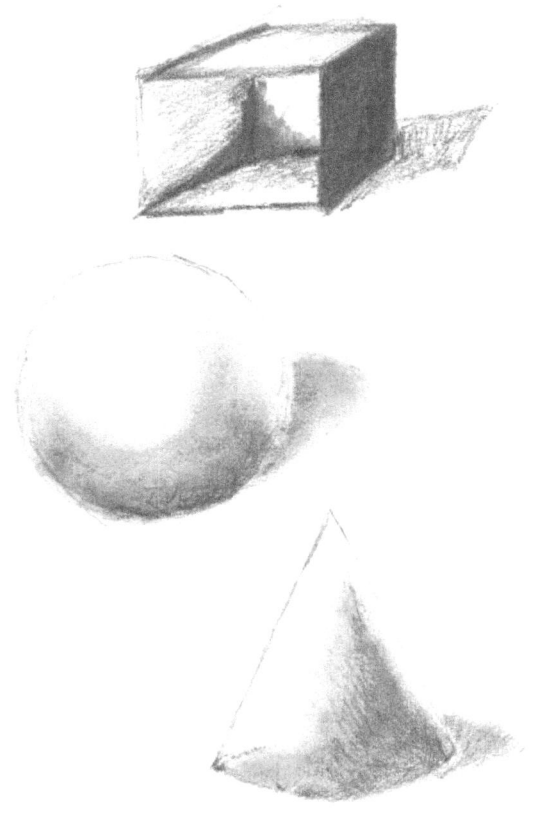

to channel their high energy levels toward productive work processes ("no funny stuff in here, guys!")

These exemplars of their work show the inmate establishing form and function through shading, tone, and line, using simple methodologies. Two-dimensional shapes are initially created and are then shaded to create three-dimensional forms. This inmate excelled in being able to visually resolve the differences between light and dark tonal work. The inmate's enthusiasm for art was noted early in the program and was also captured in their response to Question 6.1: How do you feel when you do art? (see Fig. 10.3).

For the pretest inmate's baseline artwork, prisoners are offered one of two options to draw in a playful manner: a tree or a safe place. This inmate generated an elaborate image of a safe place during their lunch break (Fig. 10.4). The safe place imagery provides a mental anchor and reference point for future therapeutic work.

Given that inmates do not have easy access to magazines or pictures from library books, teaching them geometric shapes becomes an essential part of their basic skills. This enables them to draw anything they see in their immediate prison environment.

The program workbook offers simple instructions. Learning how to draw faces can help participants understand other people's emotions and is a simple stepping

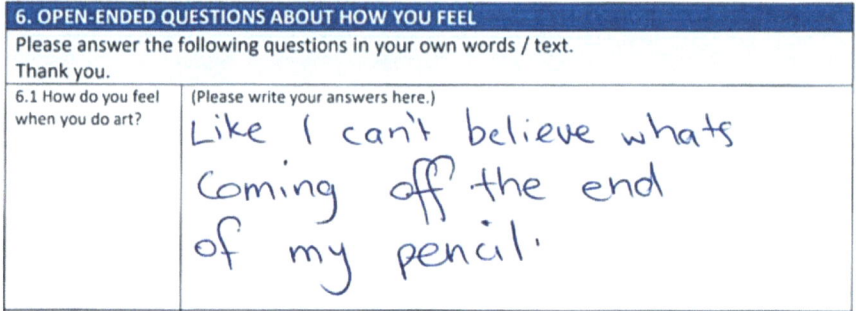

Fig. 10.3 Questionnaire answer reflecting the program participant's excitement and high motivation

Fig. 10.4 Inmate sketch of a "safe place"

stone to developing more complex skills. This basic measuring system used to illustrate facial anatomy is broken down in the class session and adapted to include the alternate features of a multicultural society; this topic is covered in subsequent program sessions and group discussions (Figs. 10.5 and 10.6).

In this example, the inmate used the facial measuring system to produce proportional facial anatomy (Fig. 10.6). Developing confidence in visually depicting facial features is significant to people who have suffered from extreme life traumas and may struggle to read and appropriately interpret facial expressions, body language, and emotive communication. When inmates have the artistic prowess to re-create characters that have caused challenges or even abuse, they are reinstated with power over that event, thus aiding their ability to process and integrate traumas (Sanderson, 2009). According to Maffei et al. (2023), "the occipital and temporal cortices … are critical for building a holistic perception of a face from its basic visual features"

10.1 Vignette: Case Study of an Inmate's Progress in Therapeutic Art

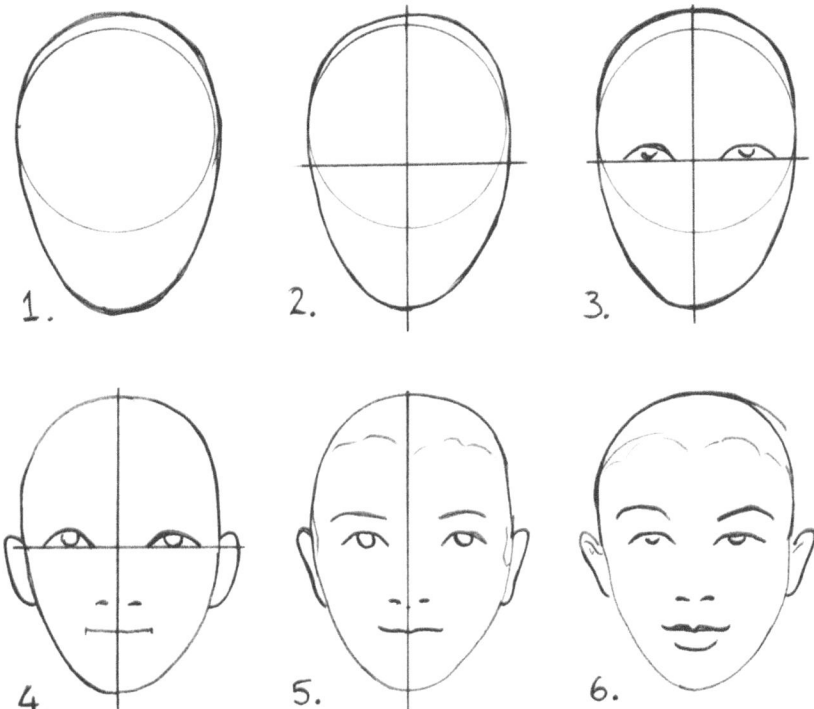

Fig. 10.5 Drawing facial shapes

(p. 2). Teaching prisoners to recognize facial expressions aids them to communicate more effectively with their institutional environment. Crucially, it addresses disparate interpersonal literacy rates, transcends educational inequalities (Sect. 3.1), sparks curiosity, and encourages further education (Giles, 2016; Giles et al., 2016).

Templates drawn by the facilitator are used in the workshops to support inmates in developing their skillsets to illustrate expressive facial features. These templates were developed over many years while the principal researcher was contracted by correctional services to deliver art programs to groups of prisoners in maximum security units (Figs. 10.7 and 10.8). Prisoners tend to respond well to simple art methods because such techniques enable them to produce quality artwork with minimal resources, such as ballpoint pens. Having these skills offers them a therapeutic outlet during situations when they may find themselves confined to their cells during lockdown periods (Cohen-Liebman, 2023; Gussak, 2016, 2017, 2019; Rothwell, 2016).

In this example, the inmate uses two grades of pencil as they implement different tonal techniques using an advancing set of tools (Fig. 10.9). As highlighted in Appendix 4, inmates are all provided with the same range of art supplies, usually self-funded by the art facilitator or sponsored by external charities.

Fig. 10.6 Inmate developing facial features

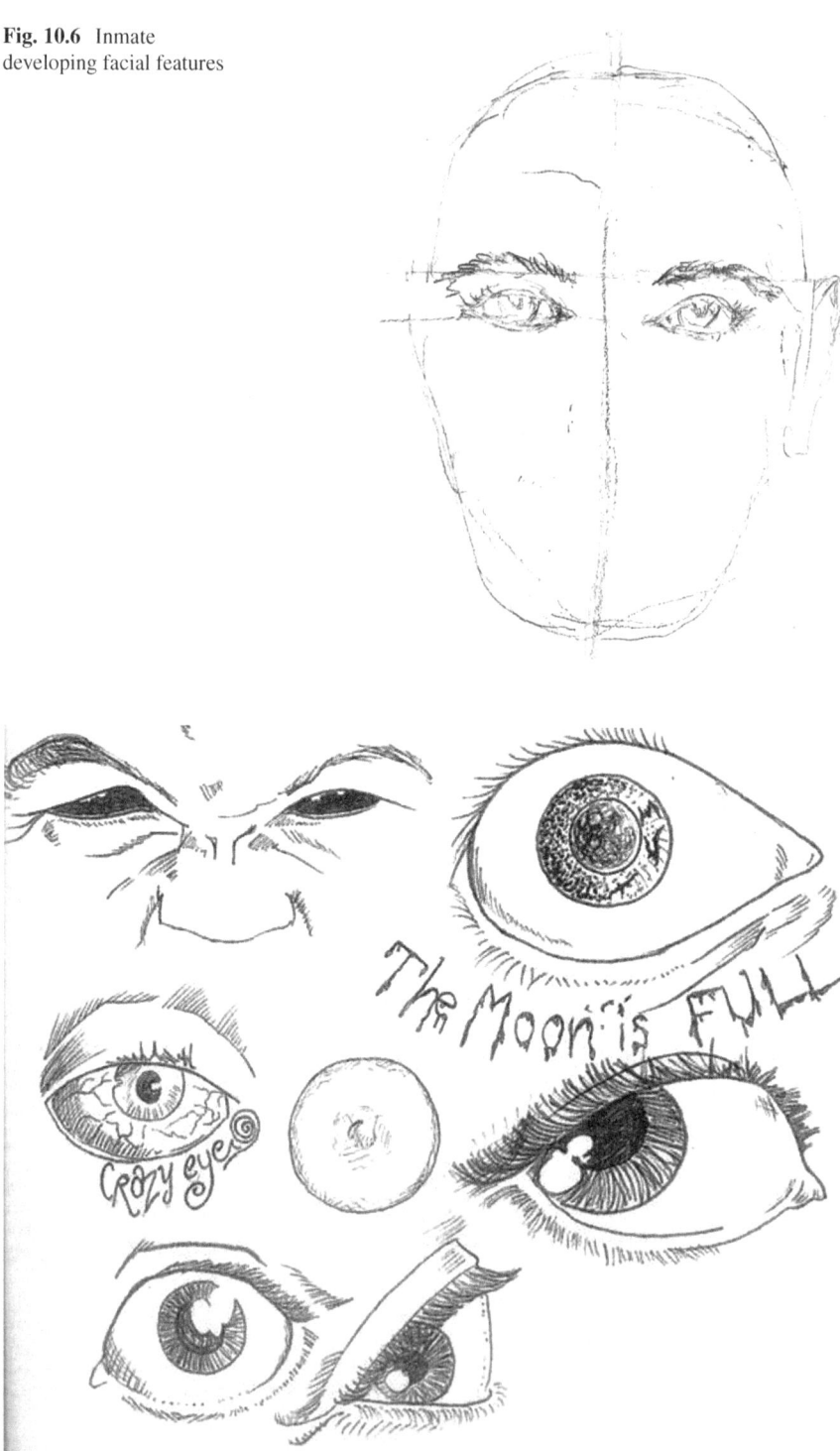

Fig. 10.7 Exercises focusing on eye details

10.1 Vignette: Case Study of an Inmate's Progress in Therapeutic Art

Fig. 10.8 Exercises emphasizing other facial features

A crucial aspect of the CDL program is nurturing a worldview that cultivates compassion. Understanding life and death promotes personal accountability for actions and reactions. Metaphorically, the human anatomy can serve as a useful scaffold whereby art theory can be meaningfully explained. Skeletal structures can play a helpful role in this endeavor and may foster self-respect for human bodies, needs, health, self-care, and overall sustenance (Fig. 10.10). For this reason, artistic interpretations of skeletal structures, facial features, and human skulls can become good group discussion openers and helpful metaphors. The following sketches build on this focus on human anatomy. While the facilitator uses the classroom whiteboard, the participants can replicate and mirror the illustrations and apply them in their own artistic development.

After a full day session, inmates return to their cells with one center-approved pencil, sketchbook, eraser, and pen. They are encouraged to do in-unit and in-cell work (in lieu of "homework"). In this example, the inmate has responded to the facilitated in-class instruction (Fig. 10.11).

These basic template illustrations (Fig. 10.12) are used to reinforce anatomical proportions and can be adapted to cultures, genders, and ages in facial expressions.

In this set of examples produced by the inmate (Fig. 10.13), art therapists will readily notice the participant's growing aptitude to master shade and tone.

Female inmates responded well to instruction on artistically reproducing female figures that exhibited confidence, agency, and independence, thus reinforcing their sense of self-empowerment (Fig. 10.14).

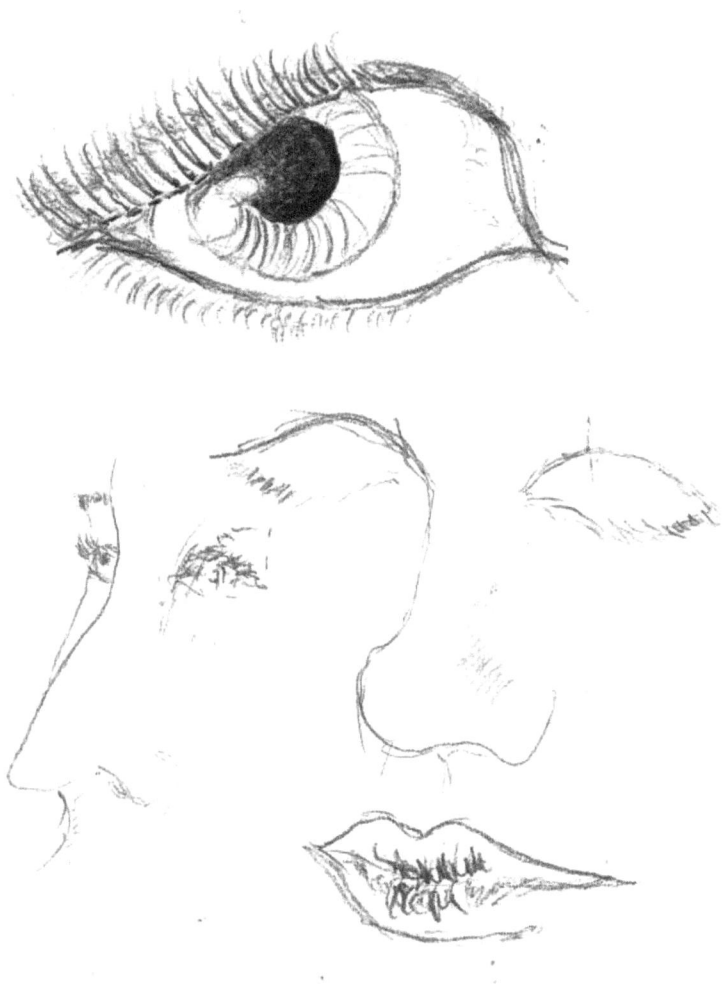

Fig. 10.9 Inmate demonstrating their expanding skills

These inmate sketches (Figs. 10.15 and 10.16) demonstrate active engagement in these exercises, reflecting moments of "epiphany" in relation to female role models. This is captured particularly well in Fig. 10.16, which shows a sketch of the program facilitator produced by the inmate.

As inmates develop their skills in facial form, they build confidence, understand their social roles, reactivate neural circuits involved in perception and self-reflection, and ultimately, enhance their locus of control. The next step then invites them to step out of their comfort zones and be challenged to develop new skills that are fundamentally different. By reversing traditional concepts of drawing, they are invited to upskill their ability to problem-solve. Traditionally, illustrating with charcoal or lead on white paper involves focusing on the darkest areas of the image.

10.1 Vignette: Case Study of an Inmate's Progress in Therapeutic Art

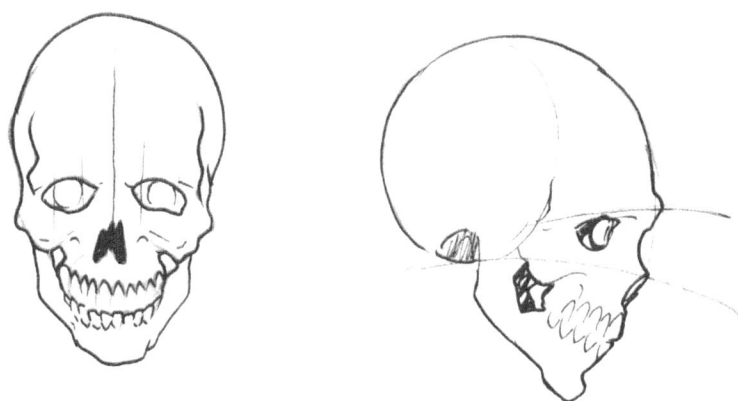

Fig. 10.10 Exercises focusing on human skulls

However, when illustrating with white chalk or polychromes on black paper, one must focus on the lightest areas. By breaking down visually complex images into smaller tasks, inmates practice vital problem-solving skills. Moreover, by bringing to completion complex tasks in art, prisoners are encouraged, metaphorically, to tackle and overcome life challenges with growing confidence (Abbing et al., 2023; Malchiodi, 2020; Tallent et al., 2022). In the workbook, inmates are invited to replicate the image shown in Fig. 10.17. They are encouraged as follows: "Your next challenge is to illustrate this on black paper! You will *not* get it right the first time. This is difficult; you have to observe the highlights!" (Tucker, 2021, p. 29)

Art therapists who understand the Expressive Therapies Continuum (ETC)[3] will relate to the use of alternate methods to shift clients from the Cognitive/Symbolic level into the Kinesthetic/Sensory level, allowing them to process traumas (Hass-Cohen & Carr, 2008; King, 2016). Successful attempts at this exercise indicate a potential for changing ingrained habits and behaviors. Shifting habits offers new ways of problem-solving (Arjona & Van Lith, 2024; Cohen-Liebman, 2023; Gussak, 2016, 2017, 2019; Hass-Cohen & Carr, 2008; Rothwell, 2016; Siegel, 2020). The current example (Fig. 10.18) reflects the complexity of the exercise and the challenges involved.

The first example of the cat image highlights the complexity of the challenge (Figs. 10.17 and 10.18). The inmate was then given a new challenge with a portrait (Fig. 10.19).

Despite clear instructions to replicate the image (Fig. 10.19) using the same method—white pencil on black paper—the inmate naturally reverted to the traditional illustration technique where lead is used on white paper (Fig. 10.20). When

---

[3] The Expressive Therapies Continuum (ETC) is a framework that identifies different levels (e.g., Kinesthetic/Sensory, Perceptual/Affective, and Cognitive/Symbolic) of creative expression, ranging from simple sensory experiences to complex cognitive processes, used to assess and guide therapeutic art activities (Lusebrink, 2015).

Fig. 10.11 Inmate sketching an anatomic form

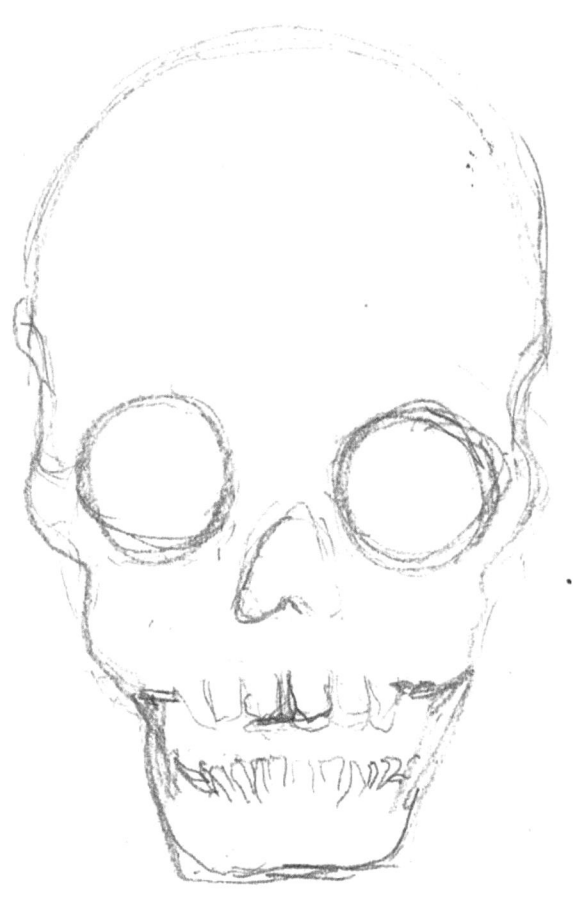

this was pointed out, the participant made a subsequent effort. This resulted in a more thorough integration of line, tone, and form (Fig. 10.21).

As reflected in Fig. 10.21, the inmate showed vast improvement in control over the illustration. This was achieved by improving their focus through breathing and relaxation techniques.

The CDL program cultivates ethnocultural inclusivity and always learns with and from the people who participate in it. It also encourages inmates to explore the distinct individual features of Indigenous communities. The program's participatory facilitation invites group discussion and addresses key contemporary themes that affect prisoners, including the hyper-incarceration of First Nations people (Sect. 7.4), Australia's historical context and colonization (Chap. 2 and Sect. 7.4), social issues, gender inequality, and domestic violence, among others. It also embraces social empathy and respect among all races and genders within the prison environment.

10.1 Vignette: Case Study of an Inmate's Progress in Therapeutic Art

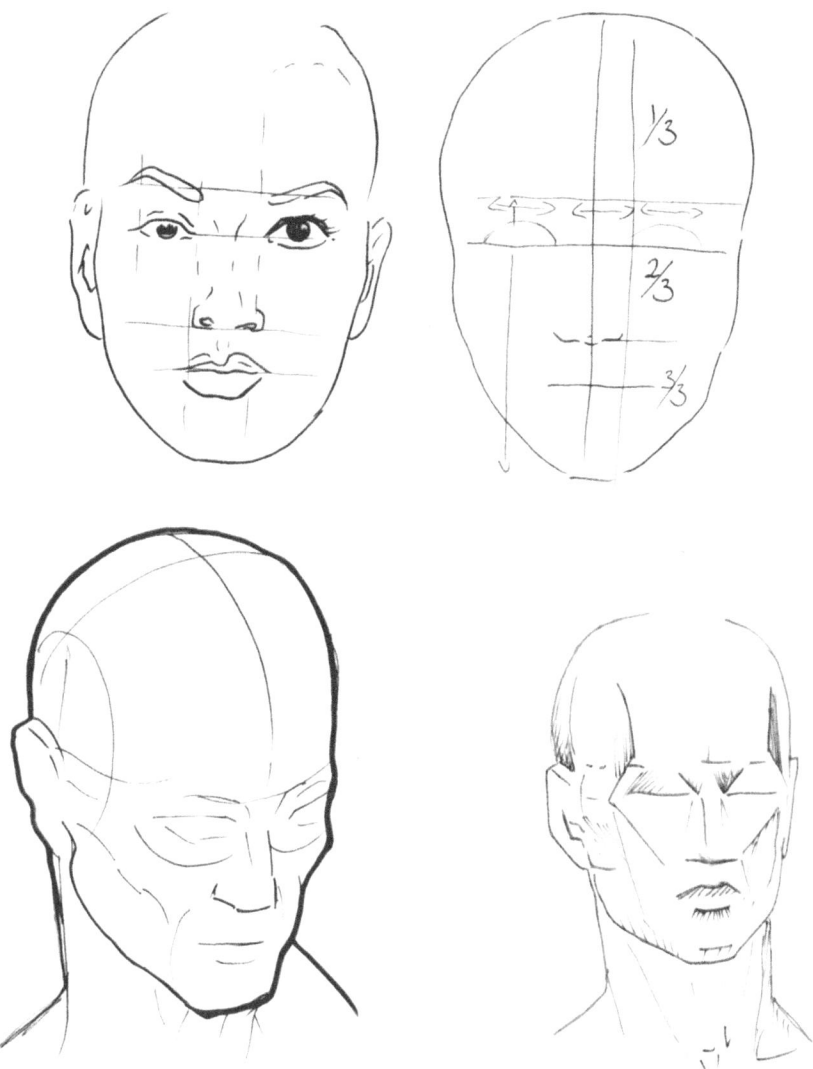

Fig. 10.12 Exercises focusing on expression and facial and neck anatomy

This illustration of a First Nations male Elder (Fig. 10.22) was produced by the female program facilitator and replicated by the participant in an exercise to help improve their skills in facial interpretation. Although it is not culturally condoned for women to draw pictures of male Elders, on this occasion, it was essential considering the prison environment and limited resources available therein. Importantly, processing imagery of men constructively may help participants overcome past experiences with significant figures in their lives.

Fig. 10.13 Inmate responses focusing on expression and facial and neck anatomy

Taking up a new challenge, the inmate's response follows a sequence that moves through the Expressive Therapies Continuum (ETC), showing progress in varying stages (Figs. 10.23, 10.24, and 10.25). The varying changes in styles reflect attempts at trying out new problem-solving approaches, finally landing on a style that integrates the techniques. The inmate's first attempt reflects a default style that focuses on line work that is somewhat rigid and controlled (Fig. 10.23).

10.1 Vignette: Case Study of an Inmate's Progress in Therapeutic Art

Fig. 10.14 Exercises focusing on diverse styles and emotional expressions

Fig. 10.15 Inmate showing improvements in illustration skills

Following feedback from the program facilitator, the inmate noticed the lack of shading and contrast to achieve depth. The image shows how the participant focused intently on this directive (Fig. 10.24).

Fig. 10.16 Portrait of program facilitator produced by inmate in class

The inmate's third attempt shows an integration of the two techniques, incorporating both line work and shading to achieve a more balanced, focused, and relaxed approach, giving the inmate a stronger sense of satisfaction (Fig. 10.25).

Given that the program seeks to meet prisoners in the context of their daily prison environment, it intentionally accommodates an element of alternative resource use. This is to ensure that in times of loneliness and distress (and no ready access to art supplies), inmates can use staples to find solace in creativity. The image (Fig. 10.26) is a standard image used in the program to demonstrate the potential of using instant coffee to paint or draw. This technique mixes instant coffee powder with a small amount of water to create layers that build up tone and contrast. The same can be done with tea bags.

In cell time after class, the inmate stained a cut piece of canvas used here (Fig. 10.27) with coffee initially and then built upon the technique with their own improvisation, also using supplied white acrylic paint (mixed with coffee and tea) to create an interesting array of alternate tones and contrasts.

Fig. 10.17 Exercise to illustrate white on black

This image (Fig. 10.28) used in the program is an overall summary of how the golden ratio[4] continually reproduces patterns in the natural environment. This concept helps the prisoners to understand how everything can be recreated in art using geometric shapes. Understanding these organic phenomena of natural patterns and architectural designs allows the inmates to create imagery without needing additional reference materials. Teaching the prisoners concepts of existentialism[5] helps them understand their place in the world in a positive light. In other words, being *in* the world signifies "that a person and the environment are an active, fluid unity" (Prochaska & Norcross, 2018, p. 79), thus giving prisoners access to their inner worlds. This opens up an interesting group discussion space, which leads the program toward their final piece: a discussion around their life and its impact.

---

[4] The golden ratio, also known as the divine proportion, is a ratio between two numbers that equals approximately 1.618. Usually written as the Greek letter phi, it is strongly associated with the Fibonacci sequence, a series of numbers wherein each number is the sum of the two preceding numbers. The Fibonacci numbers are 0, 1, 1, 2, 3, 5, 8, 13, 21, and so on, with the ratio of each number and the previous number gradually approaching 1.618 or Φ.

[5] Existentialism is the philosophical belief that we are each responsible for creating purpose or meaning in our own lives (Prochaska & Norcross, 2018).

Fig. 10.18 Inmate's first attempt at white on black technique

This simple exercise of color placement in a pattern (Fig. 10.29) helps introduce color theory, which on the ETC scale introduces sensory and kinesthetic levels of creative engagement. Simple and playful activities like coloring patterns pave the way for more complex color theory exercises. The color theory (Chap. 9) assists inmates in creating any color they require from the basic art supplies provided within the correctional setting (Appendix 4).

The color theory component begins to introduce expressionistic and emotive uses of colors. During group discussions, participants associate colors with specific emotions and affective states. This is a joyful and relaxing way to introduce the program participants to the arduous work ahead. Exercises reflected in Fig. 10.30 cover two pages of the participant's visual diary. Inmates were given warm primaries, cool primaries, and black and white acrylics. (The color theory topic is usually covered during Sessions 3–4; see Table 6.1)

Notably, the exemplars shown in Fig. 10.30 were created freehand without any rulers, protractors, or measuring implements. Instead, prisoners improvised using plastic prison plates and book edges. The exercises culminated in each participant creating their own full spectrum color wheel for their own future use.

10.1 Vignette: Case Study of an Inmate's Progress in Therapeutic Art

Fig. 10.19 White on black portrait exercise

Fig. 10.20 Inmate's first portrait attempt (black on white)

Fig. 10.21 Inmate's second portrait attempt (white on black)

Fig. 10.22 Illustration of an Indigenous male Elder

10.1 Vignette: Case Study of an Inmate's Progress in Therapeutic Art 125

Fig. 10.23 Inmate's first response to the exercise

The two pages from the inmate's visual diary (Fig. 10.31) highlight the self-reflective work around personal states, reactions, and associations. Self-awareness and accountability emerge from the participant's inner worlds more seamlessly through creative association. Many participants select words that have been used in the past to label them, including during trials. Using art and color, the associations temper or even neutralize the impact and power that these words hold over their lives.

At this point in the program, prisoners are reminded that there are only three sessions remaining. Participants are encouraged to begin working in earnest on their final pieces. More specifically, inmates are creatively supported to consider their background, life development interruptions, and social and cultural factors that have contributed to their current situations. Participants are also challenged to present their parole needs in a storyboard format (see the facilitator-produced exemplar in Fig. 10.32).

The larger program aim is for prisoners to be supported to use art as a valid visual communication tool in various settings, including parole submissions. More specifically, as the program moves toward its conclusion, the program reinforces the manifold benefits for prisoners to communicate their needs, mental states, and emotions through alternative methods. This assists them in reaching for a life of successful rehabilitation.

Fig. 10.24 Inmate's second response to the exercise

Fig. 10.25 Inmate's third response to the exercise

10.1 Vignette: Case Study of an Inmate's Progress in Therapeutic Art

Fig. 10.26 Monochrome portrait produced by the facilitator using instant coffee

128   10 Supplementary Chapter 2: Visual Vignette (B): Single Case Study

Fig. 10.27 Inmate's response to the instant coffee exercise

Fig. 10.28 Golden ratio example illustration

10.1 Vignette: Case Study of an Inmate's Progress in Therapeutic Art

Colour this in with contrast colours.

Choose 3-5 contrast colours, and start at the inner star by colouring one set of triangles with one colour, then colour the next layer of triangles with a contrasting colour, and continue maintaining the structure but changing up the colours.

Fig. 10.29 Inmate's response to working with patterns and the golden ratio

Fig. 10.30 Inmate's color wheel exercises

The participant's response to the storyboard exercise (Fig. 10.33) speaks to areas of life that the inmate considers to hold a significant impact, reflected through the words "guilty," "alleged," "sentenced," and "free."

Typically, at the program conclusion, the facilitator actively celebrates the participants' achievements, including the new skills gained to produce high-quality art with minimal resources. Prisoners regularly admit that they now feel better equipped to support a level of self-soothing during highly stressful and isolating times. In addition, many finish the program with a sense of confidence and resilience, feeling up-skilled to better serve their custodial sentence during times of boredom, stress, and anxiety while exploring areas of their internal psyche and soul using art.

10.1 Vignette: Case Study of an Inmate's Progress in Therapeutic Art

Fig. 10.31 Inmate's work associating colors, emotions, and actions

Fig. 10.32 Storyboard depicting "Rodney Respect 100%" leaving prison on release day

Fig. 10.33 Inmate's response to storyboard exercise

References

Abbing, A., Haeyen, S., Nyapati, S., Verboon, P., & van Hooren, S. (2023). Effectiveness and mechanisms of the arts therapies in forensic care. A systematic review, narrative synthesis, and meta analysis. *Frontiers in Psychiatry, 14*, 1128252–1128252. https://doi.org/10.3389/fpsyt.2023.1128252

Arjona, H., & Van Lith, T. (2024). Transformative connections: Exploring relational art therapy in a women's prison. *Art Therapy*, 1–7. https://doi.org/10.1080/07421656.2024.2354630

Burger, N. (2023). *Naïve art: The movement of childlike whimsy*. artfilemagazine.com/naive-art/

Cohen-Liebman, M. S. (2023). *Forensic art therapy: The art of investigating, interviewing and testifying*. Routledge.

Giles, M. (2016). Study in prison reduces recidivism and welfare dependence: A case study from Western Australia 2005–2010. *Trends and Issues in Crime and Criminal Justice, 514*, 1–9.

Giles, M., Paris, L., & Whale, J. (2016). The role of art education in adult prisons: The Western Australian experience. *International Review of Education, 62*(6), 689–709. https://doi.org/10.1007/s11159-016-9604-3

Gussak, D. E. (2016). Art therapy in the prison milieu. Part V: Practicing art therapy in interdisciplinary settings. In D. E. Gussak & M. L. Rosal (Eds.), *The Wiley handbook of art therapy* (pp. 478–486). Wiley.

Gussak, D. E. (2017). The continuing emergence of art therapy in prisons. In B. Elger, C. Ritter, & H. Stöver (Eds.), *Emerging issues in prison health*. Springer. https://doi.org/10.1007/978-94-017-7558-8_5

Gussak, D. (2019). *Art and art therapy with the imprisoned: Re-creating identity*. Routledge.

Hass-Cohen, N., & Carr, R. (2008). *Art therapy and clinical neuroscience*. Jessica Kingsley Publishers.

King, J. (2016). *Art therapy, trauma and neuroscience. Theoretical and practical perspectives*. Routledge.

References

Lusebrink, V. B. (2015). Expressive therapies continuum. *The Wiley handbook of art therapy* (Ch. 6; pp. 57–67). https://doi.org/10.1002/9781118306543.ch6

Maffei, A., Coccaro, A., Jaspers-Fayer, F., Goertzen, J., Sessa, P., & Liotti, M. (2023). EEG alpha band functional connectivity reveals distinct cortical dynamics for overt and covert emotional face processing. *Scientific Reports (Nature Publisher Group), 13*(1), 9951. https://doi.org/10.1038/s41598-023-36860-4

Malchiodi, C. A. (2020). *Trauma and expressive arts therapy: Brain, body, and imagination in the healing process*. Guilford.

Muran, J. C., & Safran, J. D. (1998). *The therapeutic alliance in brief psychotherapy*. American Psychological Association.

Prochaska, J. O., & Norcross, J. C. (2018). *Systems of psychotherapy: A transtheoretical analysis*. Oxford University Press.

Rothwell, K. (Ed.) (2016). *Forensic art therapies: Anthology of practice and research*. Free Association Books UK.

Sanderson, C. (2009). *Introduction to counselling survivors of interpersonal trauma*. Jessica Kingsley Publishers.

Siegel, D. J. (2020). *The developing mind: How relationships and the brain interact to shape who we are*. Guilford.

Tallent, J., Phillips, J., & Coren, E. (2022). PROTOCOL: Arts-based interventions for offenders in secure criminal justice settings to improve rehabilitation outcomes: An evidence and gap map. *Campbell Systematic Reviews, 18*(3). https://doi.org/10.1002/cl2.1255

Tucker, S. (2021). *Eight-session CDL art therapy workbook*. [Unpublished workbook used to facilitate therapeutic prison art program. Produced in conjunction with Uniting Care Prison Ministries, Chermside, Queensland, Australia.]

Open Access This chapter is licensed under the terms of the Creative Commons Attribution 4.0 International License (http://creativecommons.org/licenses/by/4.0/), which permits use, sharing, adaptation, distribution and reproduction in any medium or format, as long as you give appropriate credit to the original author(s) and the source, provide a link to the Creative Commons license and indicate if changes were made.

The images or other third party material in this chapter are included in the chapter's Creative Commons license, unless indicated otherwise in a credit line to the material. If material is not included in the chapter's Creative Commons license and your intended use is not permitted by statutory regulation or exceeds the permitted use, you will need to obtain permission directly from the copyright holder.

Chapter 11
Supplementary Chapter 3: Research Instruments and Additional Resources

The final supplementary chapter comprises a compendium of resources from this research. Featured resource materials include the mixed-methods research instrument that also invites visual responses from the participants (Appendix 1), the AART Instrument, which was used to collect data in the public art exhibition (Appendix 2), the Certificate of Completion that program participants received on the day of graduating from the program (Appendix 3), the list of art supplies used in this research (Appendix 4), and selected commentary from members of the public (Appendix 5). These resources are useful for educators, art therapists, prison managers, and other stakeholders seeking to implement similar future therapeutic art programs in a variety of national and international justice settings.

Appendix 1: Questionnaire Used in this Research

1. Background questions	
Correctional centre:	
Today's date:	
First name or IOMS number:	
Age:	
Gender:	
Is this your first time in custody/prison?	
Highest level of schooling completed:	

2. Questions about self-awareness

Please tick how much you agree with each sentence. ☑	Strongly Agree	Agree	Neither	Disagree	Strongly Disagree
2.1 I enjoy art.					
2.2 I feel good about myself when I am creative.					
2.3 I think beautiful art can be calming for people when upset or in distress.					
2.4 Creative hobbies like colouring in or writing letters help me to feel peaceful.					
2.5. I think art and being creative can lift my emotional well-being.					
2.6. Learning art and craft skills can stop me from feeling lonely.					

3. Questions about the prison environment

Please tick how much you agree with each sentence. ☑	Strongly Agree	Agree	Neither	Disagree	Strongly Disagree
3.1 I would like to use art for my parole application.					
3.2 I would be interested to learn more about art while I am in prison.					
3.3 Creative activities can help to reduce anger in prison.					
3.4 I would feel less lonely during lock downs if I could do art.					

4. Questions about the past 8 weeks

Please tick how much you agree with each sentence. ☑	All of the time	Most of the time	Some of the time	A little of the time	None of the time
4.1 In the past eight (8) weeks, about how often did you feel worried?					
4.2 In the past eight (8) weeks, about how often did you feel discouraged/put down?					
4.3 In the past eight (8) weeks, about how often did you feel restless/fidgety?					
4.4 In the past eight (8) weeks, how often did you smile?					
4.5 In the past eight (8) weeks, about how often did you feel idle/useless?					
4.6 In the past eight (8) weeks, about how often did you have happy dreams?					
4.7 In the past eight (8) weeks, about how often did you find it easy to focus?					
4.8 In the past eight (8) weeks, about how often did you feel that your future could be more positive/happier?					

Appendix 1: Questionnaire Used in this Research 137

5. Visual questions

Please answer the following questions in your own artwork/drawing/graffiti.
Thank you.

5.1 Please picture your biggest dream	(visual response here)
5.2 This is how I feel right now	(visual response here)

6. Open-ended questions about how you feel

Please answer the following questions in your own words/text.
Thank you.

6.1 How do you feel when you do art?	(Please write your answers here.)
6.2 What have you learned about yourself/culture/life/others through art/song lines?	(Please write your answers here.)
6.3 What other creative activities do you enjoy? (For example, writing, sculpting, building, sewing, designing, gardening, making music, mechanics, etc.?) Please list the first five that come to mind.	(Please write your answers here.)
6.4 If you had an opportunity to speak to the Minister for Corrections about art, what would you say?	(Please write your answers here.)
6.5. Is there anything else you would like to say?	(Please write your answers here.)

[The original questionnaire also includes a blank page at the end. It is intentionally left blank to give participants additional space to express themselves creatively.

Program participants are encouraged to use this empty page to draw or write their your own additional responses.]

The original questionnaire (with blank spaces for visual responses) is available here: https://journals.sagepub.com/doi/suppl/10.1177/0306624X231165350/suppl_file/sj-pdf-1-ijo-10.1177_0306624x231165350.pdf

Appendix 2: Anonymous Art Research Tool (AART)

Visitors to the public art exhibition used this instrument to score the prisoner artwork.

Please complete one evaluation for each artwork according to your personal response. Please complete as many assessments on individual artworks as possible. Thank you ☺

Very Realistic	Realism/Expression										Very Abstract/Expressive
	1	2	3	4	5	6	7	8	9	10	
Bright	Colour usage										Dark
	1	2	3	4	5	6	7	8	9	10	
Multiple/Chromatic	Colour Variety										Monochrome
	1	2	3	4	5	6	7	8	9	10	
Positive	Subject Matter										Negative
	1	2	3	4	5	6	7	8	9	10	
Emotional	Themes										Unemotional
	1	2	3	4	5	6	7	8	9	10	
Filled	Use of space on canvas/paper										Empty
	1	2	3	4	5	6	7	8	9	10	
Positive	Symbolism (If any)										Negative
	1	2	3	4	5	6	7	8	9	10	
None	Words/Text in artwork										Heaps
	1	2	3	4	5	6	7	8	9	10	
Flat	Perspective/Dimension										Dimensional
	1	2	3	4	5	6	7	8	9	10	
One	Mediums/art supplies used										Many
	1	2	3	4	5	6	7	8	9	10	

The original questionnaire tool is available here: https://journals.sagepub.com/doi/suppl/10.1177/0306624X231165350/suppl_file/sj-pdf-2-ijo-10.1177_0306624x231165350.pdf

Appendix 3: Certificate of Completion

Change the Design of your Life

Certificate

OF ART THERAPY RESEARCH

[Participant Name]

Successfully completed all components and homework requirements, showing dedication and hard work through adversity.

Sarah Tucker (Principal Researcher)   Dr. Johannes Luetz (Associate Researcher)   (Uniting Care Prison Ministry)

Appendix 4: List of Art Supplies Used in this Research

Choosing art supplies was carefully deliberated, considering fundraising and budget constraints. Despite the principal researcher's deep appreciation for high-quality art materials as an artist, her significant experience within prison settings expressed itself in a good understanding of what art supplies are both ethical and appropriate for the environment. This consideration took into account the art supplies that prisoners can legally purchase within the prison—if they have a job or funds provided by family or friends externally. Prisoners were permitted to use these supplies in their cells to engage in activities that alleviated boredom. However, this provision excluded any access to dedicated art spaces. The process of purchasing art supplies in prison uses the so-called prisoner buy-up forms (Fig. 11.1). The prison sources supplies only from security-approved suppliers.

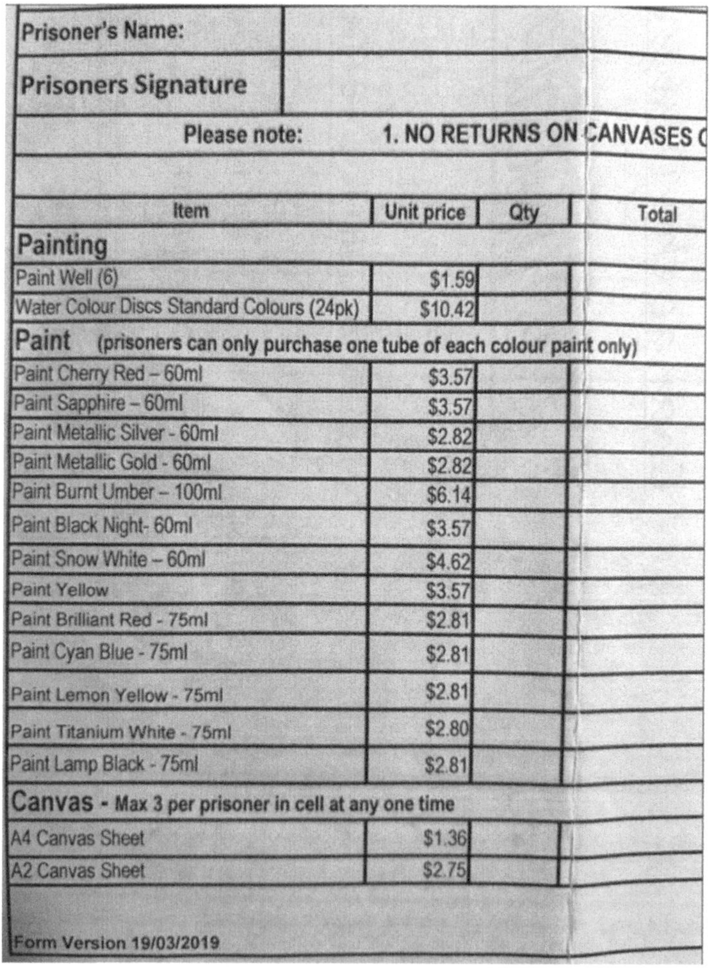

Prisoner's Name:		
Prisoners Signature		
Please note:	1. NO RETURNS ON CANVASES	

Item	Unit price	Qty	Total
Painting			
Paint Well (6)	$1.59		
Water Colour Discs Standard Colours (24pk)	$10.42		
Paint (prisoners can only purchase one tube of each colour paint only)			
Paint Cherry Red – 60ml	$3.57		
Paint Sapphire – 60ml	$3.57		
Paint Metallic Silver - 60ml	$2.82		
Paint Metallic Gold - 60ml	$2.82		
Paint Burnt Umber – 100ml	$6.14		
Paint Black Night- 60ml	$3.57		
Paint Snow White – 60ml	$4.62		
Paint Yellow	$3.57		
Paint Brilliant Red - 75ml	$2.81		
Paint Cyan Blue - 75ml	$2.81		
Paint Lemon Yellow - 75ml	$2.81		
Paint Titanium White - 75ml	$2.80		
Paint Lamp Black - 75ml	$2.81		
Canvas - Max 3 per prisoner in cell at any one time			
A4 Canvas Sheet	$1.36		
A2 Canvas Sheet	$2.75		
Form Version 19/03/2019			

Fig. 11.1 Sample prisoner buy-up form showing art supplies available (2019). Prisoners need to fill in the form as shown and submit it for approval to the administration

Appendix 4: List of Art Supplies Used in this Research

Considering the limited finances of most prisoners, the administration seeks the basic and cheapest options for inmates. Although each prison alters its provision of these approved lists according to security ratings, primary colours are typically available across the State as a basic supply. Therefore, the significance of Session 3.5 (see Table 6.1) is foundational to inmates obtaining future skill sets in art by utilising the materials at hand. Changing management may additionally alter the buy-up lists (Sect. 7.1).

Table 11.1 shows the art supplies purchased and self-funded by the principal researcher and program facilitator to offer the course. In selecting, sourcing, and distributing these supplies, the facilitator carefully considered their limited propensity to be misused for other purposes, including as weapons, drug utensils, and/or quality/archival jail tattoo art,[1] among others.

Table 11.1 CDL art supply list

Amount per inmate	Art Supply description	Shared supplies
1	Pencil case[a]	1 × jar of modelling paste
1	HB pencil	Spray bottle (for water paint, expression & backgrounds)
1	2B Pencil	Oil pastels
1	4B Pencil	Ream of 120 GSM Cartridge paper
1	6B Pencil	Ream of A3 copy paper
1	Graphite woodless pencil	Book of A4 Black illustration paper
1	Pencil sharpener	4 × Glue Sticks
1	Kneadable eraser[b]	
3	Nylon paint brushes	
3	Course-hair brushes	
1	White wax illustration pencil	
1	Red Fineline marker	
1	Green Fineline marker	
1	1 .04 fine line black felt tip pen	
1	Plastic paint tray	
1	75 ml tube acrylic warm red	
1	75 ml tube acrylic cool red	
1	75 ml tube acrylic warm blue	
1	75 ml tube acrylic cool blue	
1	75 ml tube acrylic warm yellow	
1	75 ml tube acrylic cool yellow	

(continued)

---

[1] Queensland prison tattoo art is referred to as 'fruities'. The program facilitator's lived experience includes an extensive previous career in tattooing. She has an in-depth knowledge of pigments and their archival application in tattoo art. Despite many inmates' repeated demands to learn tattooing skills, the CDL program is not designed with tattooing in mind but rather introduces expressive art conducive to fostering self-development.

Table 11.1 (continued)

Amount per inmate	Art Supply description	Shared supplies
1	75 ml tube acrylic warm yellow	
1	75 ml tube acrylic black	
1	75 ml tube acrylic white	
1	Manilla folder	
1	A4 Visual diary	
1	25 ml tubes water colour × 18 variety[c]	
1	12 watercolour pencils	
1	Change the design of your life workbook	

[a]The pencil cases issued were sewn by inmates at a women's low-security prison, St Helena Jones, and were donated to Uniting Care Prison Ministry, then donated to the facilitator/researcher for the sole purpose of being used in the CDL program

[b]Kneadable erasers are versatile and long lasting. They collect all forms of pencil from the page with minimal damage and can be reshaped for finely detailed areas

[c]These small tubes of paint were kept by the facilitator, and inmates were not permitted to take them back to cell for their potential in other uses, i.e. metal tubes

Appendix 5: Selected Commentary from Members of the Public

Appendix 5 features selected commentary shared with the principal researcher at or after the public art exhibition. The three commentary authors have given permission for their text to be included in this research. All commentary has been de-identified.

1. Sarah,

I was moved by your art exhibition today. I reflected about it on the train on my way home.

I was particularly struck by the huge leap in the participants' self-belief and commitment to the art project as revealed between their first base-line images and final art works just eight sessions later.

With the exception of one or two base-line images (including the intriguing portrait crammed into the top right hand corner of the page, as if the participant didn't feel they had the right to own the whole page), the base-line images evoked the participants' listlessness and shoulder-shrug attitude of 'whatever'. The base-line images told me that the participants were exhausted with telling and re- telling their stories which continued to be ignored or diminished. The baseline drawing of two amoeba-like ovals was especially confronting for me. A chilling snapshot of exhaustion & despair.

But then! The final art works! 🙌 Without exception, they illustrated the participants' commitment - and perhaps sense of personal urgency - to showing their past experiences, emerging insights, and hopes for their future.

Appendix 5: Selected Commentary from Members of the Public   143

The standout dramatic art experience apropos growth and courage was the final art image made by the participant who started off with the amoeba-like ovals. So stunning.

I also appreciated witnessing the participants' commitment to developing their art-making skills over the eight sessions. All the final works are images which the artists can be proud of. I'm especially thinking here of the artist who did a collage of freedom, and also the artist who created a dual profile with two faces pulling in opposite directions.

Such growth in art-making skills as well as expressive insights plays to my belief that art therapy conventionally pays insufficient attention to the importance of supporting clients to be effective in their art-making skills. Even the way art therapy education is promoted underscores this lack ie 'You don't need art skills to be a therapist!' 😀

(Compared with music therapy in which tertiary qualifications in music are mandatory).

I wish you continuing success. 😀

[Name redacted]

2. **Hi Sarah Tucker**

I just Wanted to drop you a email to say the art show was absolutely fantastic. I wish I had more time this morning to look at the art.

It was so inspirational to think of the gift this gives to the artist and a great outlet for them. I have been thinking of the art and the words/ stories all day.

Thank you for sharing [Name redacted] 😊

3. **Hello Sarah**

Just reflecting on the fantastic art project - was looking through some photos I took - thank you.

You may or may not recall that my son [redacted] and I (extended family members of [redacted] attended.

My family is now writing regularly to [redacted].

Please let us know if you require any further support with the Project. Thanks for all that you've done and continue to do...We need way more people like you in this World! 🙏

Kind regards

[Name redacted]

Open Access This chapter is licensed under the terms of the Creative Commons Attribution 4.0 International License (http://creativecommons.org/licenses/by/4.0/), which permits use, sharing, adaptation, distribution and reproduction in any medium or format, as long as you give appropriate credit to the original author(s) and the source, provide a link to the Creative Commons license and indicate if changes were made.

The images or other third party material in this chapter are included in the chapter's Creative Commons license, unless indicated otherwise in a credit line to the material. If material is not included in the chapter's Creative Commons license and your intended use is not permitted by statutory regulation or exceeds the permitted use, you will need to obtain permission directly from the copyright holder.

Postscript

Sarah Tucker's research, which included a multi-year pilot conducted across several prison centers, examined whether art programs in prisons have therapeutic benefits. There have been numerous attempts to make prisons conform to human rights, to be 'healthier' and to be 'therapeutic communities' in Anglo-colonial countries, with some small measures of success; but those experiments rarely last, and prisons revert to their harsher state; for example, the Barllinnie prison (maximum security), Glasgow Scotland rehabilitation unit (1970s–80s) that ran successful therapeutic art amongst other humane programs. In Australia, prisons are closed, brutal institutions that exclude those confined in them from society and normal human social interaction. Although prisons are not supposed to mete out punishment (going to prison is the punishment), they are inherently places of punishment. They are supposed to enable rehabilitation so that people returning to the community can live better lives, but they rarely do so. Recidivism is high, and most people exit prison into the same or worse disadvantageous circumstances from which they came.

Society should be supporting policies and social services that prevent people, First Nations' children in particular, from being criminalised and incarcerated in the first place. Over 90% of people in prison today come from poor and disadvantaged families and communities, have poor levels of education, have been homeless or in unstable housing, have experienced abuse and violence, have mental and/or cognitive disability, and have had early contact with police as a victim. These social determinants mean that our prisons are full of the most disadvantaged people in Australia who have had little opportunity to grow and flourish or to express their humanity.

Until substantial progress is made in preventing criminalisation and reducing the numbers of people being incarcerated, people will continue to be sent to prison. So, we must try to make prisons places where those incarcerated have their rights respected and are supported to live more fulfilling lives.

Back to the question of whether art may be one way to make prison less brutal and traumatising. The expressive arts: painting, drawing, weaving, clay work, drama, singing and writing, have very long traditions in prisons. But as Sarah Tucker and Johannes Luetz point out, there is a paucity of research and evaluation of art programs in prisons in Australia and diminishing approvals or opportunities for prisoners to participate in the arts. Art, in this case drawing and painting, have demonstrated therapeutic results in our broader society, but we know so little about its therapeutic effect in prisons.

Sarah's research approach is powerful: she has lived and living experience of criminal justice, including imprisonment, and this, combined with her skills as an artist and art teacher and her Aboriginality, makes her a unique insider–outsider researcher and teacher. She understands the complex support needs of prisoners and the positive impact self-expression through art potentially can have. But she is also alert to the need for skilled therapists to be involved as well as making the art experience accessible given the high level of trauma and cognitive and other disabilities among prisoners. Her sample is very small, not because she organised it that way, but because in some jurisdictions in Australia and internationally, prison authorities are risk averse and restrict or even close down research on programs like this, unlike in open and successful systems like Finland and Norway. So, although the data are not quantitatively valid, she notes the positive effect of the art program on those in the art group as well as in the 'control group' despite the control not participating in the art program. The authors speculate that this could be an emotional, calming ripple effect from those who participated in the program on those in their prison wings. This is supported by evidence from more open systems where participation in many kinds of programs like art, and especially the difference in the way prison officers treat prisoners respectfully, result in significantly calmer prisons, lower recidivism rates and higher well-being for prisoners and those leaving prison. This is especially the case for women.

Although a women's prison was included in the program initially, the women's prison could not continue its involvement. The authors are enthusiastic to include women in the next iteration of the program. I agree wholeheartedly, but also wonder about youth detention centres in which First Nation children comprise well over 50% of incarcerated children and in which some of the most vulnerable children in Australia are imprisoned. The youth detention to adult prison pipeline is shockingly embedded. No child should be in prison, but as long as Australian states and territories continue to lock them up, therapeutic programs such as this one should be available to children.

The authors' observations in the concluding synthesis suggest a new framework for future art programs in prisons. Ensure:

- one of the members of the team has lived and living experience of incarceration and is supported by another team member;
- one of the members of the team is skilled in therapeutic work with people with trauma and complex support needs;
- the program is sensitive to each person's needs and context;
- openness by prison authorities to support programs and work with program providers to gain the greatest therapeutic benefit;
- and that each program is evaluated and findings published.

The authors also highlight the central, holistic, and vital place expressive art has in the lives of First Nations people and the importance of art programs in prisons for them.

Corrective Services across Australia and internationally have been dominated by 'criminogenic needs' directed programs, in particular, programs developed by the 'risks, needs, responsivity' (RNR) framework. These programs are uni-directional and are not holistic. Humanistic programs like art generally are not included. The results of these programs have been woeful and negligible. Across Australia recidivism is as high as it's ever been, underscoring that 'jailing is failing' to rehabilitate.

As the late Professor Tony Vinson said when he was the reformist Commissioner of Corrective Services in 1980, 'Perhaps the best we can aim for is to do no harm and for prisoners to leave no worse than they came in.' But he hoped for better than that. He believed that treating prisoners with respect and opening prisons to programs that humanised prisons by bringing human expression and interaction, including art, and that brought people from the community into prisons would be beneficial. This applied, in particular, to women prisoners. During his time, recidivism reduced as did prisoner numbers. Suffice it to say that he resigned after 3 years for lack of support from politicians.

Let's support human and humane holistic initiatives, like this art program, in prisons.

University of New South Wales (UNSW) Eileen Baldry
Sydney, Australia
November 2024

Index

A
AART instruments, 4, 29, 30, 48, 52, 54, 62–64, 88, 135
Aboriginal, 2, 7, 11, 79, 80
Additional resources, 4, 135
Art exercises, 4, 107
Art exhibition, 3, 19–20, 29, 30, 37, 48–65, 87, 90, 135, 138, 142
Art in prison, 2, 16, 17, 73, 74, 86
Artistic expression, 3, 28, 62, 76–80, 86
Art supplies, 4, 29, 39, 53, 56, 58–60, 62, 64, 95, 111, 120, 122, 135, 138, 140–142
Art therapy, 1–3, 15–20, 25–29, 69, 70, 73, 74, 76, 85, 86, 89
Art therapy impact, 16, 74
Art therapy in prisons, 2, 26
Australian prison history, 7–8
Australian prison statistics, 11–12

C
Chaplaincy, 3, 32, 70, 85
Certificate of completion, 4, 28, 135
Change the Design of Your Life (CDL) program, 25–31, 37–41, 43–48, 54, 70–74, 76, 78, 88, 93, 107, 113, 116
Cognitive disparity, 12
Colonial incarceration, 16
Concluding synthesis, 85–91
Convict transportation, 7
Correctional agency/agencies, 1, 26, 28, 32
Correctional facility interventions, 28
Correctional settings, 16, 122
Correctional services, 93, 111
Correctional systems, viii–x
Creative intervention/s, 3, 73, 74, 85, 86, 91
Criminal justice, 16, 146
Criminogeny, 147
Criminological, 85
Criminology, 90
Cultural perspectives, 80

D
Discussions, 52, 69–80, 87, 96, 99, 110, 113, 116, 121, 122

E
Educational engagement, 12
Emotional expression/s, 119
Emotional rehabilitation, 25
Empirical research, 26, 69
Ethical art exhibitions, 19–20
Ethical considerations, 19–20
Expressive art/s, 141, 145, 147
External program feedback, 119

F
First Nations, 116, 117, 145–147
Foreword, vii

G
Group artwork, 3, 93–97

H
High-security prison, 74
Holistic prison reform, 147
Hyper-incarceration, 76, 77, 116

I
Incarceration, 1, 3, 7, 12, 15, 16, 19, 25, 69, 75–80, 87, 88
Indigenous art, 17, 18, 79, 89
Indigenous culture, 76–78, 80
Indigenous dispossession, 77
Indigenous identity, 3, 69, 76–80, 86, 87
Indigenous identity and art, 3, 76
Indigenous incarceration, 11
Indigenous inmates/prisoners, 12, 18, 76–80, 87, 91
Indigenous prisoners, 76–79
Inmate artwork, 19, 28, 29, 31
Inmate perspective/s, 87
Inmate rehabilitation, 12
Inmate well-being, 2
Introduction, 1–4, 37–39

L
List of art supplies, 4, 135
Lived experience, 90, 141
Living experience, 1, 86, 146

M
Mixed-methods research, 2, 4, 85, 135

N
Narratives and identity, 16, 71, 75, 76, 86

O
Offender rehabilitation, 70

P
Parole, 3, 26, 43, 44, 70, 76, 85, 125, 136
Participant improvements, 4
Participatory, 74, 116
Preface, 1
Prison art programs, 15, 52, 88
Prison art therapy, 1, 2, 15–20, 26, 85
Prison center/s, 3, 27, 37–40, 70, 90, 145
Prison culture, 1, 8, 17, 19, 25, 74–76

Prison education programs, 18
Prison environment dynamics, 2, 3, 17, 19, 25, 28, 29, 31, 44, 69–76
Prisoner perspectives, 20
Prisoner rehabilitation, 1, 2, 71
Prisoner well-being, 12, 73, 85, 88
Prison rehabilitation, 16, 25
Prison research, 2, 3, 17, 48, 71, 89
Prison setting, 74, 86, 90, 140
PTSD in prisons, xvii
Public art exhibitions, 3, 4, 37, 48–65, 87, 135
Punitive practices, 15

Q
Qualitative data, 26, 28, 30, 44–48, 87, 105
Quantitative and qualitative research, 87
Quantitative data, 2, 17, 18, 28, 30, 37, 40–44, 48
Questionnaires, 27–30, 37–48, 56, 71, 73, 76, 108, 110

R
Recidivism, 1, 12, 18, 25, 85, 90
Recidivism prevention, 1
Recidivism reduction, 12
Rehabilitation, 1, 15–18, 20, 25, 70, 85, 86
Rehabilitation through art, 2, 15, 16
Rehabilitation *vs.* punishment, 8
Research ethics, 88
Research instruments, 4, 28, 135
Restorative justice, 15, 16
Results, 1, 3, 37–48, 65, 67, 71, 73, 74, 76

S
Self-awareness, 1, 28, 41, 42, 45, 125, 136
Self-expression, 17, 67, 146
Self-reflection, 54, 64, 66, 114
Single case study, 4, 107–130
Social exclusion, 2, 12

T
Therapeutic alliance, 107
Therapeutic art in prisons, 90
Therapeutic art programs, 3, 72–74, 85, 86, 108
Therapeutic benefits, 2, 66, 145, 146

Therapeutic effects, 15, 146
Therapeutic outlet, 111
Therapeutic work, 109, 146
Trauma/traumatic/traumatising, 12, 15–17, 25, 76, 110, 115, 145, 146

V
Visual response/s, 4, 28, 48, 87, 135, 137

Visual vignette, 3, 93–97, 107–130

W
Workshop/s, 111

Y
Youth detention, 146

The manufacturer's authorised representative in the EU is Springer Nature Customer Service Centre GmbH, Europaplatz 3, 69115 Heidelberg, Germany. If you have any concerns regarding our products, please contact ProductSafety@springernature.com

Printed and bound by CPI Group (UK) Ltd, Croydon, CR0 4YY

23/03/2026

02076446-0006